GENERATION
ALPHA

About the authors

Mark McCrindle, a social researcher with an international following, is recognised as a leader in tracking emerging issues and researching social trends. Having developed his reputation across two decades as a bestselling author and social commentator, Mark has appeared on all Australian television networks, radio and print media, and has twice been invited to speak at TEDx. He has presented thousands of keynote addresses and workshops in all major industries. His advisory, communications and research company, McCrindle, counts among its clients more than 100 of the largest companies and leading international brands. Mark is the author of five books on emerging trends and social change: *Generation Alpha*; *Work Wellbeing: Leading Thriving Teams in Rapidly Changing Times*; *The ABC of XYZ: Understanding the Global Generations*; *Word Up: A Lexicon and Guide to Communication in the 21st Century*; and *The Power of Good*.

Ashley Fell is a social researcher, TEDx Speaker and the Director of Advisory at McCrindle. Drawing on her background in communications and as a generational expert, Ashley is regularly engaged by organisations, conferences and the media to advise on future trends, business insights, generational transitions, leadership and communication skills. Her expertise is in training and equipping leaders and teams on how to inspire across generational divides, particularly Generation Y, Generation Z and now the newest generation, Generation Alpha. She is the author of two books: *Generation Alpha* and *Work Wellbeing: Leading Thriving Teams in Rapidly Changing Times*.

Sam Buckerfield is an experienced writer. An advocate of the imagination, he is passionate about story and his desire is to champion a new generation of storytellers. Sam's written work crosses genres and ranges from children's television scripts to non-fiction books. He has written scripts for Channel 10 and has acted as a ghostwriter, writing blogs for executives in both the corporate and not-for-profit sectors. On the side he's developing several young adult novels.

GENERATION
ALPHA

UNDERSTANDING OUR CHILDREN
AND HELPING THEM THRIVE

MARK McCRINDLE & ASHLEY FELL

WITH SAM BUCKERFIELD

Copyright © McCrindle Research Pty Ltd 2021
The right of McCrindle Research Pty Ltd to be identified as the author of
the work has been asserted by them in accordance with the
Copyright, Designs and Patents Act 1988.

Originally published in Australia and New Zealand in 2021
by Hachette Australia (an imprint of Hachette Australia Pty Limited)

First published in Great Britain in 2021
by Headline Home
an imprint of Headline Publishing Group

2

Cataloguing in Publication Data is available from the British Library

ISBN 978 14722 8148 7
eISBN 978 14722 8149 4

Illustrations by Ben Duffin
Typeset in Minion Pro by Kirby Jones

Headline's policy is to use papers that are natural, renewable and recyclable
products and made from wood grown in sustainable forests. The logging
and manufacturing processes are expected to conform to the
environmental regulations of the country of origin.

HEADLINE PUBLISHING GROUP
An Hachette UK Company
Carmelite House
50 Victoria Embankment
London EC4Y 0DZ

www.headline.co.uk
www.hachette.co.uk

To Arbie, my dear wife, best friend and co-adventurer for these twenty-three years. In all I do is you. And to our wonderful tribe of Generation Zs and Alphas for whom we are so grateful: Acacia, Jasper, Zari, Brighton and Corban – it is an honour to call you our children. – Mark

To Michael, (my husband), Marja (my mum) and Antonia (my oma), for your love and support. And to my adorable Generation Alpha nieces and nephews, Noah, Sage, Chloe, Kaydence, Matilda and Kip, you bring me such joy and were at the forefront of my mind when writing this book. – Ashley

To my family, John, Christine, James, Sarah, Josiah (our own Gen Alpha!) and Kathryn for your love and support. To Ryan and Ben for your invaluable friendship. To Nooma Management for your deep belief. And to our readers – I hope this book helps you empower the children you've been entrusted with to thrive. – Sam

Contents

Prologue

I have one of the best jobs in the world. I'm a social researcher, which basically means I study human behaviour. This involves observing different trends and their impact on how people behave, work, live, shop and communicate. The types of trends I focus on are often: technology trends – like the rise of artificial intelligence and robotics. Demographic shifts – like an ageing and more culturally diverse population. And one of my favourites, social trends – like understanding the mix of generations in our society. The year 2020 will go down in history as one of massive change, because COVID-19 accelerated and highlighted many of these trends.

But even prior to 2020, I began to notice an increase in the interest the world was taking in the next generation of children. To many people, they are a bit of a mystery. As a result, I regularly get to speak to groups of parents wanting to find out more about the world shaping their children, educators, and business leaders wanting to better understand them, and some of the leading technology platforms about what they need to know in order to remain relevant. What I have noticed is that people are starting to sit up and take note that a new generation is not only coming, but they are already here.

This is precisely why I decided to write this book, along with Ashley Fell, the Director of Advisory at my research and communications company McCrindle. Between us, we have been in social research for almost three decades. Both Ashley and I take a keen interest in the topic of generations, and are regularly asked to give presentations, media commentary and advice about them, based on our research. This research takes the form of surveys, focus groups and in-depth interviews. Every day we get to speak to people from all over the world, sharing our research and hearing their opinions, stories and expertise on this topic – some of which we quote in this book. This area of research is important, because we believe great leaders are focused not on the next program, but the next generation. To tell Generation Alpha's story, we have also engaged Sam Buckerfield, a Sydney-based writer who is equally passionate about storytelling, to help us pen this book.

Across these pages we endeavour to bring you insights from our research on the world being created for children born between 2010 and 2024, a cohort that I have dubbed Generation Alpha. In this book you'll find statistics and percentages that show how different this generation is, because of the increasingly digital and global world they are being shaped in. You'll engage with stories from people who are on the ground equipping, empowering and leading Generation Alpha – people like you – parents, educators and professionals.

Over the course of my career and the thousands of presentations I have delivered, I consistently find that it is the topic of the generations that people have a great interest in.

Perhaps because it is relatable – we all fit into one. Or perhaps it is because we all have an interest in reflecting on how it was and how it will be. Our work aims to help people understand the changing times so they can better engage with the world around them. Explaining why generational labels like 'OK Boomer' (the phrase Gen Z use to describe ideas that are outdated) or 'KIPPERS' (which is an acronym that stands for Kids In Parents' Pockets Eroding Retirement Savings, used to describe adult children staying longer at home) exist, makes for fascinating social commentary. I enjoy this topic so much that I made it the focus of one of my previous books – *The ABC of XYZ: Understanding the Global Generations.* It was during my research for this previous book that something significant dawned on me. No one seemed to even be thinking about the next generation that was about to commence! There wasn't even a label to describe them. At the time, the focus was on Generation Z, those born between 1995 and 2009. And yet a new generation was about to begin. With Z completing the Latin alphabet, there was no subsequent letter to assign to them.

So, I conducted a survey on what the new label could be. Many people suggested Generation A. But knowing this generation would be the first to be entirely born in the twenty-first century (with births commencing in 2010), I felt that they are not a return to the old, but the start of something new. Using this reasoning and drawing on the scientific nomenclature of turning to the Greek alphabet, I decided to name them Generation Alpha.

We explore the various stages of life that Generation Alpha will walk through including home and community, education, the workplace, health and wellbeing. Our hope once you've finished reading the book, is that you will have a greater understanding of the world Generation Alpha are growing up in. That you will not only be informed, but inspired and equipped with the tools to help them live and thrive in today's challenging and constantly changing world.

Mark McCrindle
Principal – McCrindle Research, 2021

CHAPTER 1

Talking About Your Generation

'People resemble their times more than they resemble their parents.'

Arab proverb

When we approach the study of different generations, we often reflect on a quote by Stephen Covey, author of the acclaimed *The 7 Habits of Highly Effective People*, who famously said, 'seek first to understand, then to be understood'.[1] In this chapter, we begin by painting a picture of each generation, the social context in which they have been shaped and the different parenting styles utilised by them. This will lay the foundation from which we can begin to understand the generation who are the focus of this book – Generation Alpha.

When you envision the next generation of children, what do you think about them? Perhaps you conjure images of them always being glued to their devices, impatient, and a little entitled. Or maybe you see them as being resilient, optimistic, adept at responding to change and good at taking risks.

Perhaps a bit of both. Whatever your perspective, it is helpful to think about your assumptions for a moment.

Generational stereotypes are nothing new. Generation Y (Millennials, born between 1980 and 1994, the parents of Generation Alpha) have been labelled as lazy and entitled. Even older generations, like the Baby Boomers, were labelled in a similar way when they were growing up. In part, these stereotypes come from simply being young. But it is also true that today's younger generations look different to how older generations did at the same age.

A more accurate understanding can be gained by looking at the significant life events, social markers and formative technologies that have affected each generation. By taking the time to understand this – the context – we move away from 'generationalising' to generational analysis. Recognising the impact of the shared experiences, societal expectations and new inventions that shaped people in their formative years helps us to better understand those of different generations and overcome generational stereotyping. The stories of the different generations matter, and an understanding of the unique times, events and experiences that have shaped each generation and their era will allow parents, educators and leaders to be more relevant in these changing times.

Rather than looking at divisions among the generations, we believe it is important to develop understanding across them. This is the first step to facilitating better engagement and connection in places where different generations mix – particularly in families, schools and workplaces. An understanding of the different generations is also important because it enables us to honour those who laid the foundations of what we are building on today.

Our hope is that, through this book, parents, teachers, leaders and anyone who engages with Generation Alpha will have a more holistic overview of the context in which they have been shaped, and therefore who they are. The more these important groups of people understand Generation Alpha, the more they will be able to effectively help them fulfil their potential.

Generational change

Change is not unique to this era, but the speed, size and scope of the change that defines our current times is truly *unprecedented* (we know because, according to our research,[2] 'change' was one of the most overused words in 2020!). It is through the frame of the generations that we can best understand the shifts, analyse the trends and know the times.

We are also undergoing a significant generational transition. The median age of the global population is just under 30 years of age. The year that Generation Alpha began being born (2010) was, interestingly, the first year that generations Y and Z comprised more than half the world's population. That is, those born since 1980 comprised more than those born before 1980.[3] Generations Y and Z now also comprise the majority of the workforce, outnumbering Generation X and the Baby Boomers for the first time. This means the demographic and economic strength has shifted to the emerging generations (Gen Y and Z) and, with that, they have a new role as the dominant workers, consumers and household formers. As you will see in this chapter, these generations are different to those who have gone before, and so too are their leadership preferences, consumer expectations and parenting styles.

In order for us to understand the tech-savvy and digitally literate Generation Alpha, we first need to look at where they fit in the generational mix. It is important to gain an appreciation of the people who are most likely to be their parents (Gen X and Y), their older siblings (Gen Z), their grandparents (Baby Boomers) and their great-grandparents (Builders). It helps to paint a picture of the people who have and are building the world, at an individual and societal level, that Generation Alpha will come of age in, which is an essential part of understanding the Alphas themselves.

The current generations:

Builders (b. 1925–1945)

Baby Boomers (b. 1946–1964)

Generation X (b. 1965–1979)

Millennials, or Generation Y (b. 1980–1994)

Generation Z (b. 1995–2009)

Generation Alpha (b. 2010–2024)

Meet your generation

One of our most consistent findings is that people love to talk about the different generations. The word 'generation' describes all of the people born within a similar time range, and we have found the most helpful span to be fifteen years. People born in a similar era are influenced by the same events, social markers and emerging technologies. This shared experience, particularly in their formative years, gives those within a generation a connection and collective identity. They are shaped by similar conditions, institutions and together share the same life stage. This cohort-experience creates shared perspectives, expectations and a sense of connection among people. It also leads to differences across other generations.

You don't have to look far to see the shared experiences and differences of generations in action. All it takes is a Gen Z teenager (or rather, 'screenager') to be captivated by their device at a family barbeque for a Baby Boomer to say, 'We never had technology like that in my day. We never had computers, and to speak to someone you had to use a telephone with a dial!' While all of those in a similar age bracket nod vigorously and agree, the children of today roll their eyes. They have never experienced such times, so don't understand the older generation's perspective of life without devices.

The Builders

The generation born between 1925 and 1945 we simply call 'the Builders' because they have built the cities we know, the communities we value and the way of life we enjoy. Today, they are the world's most senior generation. They were born into the crisis period of the Great Depression and the years up to and including World War II, and these events have heavily shaped them. During World War II, 70 million people[4] fought with the Allied forces, and almost a million[5] of those were from Australia. Tens of thousands of Australians died in battle, but over 900,000 men and women returned home after their military service.[6] It's no wonder we honour these veterans around the world on Anzac Day, Remembrance Day and Memorial Day.

The Builders have been referred to as the 'greatest' generation because of the hardships they overcame and their indefatigable attitude. Hugh Mackay, in his book *Generations*, labels them the 'lucky' generation because of the years of relative comfort that followed World War II.[7] They are the generation that built the economy, infrastructure and society after the Depression. Growing up, this generation played out on the street, riding around on bikes or rollerskates; their parents drove Model T Fords and listened to their music on record players or the wireless. Screen time for this generation involved watching movies at the local cinema, or 'picture theatre' as it was often referred to. The Builders started their families as young adults during the post-war boom and they had a more authoritarian parenting style, intent on keeping order in the home.

While society is constantly evolving, the amount of change that the Builders have seen is truly phenomenal. They have lived through the introduction of electric ovens, refrigerators, washing machines and televisions and the invention and adoption of most of the technologies that we take for granted today.

The vast difference between the Builders' experience growing up and that of the Alphas is clearly seen when we interviewed Shirley, aged eighty-two.

'When I was seven, my mother assigned me the clothes-washing duties. Back then, without electricity, washing was a lengthy affair. My mother taught me to soak the clothes overnight, then the next day I had to soap, boil and rinse them, wring them out, put them through the mangle and hang them out to dry. If the clothes were especially dirty, I'd have to do this process three times. Technology has come a long way in my lifetime. I am concerned that young people are becoming increasingly sedentary. But, that said, I love FaceTiming my granddaughter, Daisy. Although she lives fourteen hours' drive away, I feel more connected to her than I did my own brother, who I grew up with.'

It's extraordinary how the older generations endured physical hardship to do daily chores around the home, compared to today's click-button appliances, robo-vacs, outsourced services and Uber deliveries.

The Baby Boomers

The Baby Boomers are the children of the Builders, and were born between 1946 and 1964. They were the last generation to span longer than fifteen years and be named after a sociological event – the post–World War II population and economic boom. This was a time of return to family and local community, with a subsequent boom in the fertility rate, which began its rapid rise in 1946, peaking in 1961. Interestingly, by the time we reached 1965 the rate dropped to the low levels of the war years and the baby boom was complete.[8] In Australia, our population increased by more than half, from 7.4 million at the end of World War II to reach 11.4 million by 1965.[9] While natural increase (number of births minus number of deaths) contributed to this, so too did changes in immigration, with millions of migrants arriving to settle in Australia after World War II. This was certainly an exciting time in the formation of what Australia has become today, a globally connected land of diversity and opportunity.

A defining event for the Baby Boomers was the United States' efforts to land humans on the moon. We are all familiar with Neil Armstrong's now-famous declaration as he set foot on the moon, 'That's one small step for man, one giant leap for mankind.' This cultural event was one of the greatest achievements of the twentieth century, especially for the Baby Boomers as it instilled in them a sense of possibility and can-do spirit.

Baby Boomers would have played frisbee on the streets with their neighbours and listened to music in vinyl form and later audio cassette, while their leisure time at home was spent watching television at first in black and white, and by the mid 1970s in colour.

The Baby Boomers had a carefree childhood. When we speak to people of this generation, they often say things like, 'Back in those days, we would be out all the time, we would be on our bikes exploring the area with the only requirement to be back by sunset.' They were innocent days where there was high trust in the community, and parents felt their children were safe in the local area. From exploring the bushland to spending hours up at the park, Baby Boomers had far more free rein in their childhood than children do today.

Generation X

Generation X is a massive generation, comprising one in five Australians. Born from 1965 to 1979, Generation X are currently aged in their early forties to their mid-fifties and are in their mid-family years, mid-careers and mid-life. Their teen years were the 1980s and 1990s and they were the generation to first see computers enter their schools and homes. They were also the first to commonly have both parents working and experience higher rates of parental divorce than the generations before them. They were labelled 'latch-key kids' and the 'home alone generation' and became a more peer-orientated, independent and flexible generation. In 1991, Canadian author Douglas Coupland mused this emerging generation was different from the Baby Boomers, but weren't in need of a grandiose label. 'Call us X,' he wrote in his book *Generation X: Tales for an Accelerated Culture*.[10] Ironically, the anti-label ushered in the generational labelling regimen for the next thirty years.

Today, Generation X are often labelled the 'sandwich generation', as many are sandwiched between caring for their elderly parents and their dependent children. And now, at the time of writing, after quite a wait, Generation X have one of their own as prime minister. Scott Morrison (born 1968) is the first post–Baby Boomer to be an Australian PM after a run of four Baby Boomer prime ministers. Australia joins countries like Canada (with Justin Trudeau) and France (with Emmanuel Macron) in having a Gen X-er at the helm. New Zealand took generational change to a new level in 2017 by electing a Gen Y to lead their nation (Jacinda Ardern was born in 1980).

In Australia, Generation X comprise more than a quarter of all voters and around a third of the workforce. This is the generation that grew up under Malcolm Fraser and Bob Hawke in Australia, and with Ronald Reagan in the White House and Margaret Thatcher as the British Prime Minister. They are the original computer generation, shaped in the audio cassette era, using the first VCRs, watching *Hey Hey It's Saturday* and the early days of MTV, and wearing acid-wash jeans, hypercolour T-shirts and the occasional turtleneck knit. They were tuned into the hype of Halley's Comet, impacted by the 1987 stock market crash and the resulting 'recession we had to have', and witnessed in real time the fall of the Berlin Wall in 1989 and, with it, communism in Europe. This was the generation that experienced the rise of the two-income family, with both parents often working in order to be able to pay their mortgage and achieve a more aspirational lifestyle than their parents.

Having lived their formative years in the twentieth century, and many or most of their adult years in the twenty-first, Generation X are a unique hybrid of traditional, structural and analogue approaches combined with the adaptive, collaborative and digital thinking of today. They were shaped in a hierarchical world but they lead with a more participative style. Education for them was conducted with pen and paper and required closed-book exams, yet now they lead teams who interact on touch-screen devices and teach in an 'open-book' world, just a few clicks away from any piece of information on the planet. Their world began when Australia still looked to England, but amid several decades of cultural change and migration growth, they now see the strong connections to Asia and have a global outlook. Their parents were shaped in the post–World War II years while their children – Generation Z – have been shaped in an era of smartphones, social media and the gig economy.

In addition to all this, they are the Commodore 64, Nirvana, Rubik's Cube, Ferris Bueller generation. Like every generation since, their music came portable – for them it was analogue not digital, and via a Walkman.

While their childhood wasn't the total separation of the 'children should be seen and not heard' era, Generation X grew up in a world where adults lived in their adult world and kids lived in their own world. While parents cared for and guided their children, they didn't feel the need to inhabit their world. Gen X kids consequently had more freedom, and felt independent from their parents.

Generation X brought about some significant changes. Through a subtle shift in values, they set new social behaviours. They were the generation to push marriage back from the mid to late twenties (which we see continuing today among Gen Y). Although Generation X were given much materially as children, some felt they lacked the more important things, such as valuable time with Mum and Dad. Consequently, as parents, this generation has tried hard to balance family and work life, and to keep the family unit together.[11] Statistics for divorce show this. The divorce rate in Australia is now half of what it was in the mid-1970s,[12] during the childhood years of Generation X.

Generation Y

Generation Y describes those born between 1980 and 1994, which means they are now in the key family-forming life stage and are the next generation of parents, the ones most likely to be the parents of Generation Alpha. Because they have 'come of age' during the approach of, or in, the new millennium, they are also sometimes referred to as the Millennials.

Gen Y are often labelled as the tech-savvy and entitled generation that has been locked out of the housing market. They have different expectations around careers, family life and lifestyle, and most will admit they seek home ownership as well as enjoying a good smashed avo at the local café. They are most likely parents of Generation Alpha, and also the aunties, uncles, teachers and leaders of this emerging generation.

Generation Y grew up during some of the best economic times the world has ever seen, and for Australia, the Global Financial Crisis (GFC) was a blip rather than a crisis. In 2020 Australia experienced its first recession in thirty years, the same year the oldest Gen Ys turned 40. This means that, throughout their formative years, most Gen Ys hadn't experienced economic hardship, high unemployment or inflation. Instead, they were used to everyday luxuries, like two or more cars per family, dinners out and huge family homes. As a result, Gen Y are an optimistic generation and enjoy life's smaller indulgences, such as a weekend brunch and boutique espresso coffee, as well as the bigger-ticket items of overseas travel. These lifestyle priorities are often described as a pitfall of this generation, who have struggled to enter the property market and obtain the 'great Australian dream' of home ownership. While they have been criticised for expecting to start their economic life in the manner in which they have seen their parents finish theirs, we must consider that the national average house prices are more than ten times the average annual earnings, compared to roughly five times what they were for their parents' generation.[13] No wonder this generation are opting for the smaller luxuries in life when breaking into the housing market has been so unattainable in recent times!

During the GFC, which coincided with the start of their working life, Gen Y's confidence in the economic security of the future was impacted for the first time – just as they were beginning their careers. Their lives were affected a second time during COVID-19, with many Gen Ys experiencing this global pandemic as they were beginning their key family-forming years.

One of the most significant events that shaped Generation Y was the September 11 attacks, a series of four coordinated terrorist attacks against the United States on the morning of 11 September 2001. Each generation has social markers that influence their worldview and expectations. The September 11 attacks changed the world as we knew it, with the impacts being evident in changes to airport security, the wars in Afghanistan and a global focus on counter-terrorism. In Australia, the acting prime minister at the time, John Anderson, was ushered to a safe house from where he addressed the nation, with intelligence briefings advising that there might very well be a series of attacks targeting other countries including Australia. Prime Minister John Howard invoked the ANZUS treaty (Australia, New Zealand and the United States) which meant that an attack on one would be an attack on all. So Australia went onto a war footing.

While other generations also experienced this event, it did not occur during their formative years like it did for Gen Y. This historic moment happened when Gen Y were coming of age, and signified a loss of innocence for this generation. As Bret, now twenty-seven, says, 'It was the first time we started to see that the world was a darker place. It opened my eyes a bit, and was the first time I realised, *Things can be pretty serious out there.*'[14] Coming of age during the 'War on Terror' connected Gen Y to their peers all over the world, making them a truly global generation.

Many Gen Ys were in their teen years when 9/11 happened, and so the harrowing footage of the planes flying into the twin towers is etched in their memory. As Sophie, a Gen Y, told us, 'I'll never forget waking up that September morning to see those planes fly into the twin towers on TV. At first I didn't think it was real, but then it kept being replayed over and over. I don't remember the details vividly, but I remember feeling uncertain, and could tell something really big was happening.'

Another defining trait of Generation Y is that they are a tech-centric generation. They are clever multi-taskers who can work on several major projects at once with aplomb. This generation grew up in a time shaped by the emergence of digital technology, laptop computers, the internet and the sharing economy, which had significant impacts on the workforce. Gen Y is the generation of Mark Zuckerberg (Facebook founder), Evan Spiegel (Snapchat founder), Melanie Perkins (Canva co-founder), Daniel Ek (Spotify founder) and Drew Houston (Dropbox founder), all of whom exemplify work flexibility, entrepreneurism and a belief that anything is possible.

Generation Y have invested significantly in their education and are committed to growing their careers. Far from being the 'snowflake generation', as some disparagingly label them, it turns out they are resilient and are now settling down, buying property and having a family – although this is happening later in life as they continue to push back these significant life markers. When Generation Y were born, their parents were largely in their late twenties, while today the median age of first-time mothers is the early thirties.[15]

Generation Z

Generation Z describes those who were born between the years 1995 and 2009. They have come of age in the twenty-first century and been influenced by growing cultural diversity, global brands, social media and a digital world.

This is the first generation of school leavers to emerge into the working world of the digital economy where robotics, automation, big data and machine learning are now mainstream. When we type something into Google and it answers our question before we've asked it, this is artificial intelligence in action. Those automated playlists on Spotify are examples of predictive algorithms at play. While previous generations of school leavers could set plans, make decisions and track towards the future, these days the future is coming at us with increasing velocity and often from an unknown direction. In an era that is less structured, sequential and predictable, it is a good thing that Gen Z are more aware of the global changes, technology trends and digital disruptions. This means this generation is well set to not only thrive amid these changing times, but also bring positive transformations to workplaces and communities.

In the nearly twenty-four years of their lifespan they have seen more change than any cohort before them at the same age. They began their life in the internet era but are being shaped in the world of mobile devices and social media. With the youngest entering their teen years, their lexicons are filled with terms that didn't exist at their birth: apps, tweets, memes, tablets, smartphones and cloud computing (not to mention the more colloquial slang terms like 'bae' and 'yass queen'!). These trends have transformed society so much, it is radically different to the times that shaped their parents and unrecognisable to the world their grandparents first knew.

Generation Z have been at the heart of social media, with the socialisation of their formative years taking place on online apps and platforms. This generation have grown up watching videos on YouTube, sending Snapchat messages to each other and communicating largely through social media platforms. It has helped them be more connected with each other and allowed them to express themselves through their own content, and often connect with like-minded people globally. It has, however, also led to challenges. YouTube bloggers sometimes have to deal with challenging negative comments, and growing up on these platforms can lead to people experiencing FOMO (fear of missing out). Constantly seeing your friends posting videos or photos of holidays or parties can make you feel excluded or unworthy.

Generation Z are truly a global generation, having been shaped in an era of digital devices and increasing connectivity. Global events that have happened in Generation Z's formative years are Donald Trump's 'against-the-odds' election as the President of the United States in 2016, as well as the role that celebrities and social media influencers played in the election of Joe Biden in

2020. Brexit, and the GFC, also had a big impact. However, the biggest social marker of them all was the COVID-19 pandemic and its associated impacts. Increasing awareness of climate change from activist Greta Thunberg (a Gen Z herself) has also shaped this generation to become one that is recognising they have a voice and can speak up and be heard.

When it comes to leadership, Generation Z prefer a style of consensus and collaboration rather than structure and hierarchy. Their perspectives are global. It is social influence, not just expert advice, that shapes them. This generation are tuned in to social activism but tuned out to traditional politics. This is significantly different from what politicians have experienced in the past. Understanding the worldviews of their younger constituents will be a challenge, but one that can be overcome if time is taken to understand them and engage with them where they are at.

Generation Z have experienced a change in parenting styles as well. Born to older mums and dads, they live highly organised lives with little unstructured time and have the fewest siblings of any generation. With an increasing focus on education in a globally competitive environment and with an education system focused on standardised testing, academically streamed classes and selective schools, it is unsurprising that they live largely indoors. It is clear that their parents place priority on homework, coaching and extracurricular activities over a carefree childhood. Furthermore, given fears about child predators, their parents are more cautious about letting their youngsters play with friends on neighbouring streets and in nearby parks. Their parents' style is one of consensus and collaboration, involving their Gen Z children in decisions and being influenced by their ideas around purchases and holiday destinations.

Generation Z and COVID-19

COVID-19 wasn't simply a generational social marker, it ushered in the biggest societal transformation in a century. The nearest comparable pandemic, the Spanish Flu, occurred almost exactly one hundred years before, in 1918.

The spread of COVID-19 was speedy, the effects devastating. Entire populations were effectively quarantined in their own homes. Only essential service outings, like visits to the supermarket and doctors, were permitted. In some countries you had to obtain a pass to leave the home at all and in many countries, streets were monitored by police, and the military with authority to fine those who breached the imposed quarantine. These were extreme but necessary measures to curb the spread of the virus and alleviate the impact on the nations' health facilities. In the same way that world wars, stock market crashes and September 11 shaped their predecessors, it seemed that the defining social marker for Gen Z and Generation Alpha had arrived.

For Generation Z, COVID-19 had a direct impact on them during a significant life stage – their teen years and early twenties. This life stage is normally characterised by education and study, as well as socialising with friends after school or during breaks at university. Weekends are normally filled with sport and shopping, going out or hanging at a friend's place. Goals and dreams of Generation Z before COVID-19 were to do well in exams, spend quality time with friends and work to save up for travel adventures. COVID-19 changed much of this. Their schools and universities shut, learning moved online, sport stopped, and their social lives almost ceased to exist during the various lockdowns. Many of this generation also had to forsake certain rites of passage that come with this life stage – school formals and graduations were cancelled, gap years delayed and, to the mixed feelings of parents, schoolies was cancelled. While Generation Z were not as vulnerable to the virus itself, a McCrindle national study of 1,002 Australians[16] at the time suggested individuals were more likely to feel anxious, frustrated, overwhelmed, confused and unprepared about the unfolding COVID-19 situation than any other generation. While this less-than-ideal school and social situation proved to be challenging for Generation Z, it has also instilled in them a unique resilience.

The economic impacts of COVID-19 were also felt by younger generations seeking to establish themselves in the workforce. According to one of our national surveys during the pandemic, Gen Y and Gen Z were the most likely to have felt the biggest negative impact financially (33 per cent Gen Z and 37 per cent Gen Y compared to 28 per cent Gen X, 20 per cent Baby Boomers and 12 per cent Builders).

The impacts on the Australian job market in the first few months of COVID-19 had been unparalleled since the Great Depression. The Australian Bureau of Statistics found that between March and April 2020, the number of underemployed people increased by more than 620,000 to 1.8 million.[17] These job-loss rates were highest for those under twenty, with almost one in five (19 per cent) losing their job. For those aged twenty to twenty-nine, more than one in ten (12 per cent) lost their job while just 5 per cent of those aged thirty to sixty-nine lost their job. This means that those under twenty were almost four times more likely to have lost their job than those thirty and over.[18]

Despite an uncertain outlook, Generation Z were also well positioned to stay connected during COVID-19, even from a distance. From TikTok videos to Zoom or House Party apps, their skills in connecting through online platforms proved helpful during COVID-19. For many, it also changed their education experience. For university students, their on-campus experience was vastly different due to COVID-19. As Gen Z-er Hannah told us, 'The turnaround period from in-person classes to online was less than a week, and while I know the lecturers tried their best, there was an obvious decline in the quality of teaching as we moved to a fully online classroom. Despite this, fees remained the same and I ended up having less overall contact hours with my tutors and little to no opportunity to work collaboratively with other students, which was an important part of my degree.'

Generation Z felt sharply the shift of BC (Before COVID-19) to DC (During COVID-19). The full impacts of COVID-19, and particularly the global and economic responses, will roll on for some years to come (even in an AC world – After COVID-19). Generation Alpha will also be significantly shaped by COVID-19, not in the dramatic way experienced by Gen Z, but in the ongoing adjustment to life in the new reality.

Naming Generation Alpha

Every generation since the Baby Boomers spans fifteen years, regardless of events and circumstances. They are also labelled using letters (X, Y, Z and now Alpha) – a more scientific approach to categorisation. There have been other attempts to label generations. The 'Millennials' is one example. The problem with this label is that it defines them around a single event (the start of the new millennium), but creates a vague birth range. Are the Millennials born from the mid-1980s until 2000, or are they born in the first decade of this millennium?

There has been some talk of Generation Alpha being labelled the 'Coronials' due to the COVID-19 pandemic that began in the middle of their fifteen-year span. Yet this is short-sighted; they will shape and be shaped by the next three, five or ten decades. The virus does not define them. Using a set span of birth years and a non-descriptive label allows objective analysis for each generation. Just think: when someone says 'Millennial' it's often with a roll of the eyes and a derogatory tone of voice. We wouldn't want a similar experience for Generation Alpha. So, a label like 'Generation Alpha' provides a blank canvas on which a generation can create their own identity. This is much better than having a descriptive label, relevant for just a portion of the generation or for just a period of time, pinned on them. In fact, the Baby Boomers signify the last generation defined and labelled by an external event – the post–World War II baby boom.

In our initial survey about this new generation, we asked respondents what they thought the generation after Z might be called. For many, the logical answer to our question was to 'go back to the beginning'. Generation A was suggested by a quarter of respondents. The respondents who suggested Generation A said the label also signified what we could expect of this generation and their times: a new and positive beginning for all, with global warming and terrorism controlled. Respondents made similar comments when they suggested the following labels: the Regeneration, Generation Hope, Generation New Age, the Zoomers, Generation Tech, the Onliners and Global Generation. Others suggested the Neoconservatives, because the upcoming generation will have grown up aware of their impact on the environment and the economy.

Our survey took place just after the Atlantic hurricane season of 2005. There had been a number of storms up to that point and the normal alphabetic names had been used up and so, for the first time, the Greek alphabet was engaged.

Taking into consideration these survey results, along with the scientific nomenclature of using the Greek alphabet in lieu of the Latin, and having worked our way through Generations X, Y and Z, Mark settled on the next cohort being Generation Alpha – not a return to the old but the start of something new – to signify the new world in which they will be shaped. In contrast to the domineering and entitled connotations of 'alpha' in phrases like 'alpha type' or 'alpha male', this new generation is inclusive, collaborative, global in outlook and keen to learn.

It appears as though the Greek alphabet approach is due to stick, with publications and platforms like *The New York Times*, *The Huffington Post* and the *World Economic Forum* acknowledging Generation Alpha. Following this nomenclature, Generation Beta will be born from 2025 to 2039, followed by Generation Gamma (2040 to 2054) and Generation Delta (2055 to 2069). But we won't be getting there until the second half of the twenty-first century, so there is plenty of time to reflect on the labels!

Generation Alpha

From 2010 the world saw the start of Generation Alpha, the first to be fully born in the twenty-first century. Alphas have been born into an era of record birth numbers. When this generation is complete, in December 2024, Generation Alpha births will total almost two billion globally, and they will be the largest generation in the history of the world.

Generation Alpha are the first generation to have been born and fully shaped in the twenty-first century. And most of them will live to see the twenty-second century.

Generation Alpha have only ever lived in a world where glass is linked to interaction and connection. Technology and customisation have shaped their childhood. While Generation Z experienced the rise of customisation, Generation Alpha have seen personalisation – where everything from Nutella jars and Coke cans to storybooks can be ordered featuring their name.

The younger generation, like a younger sibling, carves out an identity in reaction to the one that went before. They don't feel bound to the previous era and so have a freedom to chart their own course.

In their life so far, the biggest social and cultural marker has been the COVID-19 pandemic. As we have explored, COVID-19 also had a significant impact on Generation Z, yet Australians believe it will transform how Generation Alpha approach technology, education, work, face-to-face interaction, mental health and resilience.[19]

The oldest Generation Alphas are currently moving into tweendom, a term describing children aged between eight and twelve, the period between childhood and adolescence. The relatively new world of 'tweendom' is evidence of the 'up-ageing' (growing up faster, being 'older younger') of today's emerging generations. Tweens have emerged as their own demographic and influence the purchasing patterns of their household. It is during these years that children often get their own smartphone, change their online behaviour and begin to take on their own identity and responsibility. These young people have access to more technology, information and external influences than any generation before them, and at a younger age than generations past. As brand influencers, tweens are a unique segment to engage with. Social media has been integral to the development of tweens in the twenty-first century, who are actively engaging on websites, being creative on TikTok, uploading their own YouTube videos and connecting with friends on Instagram and Facebook. Many websites are targeted specifically to this demographic. Tweens can create virtual pets, play games and interact online with other people their age with ease.

Generation Alpha are 'up-agers' in many ways: the onset of physical maturity occurs earlier than previous generations, so adolescence for them will begin earlier. While adolescence begins earlier, it also extends later – the adult life stage, once marked by marriage, children, mortgage and career, is being pushed back. This generation will stay in education longer, start their earning years later and so will stay at home with their parents for longer than was previously the case. The role of parents, therefore, spans a wider age range, still housing (and funding!) their adult children. Generation Alpha will no doubt continue this trend. In Australia, as we've mentioned, we've labelled the stay-at-home twenty-somethings the KIPPERS, which stands for Kids In Parents' Pockets Eroding Retirement Savings.

While we're not particularly fond of well-worn phrases and clichés (and avoid them like the plague, we say!), they are often rooted in truth. Based on both research and observation we can confidently say that the *future is bright* for Generation Alpha. As author of *The Chronicles of Narnia* series C. S. Lewis stated, 'There are far, far better things ahead than any we leave behind.' That statement is not to diminish the past but to champion the future. As is true of days past, the days ahead will have their complexities and challenges, but they will also be replete with innovation and opportunity. And as you will see from the chapters that follow, Generation Alpha are living on the edge of an extraordinary age.

Busting myths about Generation Alpha

Myth: Generation Alpha won't live as long as previous generations

Some people think that Generation Alpha will be the first generation to not live as long as their parents. This is due to their increasingly sedentary lives, the rising rates of obesity and greater access to junk food. But the opposite is actually more likely to be true. Due to medical advancements, improved public health measures, pharmaceutical breakthroughs, declining smoking rates and workplace and public safety measures, Generation Alpha will live longer than any previous generation, with life expectancy for a Generation Alpha born in Australia today approaching the mid-eighties.

Myth: Generation Alpha won't work as late into their lives as current or past generations

We often hear people say that Generation Alpha won't work as much throughout their life due to labour-saving devices, leisure lifestyles and a universal basic income. People often think that these trends will enable them to work less throughout their life and enable them to retire early. Once again, the opposite is most probably the case. Generation Alpha will work later into their life than any previous generation. Why? Because they will live longer and therefore have a need to work later to supplement this longer life. With machines helping to ease the physical burden of work, they will be able to work less physically. Additionally, work will have a purpose for them beyond remuneration – it will be a place of social interaction, purpose, stimulation and lifelong learning.

Myth: Generation Alpha's future will be entirely virtual

Generation Alpha are being raised in increasingly technologically integrated times, so many people think their future will be entirely virtual. They think Generation Alpha will have no need to interact with other human beings in a work-from-home future that is full of technology and robotics. But a timeless human need is for relational connection and social interaction. During the working from home and learning from home measures that COVID-19 necessitated, we once again experienced that while digital connectivity is convenient, it's no permanent substitute for the physical interaction that is core to the human experience. As we will explore in more detail in Chapter 6, Generation Alpha will have a greater need for interpersonal skills such as communication and leadership to thrive in a more machine-assisted future.

Generation Alpha focused on personal growth

Generation Alpha are being shaped in an education system that encourages them to set their own goals and resources them through technology both in school and at home, to progress and explore beyond the classroom instruction. They are given time for personal reflection, and there is a strong focus on the development of multiple intelligences beyond just the numeracy and literacy of old, which focused on 'the three Rs' – reading, writing and arithmetic.

We've found in our research with educators and parents that Generation Alpha are both agile and adept. Educators told us that they believe the mindset of Generation Alpha is different to that of Generation Z. When faced with a challenge, educators believe Generation Alpha are significantly more likely to persist than to give up, when compared to Gen Z.

Educators think Generation Alpha are more likely to ask for help while Gen Z are more likely to struggle in silence. When they experience failure, educators think Gen Z are more likely to see it as a personal deficiency while Gen Alpha are more likely to see it as an opportunity to learn.[20] As Generation Alpha grow up it will be interesting to see how this mindset shapes their experience and approach to life.

Whether children hold a growth mindset or a fixed mindset can have a big impact on their education, achievement and success. A fixed mindset cultivates a belief that intelligence or talent is a fixed trait, so people with this mindset tend to give up when a challenge or problem arises. Whereas those with a growth mindset believe their abilities can be improved through hard work, which leads to growth, success, a love of learning and greater resilience. So how can parents develop and encourage a growth mindset in their children? Here are some tips:

- **Place value on the effort being made.** Praising children's effort and how they approach a challenge is more helpful than their intelligence, ability or how well they did. By praising their effort, it encourages more of it in different situations and gives them agency to work hard. As Carol Dweck says, 'If parents want to give their children a gift, the best thing they can do is to teach their children to love challenges, be intrigued by mistakes, enjoy effort, and keep learning. That way, children don't have to be slaves of praise. They will have a lifelong way to build and repair their own confidence.'[21]
- **Use the power of 'yet'.** It's amazing how such a small word – 'yet' – can have a big impact in shifting a child's worldview and approach to difficulty. Instead

of a child saying, 'I can't read', it's much more empowering for them to say, 'I can't read, yet'. It's encouraging to hear that teachers are incorporating this into their teaching. Helena, a primary school teacher, told us how her class has a routine where every Friday they sing the growth mindset song from *Sesame Street* called 'The Power of Yet'. Helena says that even though 'they are in year six, they love it. They sing it as they walk out the door every single Friday and remember it over the weekend. It's the difference between the mindset of, "Oh this is too hard, I'm not going to do it" and "I'm going to have a go".'

- **Avoid labelling children.** Whether the label is positive or negative, labelling children springs from a fixed mindset and can prohibit parents, teachers and leaders from encouraging effort and hard work to develop and grow. Neuroscience research shows that the human brain is continually learning and adapting – not just in our formative years but throughout our lives.

- **Reframe failure as a normal part of the process, rather than a negative outcome.** An important part of building resilience in children is to not let failure stop them from working to improve. While it might seem natural to say to a child, 'It's okay if you aren't very good at maths, don't worry about it', this can inhibit them from persevering and learning new things. Rather, encourage them to think about what they learnt from not doing well, what the next steps could be and what they could do differently next time.

- **Model a growth mindset and share examples from your own life.** As most parents know, children are like sponges, picking up the behaviours and attitudes of the adults in their life – namely their parents. By modelling an attitude of growth and an ability to learn, parents can set a positive example for their children. Sharing stories or examples of growth and overcoming challenges can also be an effective way for parents to show their children that they aren't alone in making mistakes or approaching a task or obstacle in a certain way.

Our research shows that Generation Alpha are more teachable than previous generations, as measured by the degree to which they see failure as a learning opportunity, are not afraid to take on harder tasks beyond their capacity and take constructive feedback more openly.[22] We're aware that they will be the most materially endowed, formally educated, longest-living generation – but what will their contribution be? To whom much is given, much is required, or as Peter Parker, aka Spiderman, puts it, 'With great power comes great responsibility.' This is the sense that we have around Generation Alpha – they have been set up with great opportunities in life to propel them into their future. In this privileged position, there is an expectation that they will each make a contribution to society at large. This isn't necessarily about hyper success, but making a contribution, achieving some goals and leading a life where they're an example to others. It's exciting to imagine the potential future for Generation Alpha.

Environmental consciousness

In our research, the theme of Generation Alpha being an environmentally conscious generation came up numerous times. We know that for Generation Z (Generation Alpha's older siblings) this is a key issue of concern. Many people began paying attention in 2018 when fifteen-year-old Greta Thunberg from Sweden began protesting outside the Swedish Parliament in place of going to school. Her small display of personal conviction had a ripple effect and ignited a global youth climate movement. In 2019 she was recognised as *Time*'s 2019 Person of the Year and was the 2019 International Children's Peace Prize Winner.

According to Amnesty International's survey of more than 10,000 people aged between eighteen and twenty-five, Gen Z rank climate change as the most important issue of our time, followed by pollution and terrorism.[23] This is the generation that Generation Alpha are looking up to, and they have formed movements and organisations that encourage people to take action. These kids care. When asked about why younger generations are having such impacts, twenty-two-year-old Steph told us, 'Our generation is living in a world that is more interconnected than ever. With our online communities, we share the realities of climate change at home and can see the reality of it further abroad. Seeing and sharing these realities motivates us to take action and think about what we can do to ensure a better planet for the future. The resources and education we have at our fingertips gives us a voice as a generation of activists, developing campaigns, initiatives and putting pressure on our governments to do more.'

Generation Alpha are being influenced by their environmentally conscious older Gen Z counterparts, and both emerging generations are using their voice to speak up on broader social issues – even at home. According to a survey we conducted of parents, 80 per cent said their child/ren have

A name given to a new generation, like a name given to a new baby, is part of their identity but it is not who they are. What is more important than the name we are given is the name we make for ourselves.

influenced their actions or consumption decisions, making them more environmentally aware.[24]

In addition to the influence of Gen Z on their concern for the environment, the products, toys, shows and entertainment that Generation Alpha engage with are also increasingly focusing on environmental issues, which is also having an impact on them.

Monica Dreger, Head of Global Consumer Insights at Mattel, one of the world's leading toy and children's entertainment manufacturers, believes one of the greatest strengths of Generation Alpha is that they have the belief and action to effect change. She told us that she is seeing kids as young as seven or eight talking about environmental issues and what they can personally do, which she has never seen in a generation before. She said, 'Even though they didn't create this mess, they are still taking ownership of these issues that they wouldn't have in the past. Activism is part of their mentality of being able to do something about it, even something small. In my family, my kids are plant-based eaters, because they want to do their share for the environment. They would be mortified right now seeing me with a Starbucks cup, because it's not reusable! We are not allowed to do that anymore in our house and that is something that is really guided by the Generation Alphas.' The challenge for Generation Alpha in a post-COVID-19 world will be living with hygiene protocols requiring single use and disposability, amid environmental concerns and a desire for reusability.

We have put together an infographic (see the next page) that shows how each generation is shaped by unique social markers, iconic cars, toys, music devices, leadership styles and even screen content.

GENERATION ALPHA

Generation	Iconic toys	Music devices	Leadership styles	Screen content
BUILDERS 1925-1945	Roller skates	Record player LP, 1948	Controlling	Cinema
BABY BOOMERS 1946-1964	Frisbee	Audio cassette 1962	Directing	TV
GENERATION X 1965-1979	Rubik's cube	Walkman 1979	Coordinating	VCR
GENERATION Y 1980-1994	BMX bike	iPod 2001	Guiding	Internet
GENERATION Z 1995-2009	Folding scooter	Spotify 2008	Empowering	Device
GENERATION α 2010-2024	Fidget spinner	Smart speakers Now	Inspiring	Streaming

Parenting styles

Now that we have a better understanding of the different generations we can look at how parenting styles have changed over time. The significant people shaping a child's life – their parents, grandparents, aunties, uncles, friends and teachers – can belong to different generation. By understanding the transitions of parenting styles, we gain a better understanding of Generation Alpha.

Those tasked with the incredibly important job of parenting today's children are likely to be those of generations X and Y. They are parenting their children (Gen Z and Gen Alpha) in different ways to how they themselves were parented. Parents of today have, in general, departed from a 'one size fits all' approach to parenting. Along with changing gender roles, we have seen changes in the expectations of mums and dads in their parental responsibilities. While most Baby Boomers were shaped in households where fewer mums worked outside the home, today the majority of the parents of Generation Alpha are two-income earning. Along with the massive increase in the proportion of mums working full-time, expectations towards fathers have also changed, as many have become more actively involved in childrearing. From attendance at parent–teacher nights and class concerts to the school drop-off, pick-up, and taking parental leave, it's the dads of Generation Alpha, not just the mums, who are stepping up.

The increase in news coverage of issues around child harm and abuse have led to an increased focus on safety, with the introduction of home surveillance and 'helicopter' parenting. And beyond safety, there's the trend known as Tiger parenting, where parents drive the academic success of their children through an authoritarian approach. Tiger parents put their children in top-performing schools and pay for after-school tuition to ensure their kids are given every opportunity to get high grades, which will then lead to acceptance into a high-ranking university and a prestigious profession.

Parenting styles

Though there are different parenting trends, from our analysis we have found four different styles of parenting, mapped across two key areas – the degree to which love is expressed and care demonstrated, as well as boundaries defined and behavioural support offered.

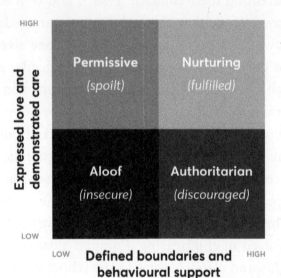

Permissive – The permissive parenting style comes from an environment where there is expressed love and demonstrated care and affection, but there are few, if any, defined boundaries. There is also no culture of discipline or attempts to modify children's behaviour. This style invariably leads to children that in the past would be described as 'spoilt' and are today labelled 'entitled' and 'undisciplined'.

Authoritarian – This parenting style is the opposite to the permissive approach. While authoritarian parents have clearly defined boundaries for their household and compliance is expected, there is a lack of expressed love, affection and care. The result is that children can be discouraged and unconvinced of their parents' love.

Aloof – The aloof parents are low in each of the key areas. There are few, if any, boundaries or behavioural expectations and nor is there a family culture of love and affection. Children are likely to become insecure because of the lack of expectations around appropriate behaviour and the absence of expressed parental love.

Nurturing – The ideal parenting style is high in both key areas. We call this the nurturing parent. These parents are clear on behavioural expectations, and their children develop self-discipline from being brought up with an understanding of boundaries and the consequences of breaching them. All of this takes place in a relationship where love and affection is repeatedly expressed and demonstrated, and the value of the child and the care the parents have for them is continually evident. This parenting style creates fulfilled children.

Societal trends are not so much a road down which we travel ever further, but rather a pendulum, which swings to an extreme before correcting back again.

Every generation has a mix of parenting styles, but traditionally, parents of the Baby Boomers tended to use a more authoritarian style. Then we saw the pendulum swing the other way to the permissive approach for parents of Gen Y. What we see emerging today is a more balanced approach, where both mums and dads show love and affection for their children – both verbally and physically. At the same time, parents recognise the benefit of raising children who understand boundaries, are emotionally equipped to make wise choices and are aware of the consequences of breaching boundaries and exhibiting poor behaviour. Today, children are asked to contribute to household tasks rather than just being told to do chores. Consequences for poor behaviour are discussed, with children taking ownership for their outcomes, rather than simply being 'given a punishment'. High standards and appropriate behaviour are expected now, as in the past, but a culture of discipline is shaped very differently to prior eras.

Generation Y, who will comprise the greatest number of parents of Generation Alpha, are parenting in different ways to those in the past. Having been shaped in their twenties by technology, this generation of parents are turning to the internet, not just family or friends, for parenting advice. As a result, they know more about child development than ever before – which, as many parents know, can be both empowering and overwhelming. This new generation of parents are documenting their kids' lives on social media, along with their family activities and parenting philosophies. Gen Y fathers are more likely to take on housework and childcare than in the past – even though women are still doing most of it.

Generation Y parents are well positioned to raise children who are empathetic, holistic and have a well-rounded understanding of the global and diverse society they live in. Their children are more often viewed as little people to be understood and guided rather than 'blank slates' to be prescribed and directed. As Emma, a Gen Y new mum, told us, 'I'm excited to keep discovering more about my son Caleb and what he is interested in and passionate about, his skills and talents, his sense of humour and idiosyncrasies. And I'm excited to watch him discover those things about himself. His whole life is ahead of him and it's full of potential.'

Baby naming traditions and trends

An important (and early) part of the parenting journey is choosing a name for your child. Parents of Generation Alpha have more access to information than at any other time in history, and are inundated with options, research and meaning when it comes to deciding on a name. Prior to the baby-name books of the 1980s, baby names were influenced by family and religious traditions. In recent years, the internet has facilitated an explosion of blogs, websites and even baby-naming apps. There are not only baby-name lists but baby-name search engines. It has never been easier to search the history of a prospective name and suitable sibling name options, assess its popularity, and get feedback on the opinions of others.

The average first-time parents of today were born in the early 1990s. These parents are likely to have grown up with several classmates named Matthew, Chris, Sarah and Jessica. In today's digitally connected world a name is more than what a teacher calls you. A name is now a social media handle, personal brand and possible web domain. For parents of Generation Alpha there is a trend to select a less common name, with names for this generation considered digital real estate in an increasingly global era. But this name will need to carry the child through a lifetime of multiple careers and jobs. That is why we see a more varied list of the most popular baby names and names that are more traditional than trendy. The top girls' names in Australia are Charlotte, Olivia and Amelia and the boys' names are Oliver, Noah and Jack.[25]

Key takeaways

In this chapter we have painted a picture of the different generations and shown how people born in a similar period display characteristics arising from shared experiences that lead to similar perspectives, and even parenting styles. We have examined both the present day and the past by looking at the characteristics of the generations shaping Generation Alpha. We've looked at parents (who are older), cultural mix (more diverse), socio-economic factors (slightly wealthier), family size (smaller) and life expectancy (longer). By looking at these characteristics we can understand the context in which Generation Alpha are being shaped and in turn predict much about their future. Then there is the research about the people most likely to be their parents, Generation Y, which gives us a sense of how they will be raised. The parents of Generation Alpha are moving homes and changing careers more frequently, are more materially endowed, more technologically supplied and are outsourcing aspects of parenting such as childcare, birthday parties and even meal provision.

In the pages ahead we will be uncovering the trends, technologies and characteristics that are shaping Generation Alpha and that will, in turn, define them. We will unpack the future of education, what work will be like, what will differ in their shopping experience and, of course, we'll look at keys to parenting this emerging generation. Our hope is that you'll not only be informed but feel equipped and inspired to play your part in leading Generation Alpha into a new and exciting world.

CHAPTER 2

Generation Alpha Defined

'Youth today love luxury. They have bad
manners, contempt for authority,
no respect for older people and talk nonsense
when they should be working.
They contradict their parents, talk too much
in company, guzzle their food,
lay their legs on the table and tyrannise their elders.'

How do you feel about this quote? Do you agree with it – or even parts of it? As many readers know, parenting is a tough gig! The lack of sleep, downtime and energy can quite easily create friction in our already busy lives. Children are, as this quote suggests, a lot to handle.

This quote could certainly be the sentiment of someone describing today's younger generation, but in actual fact it's attributed to Socrates, the classical Greek philosopher who lived around 470–399 BC, complaining about the youth of Athens. It's quite telling that so many of us can relate to a quote said over two thousand years ago.

In this chapter we explore the distinguishing characteristics of this new digital, social, global, mobile and visual generation. We also take a look at the timeless needs of human interaction and belonging, and share what kind of outlook we can expect for their future.

As the quote at the beginning of this chapter depicts, young people today often receive a bad rap from those who have gone before, yet the intergenerational divide is not a new phenomenon. As we can see from Socrates, the challenge of intergenerational harmony has been around for centuries. George Orwell, born in 1903, noted this too. He was quoted as saying, 'Every generation imagines itself to be more intelligent than the one that went before it, and wiser than the one that comes after it.' But negative stereotyping and generalising (or generationalising as we often call it) without evidence, without justified reasoning, can be a barrier to building the authentic intergenerational relationships we need for a flourishing society.

There are myriad ways for generations to work together towards a positive end. They could collaborate in the workplace to make use of the different strengths each generation brings, or people of different ages might share stories over coffee about how much life has changed over time. The benefits of the generations mixing are enormous both on a personal level and on a wider, societal level. When our perspective becomes more diverse, we can communicate better with those in our family, our workplace, our clients and our customers who might be of a different age to us.

'My son had a problem in his first two weeks of school. A couple of the kids were giving him a hard time – taking his hat and hiding it – which is kind of mean-spirited, and it was an issue for Jack. When it was brought to my attention, I was worried, but he wouldn't talk to me about it. Instead, he was going to his grandmother. Usually, my son is full of questions, he's like, "I have got a million and seven questions, and I'm going to ask you all of them even before you answered the last one. And I'm going to ask you the new one in the middle of your explanation!" But instead of me, he was going to his grandmother – my husband's mother, and telling her about what was happening to him at school. Of course, it kind of hurt my feelings, but I was just glad he had somebody to go to that's not just me and his teachers. He had an extended family.' – *a mother of a Generation Alpha*

Over the next decade, understanding and engaging with Generation Alpha will be essential for organisations, not only for their relevance but for their very existence.

Shaped by change

As social researchers, we spend a lot of time looking back at the previous generations in order to learn from the past. We study human behaviour. From focus groups and interviews to surveys, we gather data that tells a fascinating story of our communities and the world Generation Alpha are being shaped in – a world that is swiftly changing. Do you feel that sense of change too? Generally, there are incremental societal and technological shifts – such as improvements to iPhones and advancement of wireless and Bluetooth technologies, but then there are moments in time where there is forced change.

It is rare in history for massive demographic shifts, rapid social change, generational transitions and technological advancement to combine and result in an altered society. Yet, today, we are living amid one such transformation and on top of that we, as a world, have experienced forced change. The COVID-19 global pandemic has had a monumental impact on society and affected schooling, work and the way we interact with one another. Governments responded in unprecedented ways, introducing preventative measures such as social distancing and travel bans – the likes of which haven't been seen since the world wars. Various industries played their part, too, with banks freezing mortgages and providing interest-free loans with the support of the government, and communications companies increasing internet capacity to facilitate the workforce relocating to work from home and increased video conferencing and entertainment streaming. In our research of Australians during the pandemic, we found that 84 per cent believe the pandemic will play a significant role in shaping the children of today.[26] The good news story is that although it has been a trying time, it has also told of humanity's adaptability and resilience. We will explore these ramifications for Generation Alpha further in the book.

Five characteristics of Generation Alpha

'Phones off! Remember – no phones at the table!' This is a common instruction from parents, particularly when families come together around the dining table. 'Oh, she's glued to her device, I actually bribe her with money to put her phone down!' said Ruby, a mother of a Generation Alpha child. 'But this is how she connects with her friends and how she has fun, which I don't mind … it's just that she's on it all the time.' If we ask around our friends and family, we might come to a similar conclusion: that the young people of the world are dependent on their devices – on phones, laptops and iPads. The defining characteristics of Generation Alpha are very reflective of the world they have been shaped in.

Defining characteristics of Generation Alpha:

Digital
Social
Global
Mobile
Visual

Digital

'I love playing sport and playing games on my phone. I like Roblox, Chicken Scream and TikTok.' – *Trinity, aged nine*

'I would call them "Gen T" for "Generation Technology", because they are growing up with technology that previous generations didn't.' – *a mother of a Generation Alpha*

'We came into technology. They're faced with it from birth.' – *a parent of a Generation Alpha*

'Managing their screen time is a constant battle.' – *a parent of two Generation Alphas*

One of the generational labels used to describe Generation Alpha is that they are 'digital natives' – for these devices and technologies have been a part of their life since their birth, affecting how they see, engage and interact with the world. With that in mind, it would be reasonable to say that one of the defining characteristics of Generation Alpha is that they are digital.

Many of us will have seen firsthand the different approach of Generation Alpha to technology. While Gen Z children probably didn't receive their first digital devices until their late primary school years, and the device was most likely for school, Generation Alpha children have typically had access to a device from their youngest years. From asking questions of the smart speaker like, 'Hey Google, what time will the sun rise tomorrow?' to watching YouTube videos of teens playing Fortnite, Generation Alpha are true digital integrators.

From our research we have observed a significant increase in app-based play and screen time among children, leading to shorter attention spans, greater digital literacy and less traditional social formation among the emerging generations. Unintentionally, Generation Alpha have been thrown into a global experiment where screens are placed in front of children as pacifiers from the youngest age. We're sure those of us with children or those of us babysitting nieces and nephews have been guilty of that on occasion! But these devices are more than pacifiers, they are tools for both entertainment and education.

In the United States, it was recently reported that children aged eight to twelve years old (tweens) consume, on average, four hours and forty-four minutes of screen time per day for entertainment purposes. This increases to an average of seven hours and twenty-two minutes for those aged thirteen to eighteen.[27] Such is their multi-screening behaviour that this is expected to increase for Generation Alpha who will only ever know a world of devices, social media and streaming services. The World Health Organisation recommends a maximum of one hour of screen time per day for children under five,[28] yet in Australia, four- to five-year-olds average more than two hours daily.[29]

World Health Organisation recommended daily screen time for children under five	Average daily time spent on screens by children aged four to five
Maximum of one hour	More than two hours

Generation Alpha are the first generation of children to be shaped in an era of portable digital devices. As such, the new challenges for parents of Generation Alpha centre on watching out for screen addiction, cyberbullying and inappropriate content. While parents of Generation Alpha have some unique challenges, it is encouraging to remember that the Gen Y parents of today have themselves been shaped in the digital world, so are better equipped to manage these complexities, unlike their parents. It is also important for parents to remember that, despite seemingly overt differences, some basic dynamics between parents and children are timeless.

'I think it's better that there is so much more information at our fingertips,' said Jennifer, a mother of a nine-year-old. 'I help my son with science projects and the amount of information is extraordinary. You can educate yourself on anything very quickly, and that's amazing. We didn't have that level of information at our fingertips when I was a kid. You had to go to the library, dig through books and ask the librarian for help. But the drawback, I would say, is the loss of physical and social interaction.' This is something that we've heard frequently through focus groups with parents of Generation Alpha. Though the digital world provides them with many positive opportunities, there is an awareness of the negative consequences of too much technology time – social isolationism and a deficiency in relational and life skills are evident among the next generation. They have access to more information and formal education, but in turn may be less proficient in practical skills. And though they are globally connected through their devices, they appear less socially engaged. 'Being social and being with other kids and making friends, back in my day, it was no effort. Technology was a luxury,' says Dinusha, the mother of a six-year-old. 'Now it's the other way around. It's no effort at all to get on technology and become proficient in it, but it's almost as if socialisation is the luxury – one that requires a lot of effort.'

Social

'My son never ate cereal, he didn't like it. But because Ryan from the YouTube site Ryan's World ate it, my son wants to eat cereal!' – *Cassie, a mother of a seven-year-old*

'If my child didn't have a social media account she would be bullied at school.' – *a mother of a Generation Alpha*

It's interesting to note that although in-person social interaction may be an area that we need to work on as we parent and nurture Generation Alpha, today's youth are – more than any other generation – extensively socially connected to, and shaped by, their peers. Due to social media platforms such as Instagram, Snapchat, TikTok and YouTube, young people are influenced by a network that is connected 24/7 across social, geographic and demographic boundaries. This is why, from our research, we see 'social' as being the second characteristic of Generation Alpha. This social world augments close friends and family with social media influencers as the primary sources of recommendation, information and opinion. Of course, there is a downside to this type of hyper-connected social life. In a survey we analysed of school students, a quarter of those who said they had experienced bullying at school had experienced it via social media, text messages or

When we look back
over the long arc of
history, there are eras in
which society altogether
changed. We give them
names: the reformation,
the enlightenment, the
industrial revolution,
postmodernity, and now
in the era of Generation
Alpha, this digital
transformation.

emails.[30] In response, the trend of wellbeing has been steadily increasing over the last few years, particularly in school and in the workplace. We will explore this topic further in Chapter 3.

Global

> 'I want to go to Amsterdam, but they speak a different language there, and I only know how to speak Australian, a bit of Chinese and French. I know the ones I just said but I don't know the Amsterdam one.' – *Jayden, aged nine*

The world has opened up in a dramatic fashion over the last few decades, which has led to Generation Alpha being the first generation to be truly global. A clear demonstration of this can be seen in the different words of the year announced by the Oxford English Dictionaries and the Collins Dictionary to best summarise the global trends and changes experienced in that year.

In Generation Alpha's lifetime, the words of the year have been:

2011 – App
2012 – Cloud
2013 – Hashtag
2014 – Selfie
2015 – Face with tears of joy (not even a word)
2016 – Post-truth
2017 – Fake news
2018 – Toxic
2019 – Climate emergency
2020 – COVID-19, lockdown, social distancing, iso, Black Lives Matter, cancel culture, superspreader … take your pick!

> These words of the year not only highlight the significant trends that occurred in the early years of Generation Alpha's life, but the global nature of the trends that affected their lives.

Due to the 'social' and 'digital' characteristics of this generation, Generation Alpha are more aware of what is going on in the world than ever before. This is in large part due to the influence of movies, music, celebrities and influencers, which have a reach far wider than in the previous generations. Trends make their way around the world quicker than ever before – and influence the trending fashion, food, online entertainment, social trends, communication and viral YouTube videos and memes.

One such global trend that took the world by storm was Pokémon Go. Initially released in 2016, the aim of the game was to find different Pokémon characters outside. The user looks at a map on their screen, it shows where the nearest character is, and then the player seeks it out to 'catch' it. It is augmented reality (real-world environments interacting with computer-generated characters) in action. So, for a short while people were literally running around the streets, heads down, as they hunted for Pokémon – grown men included! Cafés even had to put up signs to say 'Pokémon are for paying customers' as the game took the player to all different locations 'to catch 'em all'. It was a very clever idea to bring the essence and nostalgia of Gen Y playing with physical Pokémon cards, in the 1990s, into the twenty-first century and to a new generation. Another interesting thing about this viral phenomenon, which clearly illustrates the nature of the global and digital world in which Generation Alpha is living in, is that it grew to 50 million users in just nineteen days![31]

This is compared to television, which took twenty-two years, the internet, which took seven years and Facebook, which took three years to reach 50 million users.[32] By 2019, Pokémon Go had over a billion downloads.[33] No matter where Generation Alpha live geographically, they are influenced by the same things as their peers who live on the other side of the world. In this wireless world their technology knows no boundaries; nor do their blogs, friendships or vocabulary. But it's not just technology that's global. It's also events.

Australian bushfires go global

From September 2019 to February 2020, Australians watched as fires blazed across the southern half of Australia, following the driest period on record experienced from January to August. On New Year's Eve, a fire encircled the seaside town of Mallacoota on the Victorian and New South Wales border – the smoke so dense it turned the day to night, as four thousand people became trapped on the beach.

The fires made international news and even affected our neighbouring country of New Zealand. Australia's bushfires turned the sky orange in Auckland, and glaciers in the South Island were tainted grey/brown by the ash. In fact, the plumes of smoke were so dense that they could be seen from space.

Hollywood celebrities brought broader global attention to the fires through their social media feeds and in comments made during Golden Globe Award speeches. Then, later in the month, when the world's sporting focus was on the Australian Open in Melbourne, the poor air quality (which for the first time ever was rated as the worst in the world) as a result of the ongoing fires and smoke put the tennis into jeopardy.

One of the biggest impacts of the fires was on Australia's flora and fauna. According to estimates from the University of Sydney,[34] over one billion mammals, birds and reptiles lost their lives. Though images of fire-scorched land dominated the media, the striking images of rescued burnt koalas captivated the attention of people around the world. Monica, the mother of a six-year-old living in California, reflected on the impact these images had on her daughter: 'She watched the news here in the US and wanted to save the animals. She saw that there was a koala fund and we had to donate to them. I asked her about giving to the people affected and she replied, "The people will find a way, but we are able to help the koalas." So, she used her allowance money to adopt a koala. And now she feels like she has her own pet koala that lives seven thousand miles away, in Australia.'

This is simply one instance of the way in which a Generation Alpha child was inspired to play her part in a global response – more evidence that Generation Alpha are not only being brought up in a global era, but are behaving in a global way too.

When the only screen in the house was a television, parents could more easily monitor what their children watched. Even as the internet emerged, family computers were placed in visible sight in the house, again allowing parental oversight. Even as WiFi emerged, modems came with an off button and parents had control of internet usage. For this new digital generation, however, with ubiquitous access to portable online devices, parents are finding it hard to shield children from the wider world.

Mobile

'Because there's so many opportunities, I have no idea
what he'll end up doing for a career. He probably won't
work full-time, more part-time or casual, because there's
more flexibility and opportunities.' – *a mother raising a
Generation Alpha son*

The fourth characteristic we use to describe Generation Alpha
is 'mobile'. This generation will be more mobile in many areas
of their life, from where, when and how they will work to how
they will study, travel and live.

Today the average length of staying in one working role has
shortened to just under three years.[35] The gig economy (where
organisations utilise temporary, independent workers for short-
term contracts) plays a part in this, but so too does the changing
nature of the future of work. The World Economic Forum
predicts that 65 per cent of Generation Alphas entering primary
school today will end up working in entirely new job types
that don't yet exist.[36] Even today, students are learning skills
in robotics, coding, social media marketing, app development
and big data analytics to prepare them for these futuristic jobs,
which they will have more of across their lifetime.

Visual

'You ask kids what they want to be and they all say
YouTubers. They like watching other people play games,
it's really weird.' – *a mother of Generation Alpha kids*

'Kids today love watching YouTube and video games. They
are just watching, not reading.' – *school teacher*

The fifth and final stand-out characteristic of Generation Alpha is that they are a visual generation. In our opinion, every generation is visual, which can be seen in the timeless love of stories. Stories are inherently visual because the descriptions conjure images in our mind's eye. Yet for Generation Alpha, stories and games have come to life in new ways, facilitated by technology and the visual apps, videos and content that they regularly engage with. This visual world has changed how Generation Alpha expect to consume information. YouTube is the second most popular search engine on the internet (after Google), but for Generation Alpha it's number one. Because why would they read something when they can watch it? Though Google has 3.5 billion searches per day, YouTube has almost five billion streams every day!

One of the most popular YouTube channels for children today is Ryan's World. With well over 24 million subscribers and over 35 billion views of his channel's content, Ryan is one of the world's leading toy reviewers. Ryan the boy is nine years old. His YouTube channel started in 2015 when Ryan was just three years old. His parents took videos of him opening his new toys and then he gave his review to camera. Ryan used to watch similar YouTube channels to the one he has today, and one day asked, 'How come I'm not on YouTube when all the other kids are?' His mother, Loann Kaji, resigned from her job as a high school chemistry teacher to build and develop the YouTube channel full-time.[37] The channel is described by Verge as 'a mash-up of personal vlog and "unboxing" video, a blend of innocent childhood antics and relentless, often overwhelming consumerism.'[38] The success of Ryan's toy reviewing channel led to the establishment of Sunlight Entertainment. The company employs a team of 30 people who help to produce around 25 videos each week! Ryan's

World has grown from a video of Ryan interacting with toys, to a global brand that entertains kids all over the world.[39] It's extraordinary to see how a simple video idea has turned into an empire. Ryan's World is a favourable alternative for the visually minded Generation Alphas than a toy expert writing up their thoughts and experiences for a parent to read and make an informed purchase. It shows how we have moved into an era of peers showing and telling online.

Generation Alpha and COVID-19

> *The age at which we're exposed to a transformative event determines how embedded it will be in our psyche.*

When COVID-19 first rocked our world in early 2020, there were immediate significant changes to Generation Alpha's lives. These included being confined to their homes and not being able to visit friends, play in the park, go to school or see grandparents or family who lived outside of their home.

> How COVID-19 changed life for Generation Alpha, in their own words:
> - 'If I had a magic wand, I would use it to get rid of the diseases and viruses around the world, so that people can live happily and have a lot of fun again.'
>   – *nine-year-old girl*
> - 'I wish there was a way to play sports with my friends without worrying that we will get each other sick.'
>   – *ten-year-old boy*
> - 'We FaceTime a lot more now and play Animal Crossing or Roblox. We play and talk about it.' – *eight-year-old girl*

- 'Our new dog Anson kept me happy. I didn't mind being stuck at home so much then.' – *eight-year-old boy*
- 'Sometimes we FaceTime to play Animal Crossing and we sometimes have a movie night and set up that on FaceTime too.' – *ten-year-old girl*
- 'I often help my mum with landscaping outside and do more chores around the house since we are all at home more.' – *ten-year-old boy*[40]

Throughout history, we see transformation take place when an enabler is leveraged by a catalyst. What do we mean by this? Well, take the work-from-home and online learning transformation experienced in 2020. The enabler (digital technology), which allowed remote working and learning, had been with us for some time. Only when this enabler was provided with the catalyst for change (COVID-19 and the resulting lockdowns) did we see the almost-overnight transition, and the biggest change to work occur in a century.

As a result of COVID-19, Australians expect to see the following changes shape their future:

- technology and screens to become more integrated in their lives (90 per cent)
- more flexible working conditions (86 per cent)
- education delivered online (82 per cent)
- more resilient children (78 per cent)
- children will feel more reserved about face-to-face interaction (69 per cent)
- negative impacts on mental health (65 per cent)
- increased desire to travel and explore the world because of the current limitations (62 per cent)[41]

Generation Alpha have become the COVID-19 generation, not in terms of virus impacts but in the resulting economic, social, educational and psychological impacts for their future.

Some of the longer-term impacts on Generation Alpha that we can expect to see from COVID-19 include:

- They will be a more creative and resilient generation due to the challenges they experienced, and will want to keep the new hobbies and way of living they adopted during COVID-19 (like board games and cooking) in the future.
- Technology will remain integrated into their life, but they will also value time away from screens.
- They will appreciate the things that were lost – interpersonal relationships and going to school.
- They will value family time more, as it has become an expected and regular part of their life.
- Working and learning from home will become a regular part of their future.
- There will be a shift in who they define as aspirational in the future, from traditional superheroes to everyday superheroes like medical researchers and nurses.
- They will connect more with regional areas as work from home opens up opportunities to live outside of capital cities.

Timeless needs

While Generation Alpha are being shaped in different times and connect with the world around them in different ways to previous generations, we must also remember that anyone from any generation is a human first. Generation Alpha have the same intrinsic human needs we all have: to be accepted, to belong and to be part of a community. These are timeless yearnings, true of people in any place across any era, and, if anything, these needs are more deeply expressed by those in their formative years, even if subconsciously.

'Dear God, I bet it is very hard for you to love all of everybody in the whole world. There are only four people in our family, and I can never do it.' – *Timmy, aged seven*

Remembering these timeless needs of Generation Alpha will help leaders, parents, friends, aunties, uncles and anyone who has the privilege of shaping the next generation to engage with them on an authentic level. As psychologist Carl R. Rogers wrote, 'What is most personal is most universal.'[42]

Their future is bright

Generation Alpha are growing up in a time of increasing complexity and greater uncertainty, with greater societal anxiety and economic and social volatility. They will face an array of problems, from environmental issues to the fragmentation of once united nations – the likes of which the world has never faced before. So it might be a surprise to some that we believe the outlook for Generation Alpha is positive.

We have the opportunity to regularly speak to young people and we find, with audiences of children, that there is no other time in which they would rather be alive than this one, and there is no other age than which they would rather be in than this era of opportunity, being young, with all of their future ahead of them.

There are many aspects of their world, their era and their opportunities that are unprecedented in all human history.

Generation Alpha will be given more consumer choice, which will enable them to purchase in accordance with their values. It is likely they will experience greater gender equality and fewer gender pay discrepancies than we do now. Many will never sit a written exam, use cash, vote in a traditional polling booth or own a car in a world where transport, like entertainment, is a service.

Research also suggests that parents believe Generation Alpha will turn out well. Parents of children aged 0–12 believe they will be more tech-savvy (65 per cent), more caring about the environment (59 per cent), more curious about the world (55 per cent), more intelligent (54 per cent) and more creative (53 per cent) than previous generations.[43] In our interviews with parents and leaders, many also said that they believe Generation Alpha are more empathetic than previous generations.

'I think Generation Alpha will be more informed, open and accepting.' – *Megan, a mother of Generation Alphas*

'I think they do have more empathy. My daughter saw an ad for Oxfam and said, "That little boy has got no clothes," and I said, "Yeah and he's got no toys and nowhere to live," and she said, "Well, where does he plug in his iPad?" And I said, "He doesn't have an iPad," So I guess they are exposed to these things more and develop compassion.' – *Christina, a mother of Generation Alphas*

Being shaped in a world that is increasingly diverse and globally connected, Generation Alpha are growing up with different perspectives and a greater diversity of opinion than any other generation before them. This diversity is also being intentionally represented in many stories, books and TV shows targeting Generation Alpha. One example is the critically acclaimed book by Charlie Mackesy titled *The Boy, The Mole, The Fox and The Horse*.[44] Containing a series of quiet musings and conversations between the boy and the animals, it contains many lessons and examples of friendship and empathy, including a much-loved quote by a boy who was asked what he wanted to be when he grew up. 'Kind,' he answered.

And, if your Generation Alpha doesn't display empathy all the time, it's not a cause for too much concern, as they are still young and learning! We heard the father of a three-year-old say recently that his son's world is a two-metre sphere with him at the centre of it, and it travels with him wherever he goes.

Growing in empathy is part of the social and emotional development of children. They can, indeed must, have it modelled and taught. In simple terms, empathy is the ability to walk in someone else's shoes. The three key characteristics of empathy are:

1. That children are able to understand and value the uniqueness and difference of others.
2. That they can identify different emotions and be equipped to name them.
3. That they are able to regulate their own emotional responses and positively respond to the emotions of others.

There are some things parents and caregivers can do to help children develop empathy, including talking about and naming feelings, caring for others (including animals) and demonstrating empathy for them.

As we look to the future and the decade ahead, to best serve this next generation it's important to take the time to understand and engage with them. We've got to connect and communicate in ways that speak their language. What worked for Gen Y may not work for Generation Alpha, and what was effective in a leadership style in the twentieth century may be less effective in the twenty-first. Generation Alpha need to be equipped with the skills and the competencies that will enable them to thrive in this era of change. How we equip this generation will be different to how it has been done in the past.

People skills, not just technical skills, will be important for this generation to work, lead and thrive in increasingly diverse contexts. As we often advise, it is desirable that leaders bring intelligence to their roles, but it is essential that they exercise empathy. Leaders of head and heart are best placed to innovate amid disruption and engage across diversity.

Generation Alpha are being taught the importance of empathy from a young age. The 2017 release of the movie *Wonder* kicked off the #choosekind movement. The movie, based on the book of the same name, centres around Auggie Pullman, a ten-year-old boy who was born with a rare facial deformity. It tracks his heartbreaking troubles with peers as well as his friendships with the kind-hearted and empathetic. The message is well summed up by a quote from Dr Wayne Dyer, which features in the book and movie: 'When given the choice between being right and being kind, choose kind.'[45]

Generation Alpha don't need the same authority structures, hierarchies or traditional power approaches as previous generations because we're in more collaborative times.

'This is my second year teaching full-time. I think the relationship you get with kids is priceless. To have an impact on them and be a positive role model is a great honour. I love the learning experience and I love seeing kids change over the year. I find it really rewarding. To see kids jumping reading levels and forming relationships with them, and they come up and say hi. That's a privilege that I wouldn't want to give up.' – *Georgie, a primary school teacher*

Key takeaways

Generation Alpha are being shaped in different times to generations past. In this chapter we have explored how this generation are more digital, social, global, mobile and visual then any generation before them. While these defining characteristics may pose some challenges for how they engage with the world around them, ultimately we believe their future is bright. Understanding these characteristics is an important part of leading and parenting them across the different spheres of their life, which we will explore further in the chapters to come.

CHAPTER 3

The Wellbeing Generation

'Wellbeing is more than positive physical and mental
health. When our life has meaningful activity, when
we have authentic social connections, are aligned to a
purpose and when we make a recognised contribution,
we have a greater ability to flourish – and this is wellbeing.'

*Work Wellbeing: Leading Thriving Teams in
Rapidly Changing Times*[46]

There's no doubt that use of the term 'wellbeing' and discussion about the subject has increased in the twenty-first century. The common definition of wellbeing is 'the state of being comfortable, healthy or happy'. Today, people place real focus on wellbeing, and it's not hard to figure out why.

In this chapter we explore how wellbeing looks for Generation Alpha, their physical and mental health, the importance of sleep, as well as the challenges of bullying, online safety, pressure to achieve success, isolation and loneliness, and how we can cultivate resilience in children.

The rise of wellbeing

The World Health Organisation defines wellbeing as a 'state of complete physical, mental and social wellbeing and not merely the absence of disease or infirmity'.[47] It can also be defined as 'a complex combination of a person's physical, mental, emotional and social health factors. Wellbeing is strongly linked to happiness and life satisfaction. In short, wellbeing could be described as how you feel about yourself and your life.'[48]

Advancements in how we define wellbeing, how often we talk about it and the focus we give to it have seen a rise in strategies as to how we obtain wellbeing – or, at least, improve it. Meditation and mindfulness have gone mainstream, devices that help us track our steps are worn on our wrists and we're continually encouraged to be informed on what we feed our bodies.

When it comes to the emerging generations and their wellbeing, their top priorities reflect this focus on wellbeing. According to a Mission Australia Youth Survey, the three most highly valued items for teens today are friendships (82.5 per cent), family relationships (81.5 per cent) and school or study satisfaction (69 per cent). Around seven in ten respondents also placed a high value upon mental health (66.6 per cent) and physical health (65.6 per cent).[49] Not only is wellbeing a focus for young people themselves, but parents also want their children to be healthy, happy and fulfilled.

So, what are some of the most important factors that underpin Generation Alpha's wellbeing, and how can it be attained and preserved? Conversely, what are the greatest challenges this young generation will face in terms of mental and physical health, and how can educators and parents help them to overcome these challenges? We will look at these issues in more depth in the pages that follow, beginning with the key influences on a person's physical and mental health.

Physical health

The first and most well-known aspect of personal wellbeing is physical health. This includes physical activity, exercise, healthy eating, nutrition and one of the most overlooked but most important parts of physical health, sleep.

Children have been taught about the importance of physical health for years, with physical education taught in most schools across Australia. Physical health is important to overall wellbeing, not just to reduce the risk of disease and for the maintenance and care of our bodies for optimal functionality, but because it can have an impact on other aspects of wellbeing, like mental health.

It is widely acknowledged that Generation Alpha will face challenges when it comes to maintaining their physical health because of the shift over the last few decades from an industrial and manual labour economy to a knowledge economy. As a result of this shift, we are all living increasingly sedentary lifestyles, with greater inactivity and less time spent outside, all of which can have negative impacts on people's health and wellbeing. Throw screen-based devices into the mix and we have some real challenges to ensure Generation Alpha prioritise their physical health when they are young, and as they grow. So, let's explore areas of physical health that are important for parents and leaders to be aware of, and ways to help children to thrive in these areas.

Exercise and fitness

For many adults, exercise can seem difficult to fit into a full schedule and it is one of the first things we give up when life gets busy. In our survey of employed Australians, 49 per cent said they struggled to make physical health/fitness a priority, and 39 per cent said they always/often didn't get enough exercise.[50]

Most children, on the other hand, love to be active and play. In addition to setting good habits for the rest of their life, the immediate physiological benefits for children exercising include developing healthy bones, muscles, joints, hearts and lungs, as well as improving their coordination and strength, balance, posture and brain development. Regular exercise will also help them to maintain a healthy body weight. Additionally, there are other benefits to children exercising, like developing social skills, embracing teamwork, learning the reward of hard work and achievement and learning how to deal with disappointments or losses. There are also mental wellbeing benefits of spending time outdoors and in nature.

According to Australia's Physical Activity and Sedentary Behaviour Guidelines, children need the following amount of physical activity based on their age:

- Under 1 year of age: movement on the floor, including tummy time
- 1 to 5 years: light and fun physical activity throughout the day that amounts to at least three hours each day
- 5 to 12 years: at least one hour of moderate activity each day, which could include a variety of activities like incidental walking, playing, running, dancing or organised sports.[51]

While technology can inhibit exercise, it can also promote it. Devices and smart watches are being used by many parents to help their children track their daily steps and gamify activity through setting goals, measuring achievement and giving rewards. There has been a shift away from children's sport being about competition and success towards participation, physical movement and fun. Combined with this, parents are participating alongside their children in fitness activities. Examples of family-friendly exercise include the global phenomenon of Parkrun, and the rise of fun activity venues such as trampoline parks and rockclimbing centres.

Sleep

One of the most important and often overlooked parts of our physical health is sleep. After exercise and fitness, sleep is the second most likely aspect of our wellbeing to suffer, with two in five employed Australians (41 per cent) saying they struggle to make sleep a priority.[52] Sleep is essential for cognitive function, creativity and overall health and wellbeing, yet 39 per cent of workers say they always or often don't get enough sleep. Furthermore, only 34 per cent of workers are extremely or very satisfied with their sleep patterns. This makes sleep among the lowest ranked areas of life in terms of satisfaction.[53]

In his book *Why We Sleep: Unlocking the Power of Sleep and Dreams*,[54] Matthew Walker explains the findings of his years of research into sleep, and makes the case for why sleep is so important. Having good-quality sleep and the right amount affects our ability to relate to others, work well, be creative, have empathy, be physically fit and exercise self-control.

Sleep is important for human beings in general, but it is especially important for children and their growing minds and bodies. Although individuals can have slightly different sleep needs, children should be getting the following hours of sleep based on their age:

- 3 to 5 years: 10 to 13 hours
- 6 to 13 years: 9 to 11 hours
- 14 to 17 years: 8 to 10 hours

When children get enough sleep, it has a positive impact on their brain function, emotional wellbeing, physical health and their ability to function on a daily basis. Conversely, when children don't get enough sleep it can have a negative impact on these areas of their life, as well as negatively affect how they relate to others, their ability to learn and regulate their emotions, and can be a contributor to further behavioural problems.[55]

A recent study of ours showed that more than half (54 per cent) of Australians access their phones during the last three minutes before they go to bed at night.[56] This activity can negatively affect sleep due to the blue light exposure from the screen, which disrupts the body's release of melatonin – a hormone that influences circadian rhythms (the body's natural internal process that regulates the sleep/wake cycle).

As you might expect, younger generations are more likely than older generations to access their phones in the last three minutes before going to bed at night (82 per cent of Gen Z compared to 21 per cent of Baby Boomers) and in the first three minutes after waking up (75 per cent of Gen Z compared to 22 per cent of Baby Boomers).[57] As Steph, a 22-year-old, told us, 'I always fall asleep watching YouTube.' This confirms that technology is disrupting a crucial and important aspect of our lives and our wellbeing. (And is a good reminder that parents of young kids are doing it tough and should be extended a lot of grace for functioning on little to no sleep at times!)

Despite the negative influences, some children and their parents are now using technology to help their children get to sleep. The rise in long-play ASMR (autonomous sensory meridian response) soundtracks on YouTube, for example, or other 'white noise' sounds (storm recordings, rain or waterfall sounds) have gained a massive following, and for many people these recordings are their go-to sleep aids.

It is widely acknowledged that time spent on screens before bed can have a detrimental effect on children's and adolescents' sleep habits. This, in turn, can have a flow-on effect on their ability to learn and perform at school. A lack of sleep can also have negative effects on other areas of a child's life, including their likelihood to develop obesity, which can result in less social interaction and more time spent using screens.[58]

Ways to improve a child's sleep can include going to bed at the same time each night, creating a sleep-inducing bedroom environment that blocks out light and has an agreeable temperature, crafting a bedtime routine that involves winding down and switching technology off, monitoring caffeine intake, and finding time for daily exercise and sunlight exposure to normalise a child's circadian rhythm.[59]

Nutrition

Another aspect of physical health that is important for children is nutrition. A balanced, nutritious diet plays an important role in a child's growth and development. Eating a mix of the different food groups from a young age sets these habits for the long-term, and can help children avoid chronic diseases like heart disease and type 2 diabetes. A nutritious diet can also help to prevent obesity, which is increasingly prevalent for children today.

The parents of Generation Alpha have seen firsthand the change in children's health from their childhood to today –

from increased childhood obesity to more sedentary lives, to the increase in food allergies and the heightened awareness of anaphylaxis and special dietary needs. This, along with these parents being more nutritionally informed, is giving Generation Alpha an improved nutritional foundation. A generation of new parents have themselves been seeking healthy eating from organic food, less meat in their diets, alcohol-free days, more label reading and additive avoidance. When women today begin their pregnancies, there is far more awareness and intentionality around nutrition for the developing baby and it extends beyond just 'no alcohol and soft cheeses' to proactively choosing foods that will best support the growth of their unborn child. The move away from formula to breastfeeding, even for working mums, and the preparation of natural foods rather than just relying on processed baby foods, as infants move to solids, signifies this trend.

Additionally, parents are supported in this direction with far more choice in supermarkets, clear labelling, health star ratings and an array of allergen-free options. Even 'treat foods' such as chocolates are adding portion-size messaging to their packages and fast-food outlets are providing healthy options. For example, McDonald's has sliced apples as an alternative to desserts and have famously removed plastic toys from the child-focused McHappy Meals.

While we live in an increasingly digital world, it's important for us all to get outside, exercise, spend time off screens and get quality sleep. If we as adults can model this behaviour well, then Generation Alpha have a greater chance of developing healthy practices that can contribute to their overall health and wellbeing.

Mental health

Mental health is far more than the absence of clinical conditions such as depression or anxiety. The World Health Organization (WHO) defines mental health as 'A state of wellbeing in which every individual realizes his or her own potential, can cope with the normal stresses of life, can work productively and fruitfully, and is able to make a contribution to her or his community.'[60] WHO go on to say that, 'Mental health is fundamental to our collective and individual ability as humans to think, emote, interact with each other, earn a living and enjoy life. On this basis, the promotion, protection and restoration of mental health can be regarded as a vital concern of individuals, communities and societies throughout the world.'

Mental health has had a growing profile among communities in schools, universities and workplaces, because it's an element of every individual's life that needs management, care and help. Mental health and wellbeing challenges don't discriminate based on social status, gender, religion or financial status. As outlined by Health Direct, examples of symptoms of mental health challenges or mental illness can include anxiety, depression, unusual thoughts, unreasonable anger, poor concentration or memory, hearing voices, increased or decreased sleep, increased or low appetite, lack of motivation, withdrawing from people, drug use, thoughts that life is not worth living or suicidal thoughts, becoming obsessed by a topic, not looking after personal hygiene or responsibilities, not performing well at work or school.[61] Most people would have experienced at least a mild version of one or more of the challenges listed, but it's good to keep in mind the WHO description outlining that sound mental health means an individual, 'can cope with the normal stresses of life'.

Currently, around one in four young people aged fifteen to nineteen meet the criteria for having a serious mental illness.[62] It is concerning that there has been a significant increase in the proportion of young people meeting this criteria; data shows that it increased by more than 20 per cent in the most recent five-year period.[63] According to global research, mental illness contributes to 45 per cent of the global burden of disease among those aged ten to twenty-four years.[64]

Parents are recognising the importance of mental wellbeing in the next generation. As one parent told us in a focus group, 'I feel like self-care and mental health, those kinds of things, are going to be super-important for our kids. I think I would put that right up there next to critical thinking and compassion.'

COVID-19's impact on mental health

One of the biggest impacts of COVID-19 was on people's health – not just their physical health but their mental health, wellbeing and resilience. When asked about the biggest impacts of social isolation, Generation Z were most likely to say that boredom (51 per cent), less physical activity (47 per cent) and increased feelings of loneliness (41 per cent) were affecting them the most, and significantly more so than any other generation.[65] They also indicated that they were more likely to see the negative impacts of increased screen time. Almost half (49 per cent) of Gen Z said they felt anxious about the unfolding COVID-19 situation, with one in four (25 per cent) saying the biggest negative impact of COVID-19 was on their mental health (again, more so than any other generation).[66]

Younger generations are also more likely than their older counterparts to believe the COVID-19 experience will have a negative impact on Generation Alpha's mental health

(88 per cent of Gen Z and 71 per cent of Gen Y, compared to 69 per cent of Gen X, 50 per cent of Baby Boomers and 48 per cent of Builders).[67]

Even though the six living generations all experienced the unprecedented challenges of COVID-19, it is the younger generations, who have experienced it in their formative years without a broader reference point and who have most exhibited increased anxiety. Another reason for this increased anxiety is that they were a 'more anxious' generation even before COVID-19. According to the American Psychological Association's annual *Stress in America* report, in the year before COVID-19, Generation Z adults indicated the highest average stress level of any demographic.[68]

Why the increase in mental health conditions?

With more young people being diagnosed with mental health conditions, it does beg the question – why? Some of the reasons why people suffer from mental health conditions come down to personal factors like personality, home and family situations, and personal trauma and history. Other factors are more indicative of our changing times – the different pressures students face today, the rapid pace of change, technology and a greater awareness of mental health conditions.

In our interview with Collett Smart, she expanded on the reasons we're seeing increased mental health conditions among Gen Z and Generation Alpha. She points out that mental health issues are presenting in children earlier in their life, but it is an oversimplification to put it simply down to technology. She told us that 'Although kids seem to come out of the womb with an iPad or tablet, it's unfair to say that if anyone has an iPad or an iPhone they will be diagnosed with anxiety. It's simply not true. I often say, "If your kids are vulnerable offline, they will be vulnerable online." Children who are lonely, anxious or suffer from depression often self-medicate with technology.'

Security and stability

Collett Smart also says there is a correlation between family breakdown and levels of anxiety. She points out that 'Children need a stable base, and the lack of structure has a significant impact. For a child who is prone to anxiety, to add a new element of managing their lives spread between two homes, no matter how loving, is a challenge. "Is my uniform at Mum's or Dad's?" "What sports equipment do I need if I'm staying at Dad's on Tuesday and Mum's on Friday?"' That said, a child can experience anxiety while living in a volatile environment where their parents still live together. The best thing parents can try and do is to create a stable environment for children and cultivate a sense of safety and security.

Behaviour management

A child who is full of energy may find it challenging to sit still in a classroom in order to be taught. These children are commonly labelled as disruptive, uncooperative and prone to making poor choices, but it may not be behavioural. Today, there is a heightened awareness and understanding among parents and educators of both the Autism Spectrum and of Attention Deficit Hyperactivity Disorder (ADHD). Autism is characterised by difficulty in social interaction and communication and by restricted or repetitive patterns of thought and behaviour. ADHD is a medical condition that exists when there is a difference in brain development leading to an impaired ability to concentrate and sit still. This means that parents ought not feel blame for their child's behavioural challenges as they can be explained scientifically.

Psychologists we interviewed highlighted that medication for these conditions can be life-altering for children, and can help them to focus at school. Research shows a massive increase in prescriptions for Generation Alpha compared to any previous generation, and teachers we spoke to are seeing this firsthand. Some expressed concern that, sometimes, medication is turned to as one of the first options, rather than managing behaviour within a broader context. As one primary school teacher told us, 'It's almost like every child today has a problem and is seeing a specialist. For some, I wonder whether it's just part of growing up, rather than a problem. Parents want to label it and are quick to take action.' When a child does experience consistent challenges, however, many clinicians (and parents) advocate seeing specialists and taking medication because they see the benefits in their child's schoolwork and concentration.

Generation Alpha and mental health

While the increased prevalence of mental health challenges among the next generation is a significant challenge for our schools, families, communities and loved ones, it is a positive step that mental health is being discussed openly and frequently, rather than being something people hide, are ashamed of or suffer in silence.

As well as ensuring we maintain a good state of wellbeing for ourselves, it is vital to look out for our family, friends, colleagues and children who might be struggling in silence. Parents and carers, friends, aunties and uncles to Generation Alpha can play a significant role in helping them to not only mitigate the challenges they face, but to thrive. Healthy family relationships where children feel supported and loved, and in which their school and friendships are of interest to the adults in their life, can all contribute to a child's positive mental health.[69] Wellbeing at school is touched on later in this chapter and investigated in more depth in Chapter 6.

Removing the stigma

In 2009, the year before Generation Alpha began being born, a man named Gavin Larkin started an Australian, non-profit suicide prevention organisation, called R U OK? It revolves around the slogan 'R U OK?' (are you okay?) and encourages people to have conversations with others. The organisation has a dedicated R U OK? Day, held annually on the second Thursday of September, which encourages Australians to connect with people who have emotional insecurity, to address social isolation and promote community cohesiveness.[70]

Awareness campaigns like R U OK? Day and Movember (where men grow a moustache during the month of November to raise awareness and funds for men's mental health) are bringing the topic of mental health to the forefront of public discussion, and parents are viewing this as a positive step for the world Generation Alpha are being shaped in. As one mother of Generation Alpha children shared with us, 'I think in today's world we're seeing the value in mental health and wellness and how important it is, and how it improves all areas of your life. It is so important to value mental health and compassion, and to be more open about its importance. We weren't as open about it before, and now some of that stigma is being removed. It's valued in today's society more.'

Challenges to health and wellbeing

What are the biggest challenges that Generation Alpha is likely to face in terms of their health and wellbeing? The fact that emerging generations are growing up in an entirely new context means there are both age-old challenges for children, like bullying, friendships and pressure to achieve, as well as the impact of technology, which in many ways exacerbates the existing challenges in ways previous generations haven't had to navigate. Before parents and leaders can respond to these challenges, they need to understand them. In our research with parents and educators, the biggest challenges for the next generation are around bullying, mental wellbeing, academic pressure and up-ageing.[71]

Top five challenges for today's primary school students[72]	
According to parents *(per cent who think it is extremely/very challenging)*	**According to educators** *(per cent who think it is extremely/very challenging)*
Bullying in person (50 per cent)	Online bullying through social networks (60 per cent)
Online bullying through social networks (48 per cent)	The pressure to grow up faster (58 per cent)
Navigating their own mental wellbeing (43 per cent)	Social pressure to be a high achiever (54 per cent)
Social pressure to be a high achiever (42 per cent)	Navigating their own mental wellbeing (51 per cent)
The pressure to grow up faster (42 per cent)	Navigating loneliness and social isolation (51 per cent)

Today's teachers are finding it challenging to deal with online bullying issues that are happening external to the classroom. They believe this bullying may be affecting the resilience of their students. 'Students post something and the immediate question they ask is, okay, how many likes am I getting? Do I delete it because I'm not getting many likes now? Peer pressure has always been there but has been massively amplified in the last decade for these kids. Their resilience to deal with life is both amplified by that and then destroyed by that, depending on how they respond to these kids,' a teacher told us.

> 'Never before have we been so connected, and yet so lonely at the same time. To be human is to be relational, yet social media has now come to amplify the worst of humanity, the anti-social. Technology amplifies wellbeing issues like bullying, and we have to deal with that.'
> – *Tony George, Headmaster at The King's School*

It is a common concern that young people today are less resilient than they used to be. On the upside, however, some teachers have seen students in a complex and uncertain world overcome many hardships, which suggests that for some students resilience is increasing because of the greater challenges they are facing. 'My definition of resilience is how you respond to hardship,' said one teacher. 'I think when it comes to bouncing back from big things, I've seen them do that really well.'

Teachers and schools are working to help build resilience in today's students. They've discovered this is best done when it is embedded into learning, and through experience. 'We're not trying to just teach little mental gymnastics tricks for kids to be able to understand the principles of resilience or be able to run through the checklist of self-talk, but building genuine experiences into their lives that allow them to gain self-understanding, and gain a sense of perspective,' said Brendan Corr, Principal of Australian Christian College in Sydney.

Dr Scott Marsh, the principal at William Clarke College, is implementing a program to build leadership and resilience in students through outdoor programs. He told us that 'one of the growing concerns I have is how risk-averse our society has become and the lack of resilience and increasing mental health concerns among young people. I think we are in an age of over-compliance and overwhelming risk minimisation. We need kids to take risks, to get outside, to push themselves and realise they can do it. So, we run a six-day outdoor education program where we go hiking and canoeing. While some might struggle, at the end we celebrate that they got through it. The goal is for them to apply that resilience to other areas of their life like in their studies or in challenges with friends.'

The impact of technology on wellbeing

Technology has brought many positive changes to our lives and our sense of wellbeing. The invention of the internet brought with it an incredible ability to connect globally with family and friends and engage with any piece of information at the click of a button (or, rather, the touch of a screen). Social media allows us to share every aspect of our lives with those we love, some of whom may live thousands of kilometres away.

During the COVID-19 crisis, schools and businesses embraced Zoom and other digital meeting technologies to great effect. Most of us were grateful to have such connectivity in a period of isolation, yet it also became evident that virtual meetings had their limitations.

Along with its many benefits, technology has also delivered us some unique challenges, particularly to our wellbeing. It has blurred the lines of private and public, of school and home, of work and rest. It has made it harder for us to switch off, to connect with the physical world around us and to be present. Online communities on social media platforms such as Instagram and Snapchat provide us with so much information about the lives of others that we now spend too much time comparing ourselves to everyone else's highlight reels rather than living our own lives. While the internet and social media can facilitate increasingly connected communities, they can also make us feel more isolated and fuel comparisons to others, negatively affecting our health and wellbeing. Interestingly, many a Baby Boomer and Gen Xer has confessed to us that when looking at the frantic activity on social media it is not FOMO (fear of missing out) they feel, but rather JOMO (joy of missing out)!

Our comparison culture and the inability to switch off, combined with other life pressures and stresses, affects our mental health and wellbeing and that of the next generation. Technology not only affects our mental health but our physical health. We are sitting more and exercising less; we are working longer per week and later in life.

To help the emerging generation improve their wellbeing and ensure technology assists their life rather than takes it over, we as parents and leaders have to first practise such habits. Ironically, technology is the means we can use to gain control of their screen-time use, with features like screen-time monitoring, setting time limits on certain apps, turning off notifications and using the do-not-disturb or flight-mode setting. Screen-free Sundays, setting time in our day or week where we don't check emails or social media, putting devices aside before family meals and avoiding recharging devices beside beds are all strategies that have been a help for many.

Pressure to achieve academic success

Young people today face a plethora of challenges and barriers to their wellbeing. According to a Mission Australia Report, the top concerns for young people (aged fifteen to nineteen) today are coping with stress (48 per cent), school or study problems (34 per cent), mental health (33 per cent) and body image (31 per cent).[73]

Our Education Future Research suggested similar findings around the pressure children face today to excel academically.[74] Parents are feeling the pressure to ensure their child can succeed in an increasingly globally connected world. In the last five years more than two thirds of parents (67 per cent) believe the pressure to set their child up for success has increased. This pressure is, at times, being transferred to the child. Almost half of parents (49 per cent) feel like at some point they have placed too much pressure on their child to achieve at school. More than three in four educators (77 per cent) and three in five parents (60 per cent) believe the high pressure to do well in exams and assessments is the number one challenge for high school students today.[75]

We recently interviewed Dr Stephen Harris, the co-founder and director of learning at Learnlife Barcelona, the first in a worldwide network of learning hubs hoping to accelerate change in existing education models through personal purpose-based learning. Regarding student wellbeing, Stephen said, 'There has been a significant backwards slide with mental health issues in the last five or six years. I think it's totally linked to an overemphasis on assessments and examinations by both the media and parents. I'm not condemning parents, because in many cases, they don't know enough about the system to understand what it's doing to the kids. Yet we keep selling the idea that the only pathway is to buckle down and study all these things. I would say in the last five years there has been a pronounced increase in the volume of kids who are suffering from anxiety. And then that also tips over into kids with severe anxiety, or severe depression.'

While the academic pressure is typically higher among high school students, we also see this pressure in primary school students, with 42 per cent of parents and 54 per cent of educators seeing the social pressure to be a high achiever as a challenge for Generation Alpha.[76] One parent told us how her nine-year-old daughter was 'diagnosed with anxiety from things that are happening in her personal life and stressing about NAPLAN. I don't want my children going through school and life thinking everything's a test, so I won't pressure them about school. I say to them on Monday, "All right you've got homework throughout the week, you know when it's due, you don't do it, that's your consequences."'

Another parent told us, 'I think pressure to reach benchmarks is a challenge.' And a primary school teacher told us how 'the demands are pretty high, and I think that's one of the things that we need to watch today, because there is a high level of stress on children. I think education brings stress. They're under pressure to perform and to achieve, and can have feelings of inadequacy around assessment processes.'

Both parents and educators need to be aware of the pressure – whether intentional or not – that is being placed on the next generation. One parent told us a story of how her daughter attended an academically focused school, and how 'her kindergarten looked like a college prep course. There was no pretend play or toys of any kind. For her birthday, she didn't want to have any kids from her school come. So I went to the school at recess, which was the only time they're able to have social time, because in class she wasn't allowed to talk to the other kids, or she got in trouble. I saw that the kids were having clear difficulties being friends, yet no one was paying attention. I watched my daughter on different days either being chased by a pack of kids or, alternatively, leading a pack of kids chasing other kids. Here's my daughter, learning these really horrible behaviours at school. Because the school was so over-focused on academics. They figure, "Well, you'll do the social and emotional at home." So I took her out of that school and now she loves where she is. She used to have a lot of anxiety about going to school. She would cry every day. Now she'll say, "Bye, Mum," and walk off. I like the greater focus on the social and emotional – to look at that as separate from or less important than academics or image or whatever else is a detriment to our kids.'

Child safety and security online

'I used to ride my bike through the drain and storm pipes. I wouldn't see my parents from eight o'clock Saturday morning, because I'd sleep over at my friend's house, until six o'clock Sunday night. It's different now. I would never, ever, let my kids do what I used to do, ever. You can't even play at the park by yourself with your friends, sorry.'
– *a mother of Generation Alphas*

In recent times we have seen an increase in parents' concern for their children's safety. Parents are worried about their kids wandering free in parks and on the streets with friends, because society is perceived as not being as safe for kids as it once was. There are also additional concerns with online safety for children, who are using technology and screens from a young age. And yet this integration of technology from such a young age has some positive benefits for this generation's safety. In some ways it can enhance a child's physical safety, because kids and teens with mobile phones are more accessible and trackable. As mum Kristel told us, 'I let my daughter [go out] a little bit, but only because she's got a phone. I've got Find My Friends, so I can access exactly where she is, I can call her in five seconds and say where are you?' The only reason that many parents will allow their children the autonomy of heading outside the home by themselves or with friends is because the location of their phone can be tracked. The bus, train or Uber they are in can be monitored in real time, or the child can be sent a text at any point to confirm that all is ok. But the very real concern for parents today is how to ensure kids are safe online.

'I know there's going to be a day that my son is going to need a phone, but I'm scared about what he's going to have on it', a mum of Generation Alpha told us. 'When he is on his iPad, and he's playing a game, something will pop up to install or download, and I can see everything that he's downloaded. And I say, "Why did you download that?" And he says, "Because it looked fun." It's actually quite scary that they can just do it so easily.'

Parents today acknowledge that, in the past, even if parents didn't like something their child was watching, 'It could be a conversation. But on these devices, the kinds of things that come up on YouTube that kids don't talk about, it's really scary,' one mum told us. Another shared this: 'I was one of the first classes of kids who got the talk on how to be critical of content on the internet. We weren't allowed to use the internet as a primary resource when we were kids. Now, all the primary resources are found on the internet. I see my boys watching YouTube, and it's just some Joe Schmo talking about ten interesting facts about ancient Greece. I'm listening, and three of them are totally over-simplified, or he's saying it in a way that's really giving the wrong impression, and they don't have the critical-thinking skills and scrutiny of like, "Who is this guy?" They're just learning from random strangers on the internet, and they don't have the critical thinking. I think a lot of parents and teachers, who grew up in a different era, don't know how to go to our kids and say, "Hey, by the way, you should not just trust this stranger." Because it's the world they know.'

From an identity and self-worth perspective, Brett Murray, CEO and co-founder of Make Bullying History, says it's a challenge. 'Kids are getting their identity from online behaviour. Most people don't have the emotional and relational capacity to have more than three to five close friends. But kids think that if they don't have hundreds of Facebook friends, then they've got less value. And we actually have to dissolve that and say they're not your friends. They're just numbers. The biggest key with technology is parental engagement. Parents used to default to other people as babysitters. Now it's the screen. It used to be the TV, now it's the tablet. If parents are overwhelmed with their responsibilities, parents are abdicating their parental roles to the screen. As long as the kids aren't actually out doing drugs or vandalising or missing school, and they can see them, then they think it's okay. But they don't understand that at this developmental stage of the brain, kids can be ingesting damaging content online.'

We recommend a four-layer approach to managing the risks of technology with Generation Alpha and it spells out the acronym DCBA:

The DCBA approach to technology use

Delay and limit – delay, as much as possible, the age when a child gets their own device. While it is a battle to resist a

---

child having their own device in their childhood years, if it can be delayed until they hit their teens they'll be better for it. If parents let their child borrow their own device or a family one, they are better able to limit when it is accessed and for how long.

Communicate values – parents need to be clear with their children and consistently reinforce what their acceptable standards are in terms of what they view or access and the values that they uphold when interacting with others. As children internalise these strong values and develop their own character they will be more empowered to make wise choices about what they access online. It is important to communicate not just what is acceptable and not acceptable, but why.

Behavioural strategies – by modelling and training our children in how to manage device use, they will be able to implement tactics to help them use technology as a tool which helps them. From privacy settings to prudence around groups and networks to join, to developing impulse control and investing in offline activities, behavioural strategies will serve this generation well for their future.

Accountability – It is important for parents to remember that almost without exception, they are the internet account holders. They pay the bills and own the devices and therefore have the responsibility for their use. Additionally, they have the role as parents to see their children flourish. Keeping them accountable on their technology use is an important part of this role. For some it might be monitoring sites visited and social media posts, while for others it will simply involve checking in with them to see how they are going with their use of technology and social media.

Growing up faster

As we have explored earlier, parents and educators are concerned about Generation Alpha up-ageing (growing up faster than they need to) due to technology, and the negative impacts this can have on their wellbeing. Almost half of educators (48 per cent), and one in five parents (20 per cent), believe up-ageing is a barrier for Generation Alpha to thrive. Consistent with this, almost nine in ten parents (87 per cent) and educators (90 per cent) are concerned that children are losing their innocence too soon. At the same time, however, parents (79 per cent) and educators (84 per cent) struggle with the tension between protecting a child's innocence and educating them for their safety.[77]

'I think it's a confusing world to grow up in,' a primary school teacher told us. A senior schoolteacher also told of how 'Gen Z grew up watching YouTube, whereas Generation Alpha are being babysat by YouTube. They are focused on social media and growing up with questions about how many people are liking their posts. Peer pressure has always been there but it has been massively amplified over the last decade. Resilience is defined by that and destroyed by that. Many get very anxious about it and crumble, and others thrive and succeed. I think social media and peer pressure has had a larger and more negative impact than it has in the past.'

Loneliness

Despite the strength of today's school communities, many children are experiencing a sense of loneliness and isolation. Two thirds of educators (67 per cent) and almost half of parents (49 per cent) believe it is extremely/very challenging for today's high school students to navigate loneliness and social isolation. To a lesser extent, navigating loneliness and social isolation is also a challenge for primary school students today (according to 51 per cent of educators and 40 per cent of parents).[78]

Unfortunately, parents expect the challenge of loneliness in Australian schools to continue. More than a third of parents and two in five educators believe that student loneliness is one of the most significant challenges that school communities will face in the next twelve months.[79] The issue of loneliness has been further exacerbated by COVID-19. As one parent told us, 'my son's online learning has been pretty positive, but he misses and needs the social interaction of being at school.'

Martin Seligman, a key contributor in the realm of positive psychology, attributes the elements of wellbeing to include positive emotion, engagement, meaning, accomplishments and positive relationships. In reference to the latter element, Seligman says in his book *Flourish*: 'Very little that is positive is solitary. When was the last time you laughed uproariously? The last time you felt indescribable joy? The last time you sensed profound meaning and purpose? Even without knowing the particulars of these in your life, I know their form: all of them took place around other people. Other people are the best antidote to the downs of life and the single most reliable up.'[80]

Loneliness is an epidemic in the twenty-first century. Our research collaboration with Dr Lindsay McMillan shows that almost half (48 per cent) of people in Australia are lonely. In the Workplace Loneliness Report, Dr Lindsay McMillan says that loneliness can have the same effect on someone's health as smoking fifteen cigarettes a day.[81] For children, loneliness can affect their levels of cortisol (the stress hormone), sleep, self-care, self-esteem, mental health and outlook on life. Common causes of loneliness in children may be caused by lifestyle changes, like moving house or school, changes in family dynamics, like divorce or siblings leaving home, arguments with friends, bullying, or a death of someone they know.[82] Despite its goal of connecting people, technology, social media and gaming can also be a contributing factor to loneliness as they substitute usage for face-to-face interaction, can create unrealistic expectations and a sense of missing out (FOMO).

If a child is exhibiting symptoms of loneliness like being unusually clingy, crying a lot more or seeming more sad than usual, creating imaginary friends to make up for a lack of real friends or acting unsure of themselves, then it may be time to step in and help. Parents and caregivers can do this by talking to the children, prioritising play and connection with others, looking for opportunities for connection like in team sports or activities, making time for family and friends, or consulting a psychologist.[83]

Wellbeing at school

The trend of implementing wellbeing programs in schools has been steadily increasing over time. According to our latest Future of Education report, in the last five years, three in five parents (60 per cent) say the expectations they place on their child's school to support student wellbeing have increased.[84] This is up twelve percentage points in two years and it is Generation Y parents driving this expectation inflation, with 31 per cent increasing their expectations of schools compared to 23 per cent of Generation X parents.[85]

Teachers are noticing the increased focus on wellbeing and mental health issues within their schools – and even at the primary school level. 'When I think back to my first year three and four class who sought outside professional help from psychologists and psychiatrists compared to now, the difference is huge,' Jess, a primary school teacher, told us. 'Whether that's because diagnosis systems have changed, it's more socially acceptable, or because people are more aware. I just think, before I might have had one or two kids who are being assessed and going up for referrals, whereas now it's at least half the class.'

Senior school teachers are also noticing the difference – 'I've noticed it more this year – the number of mental health issues has increased exponentially,' one told us. Others in this particular focus group agreed, saying things like, 'The emotional demand and pastoral care for caring for students and mental illness – the emphasis it needs to have or does now have is far greater.' It seems that children today are more aware of and open to talking about their mental health. As one teacher put it, 'Kids are more aware of it and why they are behaving the way they are. They are open to it and more interactive with teachers about it.'

In response to this, it is important that mental health, resilience and a focus on wellbeing are key topics of discussion within the education sector, with an emphasis on how teachers can help. 'Education has changed over the past ten to fifteen years in the way that mental health is both brought up, but also dealt with,' one teacher told us. 'A challenge for education, I think, is that a lot of people either need to have really good intuition or pretty much be trained in counselling to effectively do their job as a teacher, just because there's so many mental health issues across the board, across every grade.'

Almost all parents believe schools should have a holistic focus and play a role in the management of wellbeing. The question is to what extent. Positively, parents and teachers are mostly aligned in their perspectives on responsibility for wellbeing. Almost half of parents believe schools should provide individualised support for wellbeing but refer on to other experts. Teachers also see themselves as the first line of defence and will then refer on to experts. 'I think we're only an identifier on a minimal level. We're the first ones to realise there's a continued behaviour or something happening and it's important that you give the [information to the] parent and suggest going to the GP. If a big thing happens on the spot and they need to see the school counsellor, they can do that, but that's the triage before they get the external help.' The challenge for schools, however, is that almost a quarter of parents believe schools should provide extensive individualised support for all wellbeing issues. Again, Gen Y parents seem to be driving this expectation, with 28 per cent of Gen Y parents agreeing that schools should provide extensive individualised support for all wellbeing issues, compared to 21 per cent of Gen X parents.[86]

'I didn't know we had a counsellor at high school,' a high school student said. When asked about how mental health and wellbeing was highlighted at his school, one student told us. 'It's more of a student-led thing. All the students got given ribbons on R U OK? Day. That was initiated by the year twelves.'

As one teacher told us, 'There has been a massive change from when I was at school. Kids talk about mental health – about resilience in overcoming things, big things in life. They don't bury it, and when they see someone struggling, they don't bully them. It's incredible to see.'

When thinking about the future challenges for schools, interestingly, education issues don't top the list. Parents believe the most significant are: addressing bullying (66 per cent), supporting students with mental health conditions (52 per cent) and improving literacy and numeracy (49 per cent). Educators have similar expectations but believe the number one challenge is supporting students with mental health conditions (73 per cent). Educators also believe improving literacy and numeracy (51 per cent) and better engaging with students in learning (47 per cent) are significant challenges facing school communities.[87]

Principals and teachers are seeing a greater focus on the holistic upbringing of students in school. More than just teaching for the test, there is a shift to education of the whole child. And as student wellbeing becomes an increasingly topical issue it can be challenging for schools to understand parent expectations and the school's role in the wellbeing journey.

Tony George, Headmaster of The King's School in Sydney, says, 'What I find from parents wanting to bring their sons to The King's School is that while they're looking at the rankings of schools based on HSC results, they're actually choosing a school based on the kind of person they want their child to become. That doesn't mean that the academics are unimportant, if you don't have the academics well then people will walk away. So, I say academic excellence is necessary, it's just not sufficient for a good education.'

Schools are responding well to this challenging issue but there is still room for improvement. Parents are increasingly expecting that their child's school will provide not just a sound education but will support their child's wellbeing throughout their school years.

Bullying

Going to school is a key shared experience. It is the bottleneck through which almost all Australians pass. Yet, despite the constant improvement in school facilities, education curriculum, teaching methods and training, bullying continues to be a serious problem in Australian schools.

We worked with the Make Bullying History Foundation to survey almost seven hundred students across a range of schools and found that four in five believe that bullying is a serious problem in their school. Both parents and educators recognise that bullying has a significant impact on student's health, with parents citing it as the most significant challenge facing school communities in the decade ahead. Sadly, one in five Australian students (21 per cent) aged fifteen to nineteen has experienced bullying in the last year.[88] Of these, eight in ten (80 per cent) reported that the bullying took place at school, TAFE or university, while a third (34 per cent) indicated they had experienced bullying online or on social media. While similar proportions of males (82 per cent) and females (79 per cent) stated they had experienced bullying at school, TAFE or university, a much higher proportion of females reported that they had been bullied online or on social media (37 per cent compared with 27 per cent of males).[89]

Jasmine, a primary school teacher, told us how, 'With wellbeing issues, in terms of bullying and things like that, technology seems to amplify, and we have to deal with that. I saw it definitely in years five and six, and even addiction in terms of being obsessed with technology and screen time and not being able to cope without screen time.'

Another primary school teacher, Anita, shared with us how Generation Alpha's use of social media from a young age can make bullying even more difficult for teachers and students to manage. 'I've found when teaching year four that students have access to applications that you have to be thirteen years or older to use, like Snapchat. Their parents let them have an account, and then bullying comes into the classroom. Then I have to deal with it, but I can't say the kids aren't allowed to use this application, because that's a parent's decision. That's what makes it hard.'

Out of the 21 per cent of respondents who had experienced bullying in the past year, more than seven in ten (71 per cent) reported that they experienced verbal bullying (e.g. name-calling, teasing). Over three in five (61 per cent) indicated they had experienced social bullying (e.g. rumours, being embarrassed or excluded), while more than one third (37 per cent) reported they had experienced cyberbullying (e.g. hurtful messages, pictures or comments). Around one in five (22 per cent) had experienced physical bullying (e.g. hitting, punching). There were notable differences in the results by gender: a greater proportion of females reported experiencing social bullying and cyberbullying whereas a much higher proportion of males reported that they had experienced physical bullying over the past year.[90]

These figures highlight the extent of this national shame. There is hope, however, with numerous programs and initiatives being undertaken at a government and school level aiming to decrease the prevalence of bullying in our society.

As Brett Murray of Make Bullying History told us, 'I have found students to not only be incredibly attentive on the topic of bullying, which is such a priority for them, but this generation of young people are also increasingly empowered to step up and stop bullying. A key component of this is empowering them to change the culture in their school, equip them with the right training and empower them to be proactive.' We saw the same phenomenon in the petitions and campaigns in early 2021 for better consent education to be included in sex education in schools. Teenagers who have been the victims of non-consensual sexual activity have become the agents to bring about change. Amid discussions of the abusive culture towards young women, it was encouraging to see the students at boys' schools step up against such abuse in various forums to pledge 'not on our watch'.

If a child you know, love or care about is being bullied, it can be upsetting for both them and you. While it might be hard for them to talk to you about their experience, encouraging them to share what is going on from their perspective can be a good first step. By staying calm and positive, you can help them to feel safe and supported, which can enable them to open up to you about the bullying.

Parents can also help by ensuring that home is a safe and supportive place for their children. While this can be difficult because of the use of digital devices (which enable bullying to occur even while children are at home), you can have conversations with your children and inform them about strategies to combat bullying. Almost all schools have a bullying policy and are required to deal with it once it has been brought to the school's attention. If your child has experienced bullying you can talk with the school and seek support. The Commonwealth Government has set up a national day against bullying and violence for school students and the community, and provides a website offering support and resources, called Bullying No Way.

As well as these practical steps, remember that a key role of parents and leaders in a child's life is to help children to know they are worthy of love and belonging, even if they aren't finding that in other spheres of their life, like at school or in a sports team, for example.

Cultivating resilience

'My son's resilience is one of my favourite things about him. It doesn't matter how many times he falls down or does it wrong, he's just as happy to do it again.'
– a mother of a Generation Alpha

The American Psychological Association defines resilience as 'the process of adapting well in the face of adversity, trauma, tragedy, threats, or significant sources of stress – such as family and relationship problems, serious health problems, or workplace and financial stressors. As much as resilience involves "bouncing back" from these difficult experiences, it can also involve profound personal growth.'[91]

In our COVID-19 research, we found that Gen Z were the least likely to say that they felt emotionally resilient during the pandemic (44 per cent) compared to Gen Y (47 per cent), Gen X (50 per cent), Baby Boomers (56 per cent) and Builders (49 per cent).[92] Resilience is an important quality for people of all ages to possess, because we all face hardships, trials and setbacks in life. In a rapidly changing world, it is important for the next generation to possess resilience so that they can adapt to the changes and thrive.

Psychologist Collett Smart believes that, 'in much of the Western world, our children have everything come very easily. They haven't been subjected to war, they have easy access to food, water, education, medication. Considering this, it's interesting that Western parents shelter their children more. What we as parents and as a society need to consider is building resilience into our children. We've swung from "children should be seen and not heard" to wrapping them up in cotton wool, but now attention needs to be given to introducing children to healthy struggles and challenges.'

The Macquarie University Faculty of Human Science in Sydney recently conducted a study led by Professor Jennie Hudson, the Director of the Centre for Emotional Health, on the importance of fathers in a child's development of resilience. The research found that fathers who encourage their children to be socially assertive and step outside of their comfort zone may help their children avoid social anxiety in young adulthood.[93] In the study, they showed how fathers play an important role in encouraging children to push themselves a bit more socially and take safe risks. Survey participants answered questions about how their own parents had behaved. In challenging parenting, a parent will encourage their child to try new things and take safe risks – and they won't step in to help out too early. Some parents, with the best of intentions, shelter their children from disappointment and give their child more help than they need, according to their age or abilities. 'This can actually increase stress or anxiety because children are led to believe they need help and protection from the outside world,' explains Anna Smout, lead author on the paper.

Smout says that traditional gender roles emphasise the idea that physical play is the domain of fathers, as is encouraging children to take appropriate risks and to be independent. Whereas parents who reinforce risk and challenge avoidance, tend to discipline children for small offences and are overly critical. 'That led researchers to believe that the challenging parental behaviour style could be more characteristic of fathers than mothers,' she says.[94]

'I often challenge my kids (aged seven, four and one) to try age-appropriate risky activities which Mum might not think are safe, like skateboards, rope swings and jumping off jetties! I think small, regular challenges are vital because I know their confidence is linked to their ability to face challenges. I throw them up into the sky but am there to catch them! While of course I want to protect and nurture them, I know that encouraging them to try new things, challenge themselves and step out of their comfort zone, even if they fail, is important to growing their resilience, character and ability to deal with life's challenges. Teaching my kids to challenge themselves is important because I don't want them to act like emotional babies forever!' – *Geoff, a dad of three Generation Alphas*

In addition to physical and mental challenging, there is also a greater understanding today of the importance of physical touch and hugs from parents, and how these positively affect mental wellbeing. 'Parental touch reduces children's attention to social threat and increases trust, particularly in socially anxious children. As a result, parental touch may reduce children's social anxiety.' These are the conclusions drawn by Eddie Brummelman from the University of Amsterdam and Peter Bos from Utrecht University. 'Children who were touched on the shoulder exhibited less implicit attention to threats,' says Brummelman. The researchers only observed these effects in children between the ages of eight and ten. This research suggests that parental touch is most important as a safety signal for children in the key developmental years as they approach the transition to adolescence.[95]

Helping Generation Alpha to thrive

Understandably, with so many new and different challenges facing Generation Alpha in the twenty-first century, managing their wellbeing and helping them to thrive can be a challenge for today's parents and carers – especially when it comes to the growing prevalence of mental health problems among them. However, there are practical responsibilities for parents and leaders – like knowing when to seek out professional advice, as well as smaller and more regular steps we can all take that can make a big difference.

In an environment where children feel safe, valued and have a sense of love and belonging, providing them with challenges and supportive encouragement are two simple ways to nurture their resilience and positively influence their mental health.

Having researched and written extensively on this topic,[96] the following is what we have found works best in looking after our health and wellbeing. To ensure Generation Alpha have good mental health, we need to take a holistic approach to wellbeing, incorporating aspects of our relational, social, physical and spiritual health.

Four factors that support mental health

Relational – invest time with loved ones, serve and give to others.

Social – connect with those around us, do fun activities with friends.

Physical – partake in moderate exercise, eat well and get adequate sleep.

Spiritual – take time out to be reflective and aware of our emotions. Practise mindfulness, meditation or prayer.

As much research has shown, the emerging generations are growing up with a greater awareness of mental health conditions. They are being taught from a young age to talk about their emotions, and understand that they are more than their emotions: to know that just because they *feel* sad, does not mean that they *are* sad. For example, there are books about emotions which teach them to say 'my heart feels happy' or 'my heart feels sad'. As well as books, there are many fun and creative ways of introducing mindfulness and self-awareness to kids when they are young, including online activities and apps.

Psychologist Collett Smart advises that if parents want their children to be well, then parents need to model life balance and replenishing practices – something many parents may think is important, but rarely prioritise. 'It's actually modelling to our kids that we aren't just work focused and worried about paying the bills, we actually do set aside time for self-care personally.'

While Generation Alpha will grow up in a world that has radically changed from the one previous generations grew up in, there are also timeless truths that still apply to them and their wellbeing. One is that every child and every person wants to know that they are worthy of love and belonging. This not only leads to a sense of worthiness, it can also translate into other positive character qualities, such as generosity and compassion.

By modelling the behaviour we want them to adopt, helping them to know they are loved and respected, engaging in dialogue around these various challenges and ensuring we as parents and leaders look after our own wellbeing, we can equip this generation to thrive and be resilient for their teenage years, and the many years of life they have yet to lead.

Providing opportunities for children to serve not only helps the wellbeing of others – it is also key for their own wellbeing.

'When children have dignity, they know that they have worth, and that they deserve to be treated with respect, then they have more of an ability to love others and to care for others. When children are involved in working in the community, we see that they develop empathy and self-worth. It's proved to be the two big factors that come out of community service. And when children are anxious or depressed, one of the things we might do is ask them who they can help, because then the focus comes off themselves and onto somebody else. It's not to minimise their pain, but to put it in perspective. Their own problems tend to fade into the background for a little while, while reaching out to somebody else. In my parenting seminars I ask, "What do you want for your child? And please don't say, "I just want my child to be happy." Then parents look up and say, "But you're a psychologist. Isn't that your job? To help a child be happy?" Well, actually no. It's more than that. Now of course I don't want your child to be sad, but when we teach children to pursue happiness, at all costs, then they will step on and step over anybody and anything to get that feeling. Yet, when we teach children that all emotions are important and valid at specific times, we teach emotional intelligence. And emotionally intelligent children have empathy. Empathic children learn compassion. Isn't it interesting, then, that when we are compassionate and we look outward and we reach out to others, we actually end up happier? And so, the very thing we weren't pursuing, happiness, we actually end up finding anyway.' – *Collett Smart, psychologist*

Key takeaways

In this chapter we have explored the areas to consider when addressing the topic of wellbeing for Generation Alpha: from the importance of their physical and mental health to the challenges posed by the risks of technology, pressure to achieve academic success, child safety and security, growing up faster, loneliness, wellbeing at school, and bullying. While this generation will face some unique challenges across these areas, we have also explored what contributes to their wellbeing, and ways parents and caregivers can lead, love and look after the wellbeing of Generation Alpha in a way to build resilience. By modelling the behaviour we want them to adopt, helping them to know they are worthy of love and respect, engaging in dialogue around these various challenges and ensuring we as parents and leaders look after our own wellbeing, we can equip this generation to thrive and be resilient for their teenage years and beyond.

CHAPTER 4

The Great Screen Age

'I love being a kid because when mum was a kid, she didn't have much things to do and now we have more technology and cool stuff to eat.'

George, aged eight

All things digital have defined the formative world of Generation Alpha, and much of their interactions, expectations and even aspirations. In this chapter we look at the profound impact that access to so many smart devices is having on Generation Alpha and their future – the uncertainty technology brings, how it affects child development, the increase in sedentary lifestyles, social media's sociability, online bullying and the growing importance of values-aligned technology.

Generation Alpha are at the forefront of the digital age. In 2010, when the first of their generation began being born, the iPad was released, Instagram was launched and 'app' was awarded 'Word of the Year' by the American Dialect Society.[97] These transformative technologies, apps and platforms are all this generation have ever known, and these devices and platforms will define Generation Alpha more significantly because of it.

For Generation Y, the parents of Generation Alpha, the world of devices and apps was not the world of their upbringing, but computers, digital technology and the worldwide web was. While there are always technological generation gaps, that which exists between today's children and their parents is not as great.

The tension of technology

Do you remember the days of dial-up? The whirring sound of your landline connecting to the internet so you could surf the information superhighway? Whenever we see people in movies having to connect to the internet in this way, it can take us back to those days where the internet – and therefore the world – wasn't in our pockets. In the last two decades technology has advanced at lightning speed, and it can be challenging for all of us – no matter what generation we are a part of – to keep up. Especially since something we were once a little unsure of, perhaps sceptical of, is now our everyday experience at home, at work, at school and throughout society.

When we speak to parents and educators on the issue of generational differences, technology comes up as the consistent answer as to how Generation Alpha are different to generations past. Screens also come up as a source of tension. On the one hand, parents want to ensure their children are equipped with the necessary digital skills to thrive in an increasingly technological world. On the other hand, they also want them to develop resilience, interpersonal and life skills that come from activities and interactions away from screens. In a recent survey we conducted, more than four in five Australians (83 per cent) agree that for children aged eleven and under, the use of screens causes more harm than good.[98]

Yet there can be positive aspects as well. When asked about the impact of technology and screens, Megan, a mum of two Generation Alphas, told us that she thinks 'it's positive. They're going to have to learn it anyway. If they don't learn it when they're kids, then they'll be left behind. I think it's good, but you can't always monitor what they're doing. If they're left alone with a device then they can find anything on YouTube. You don't know what they're watching or what the content is.'

One primary school teacher, who has been teaching for more than forty years and has seen many trends come and go, told us she has observed some new challenges with Generation Alpha: 'Kids find it difficult to focus and just use the iPad or laptop for the purpose which they were meant to be using it. It's certainly got lots of advantages. I love children writing on it because it's not such a tedious process. And that's the way the world's heading, so there are lots of benefits to that. But it does have some negatives associated with it too.'

Blessing or curse?

'The internet is either the greatest blessing or the greatest curse of modern times, sometimes one forgets which it is.'

With technology, there is an undeniable mix of opportunities, benefits and challenges. Many parents struggling to get their children's screen time under control may agree with the sentiment expressed above. This quote is from E. F. Schumacher, who wrote about economics for London's *The Times* after World War II. But it isn't the original wording. We have put the word 'internet' in place of his original words 'printing press', to highlight that people of every era can be

———

While the times affect
us all, the impacts are
greater when experienced
in our formative years.
Our research consistently
shows that the age at
which we're exposed
to a new technology
or transformative
event determines how
embedded it will be in our
psyche and lifestyle.

———

uncertain about the revolutionary technology of their times. No doubt, very few people today worry about the negative impacts of the printing press, and over time we will see today's digital equivalent of the printing press overwhelmingly used to promote human flourishing as well. It's okay to be cautious of technology, especially when it comes to how our youngest generations use it. But we shouldn't fear it, as it can be harnessed for good, for transformation and for the benefit of the next generation.

Some of the benefits of technology include greater access to information and the speed at which we can retrieve it. We can easily connect with people around the world and collaborate, even when we are in different places. During COVID-19, digital technology was transformative in reducing the impacts of the pandemic. From telehealth medical consultations during lockdowns to the ease of accessing medical and pharmaceutical records through e-health, from the digital notification of testing results via text message to digitally 'checking in' at public places, technology is key to managing public health. Technological advancements in pharmaceuticals, medical therapies and medical devices will continue to advance the life expectancy and quality of life for Generation Alpha.

'My daughter uses technology for educational reading because of her Cochlear implants. We plug in the iPad to her Cochlear, and then she will read books, but she'll hear them straight into the implant. And so for me, I don't count that as screen time, because she needs that. I think it would be beneficial for a lot of kids, with Cochlears or not, to have that.' – *a mum of a nine-year-old*

How technology helped Generation Alpha during COVID-19

While the role of technology in the lives of Generation Alpha has been mixed, ultimately it will be used to achieve what it has done through the ages – facilitate human connecting and flourishing. The importance of the internet was highlighted during the COVID-19 pandemic. It kept the world, though individuals and families were isolated in our own homes, connected. It meant we could continue to work and study, and our children could continue to be educated.

The COVID-19 restrictions often meant maintaining relationships with friends, family and colleagues via video call. This is the brave new world Generation Alpha are being born into, and with the oldest of them born in 2010, they are already actively participating in it, too. Children as young as five had to learn from home, but they also couldn't go to the park or see their friends. As we discussed in Chapter 3, social isolation and loneliness is a key challenge parents need to be watchful of, and, had it not been for FaceTime, Zoom, online games and other platforms that kept children connected, this could have been a significant issue for many people, especially the one million children in Australia[99] who are, only children and don't have siblings to play with.

During the pandemic, many of us were thankful for technology, which made the need for social connection relatively easy. We recognised that this was something that we couldn't have accessed in previous eras. One mother we spoke to said that online games meant that her children could interact with their friends, in a way that wouldn't have been possible in previous eras. She said, 'My teenage sons' vice-principal admitted on one parent–teacher Zoom meeting I attended that he never thought he'd utter the words "Thank goodness for Fortnite", but that's exactly how he felt during lockdown in Melbourne. I had to agree!' she said.

Although some Generation Alphas will be too young to remember the pandemic itself, this generation will remember COVID-19 and be affected by the widespread changes to life, work and education it brought about. Our research during the pandemic showed that 84 per cent of Australians believe COVID-19 will play a significant role in shaping the children of today. When we delved deeper into where they think this impact will be most felt, we found that 90 per cent of Australians believe the experience will cause technology and screens to become more integrated into their lives.[100]

One Gen Y told us she was taken aback when her Generation Alpha nephew wanted to FaceTime her. 'Firstly, because this is something I normally do with people my own age, and secondly because my six-year-old nephew was the one initiating it! When we FaceTimed, I asked him about school – which he was doing from home, if he missed his friends and what else he had been up to. Although it wasn't the same as seeing him in person and giving him a big hug, technology still enabled us to connect during a time where many of us felt physically isolated from those we loved.'

The fear of the unknown

Despite the fact that we have been living with and utilising computer technology for decades, parents of Generation Alpha continue to feel unsettled by the impact robotic technology may have on their children's future. Will robots take their children's jobs? Do robots have the capacity to go rogue, like Hollywood depicts in movies such as *iRobot* with Will Smith? What kind of future will this be for Generation Alpha?

As we saw with the comment about the printing press, while the unknown can create a sense of fear and it will take time for people to see the benefits of artificial intelligence, Generation Alpha will simply accept this as part of their life. Many young children already engage in coding classes and interact with different forms of artificial intelligence in their everyday life, and so it is not something they need to adapt to – rather it is something they will have always known. Not only does this mean they are less likely to fear it, they will also be well positioned to handle the opportunities and challenges presented by it. As technology becomes more and more part of everyday life, as robots become more 'human', the ethics around this sort of technology will be a conversation for Generation Alpha to engage in.

The changing face of technology

The year 2019 marked half a century since the July 1969 moon landing by the Apollo 11 crew. The technology NASA used for this momentous achievement required a series of mainframe computers, each the size of a car! In the decades since then we've seen the invention of Magnetic Resonance Imaging (MRI), the personal computer, Global Positioning System (GPS), DNA fingerprinting, the World Wide Web, DVDs, International Space Station, Bluetooth, Facebook, Google Maps, Siri and the Tesla Model 3 – just to name a few! It's amazing to think that even early-model iPhones had computational power hundreds of thousands of times greater than the processing powers of those first-generation computers. In the decade since the first iPhone, the capability and availability of digital devices has further multiplied. There are now seven times the number of connected devices on the planet as there are people! These devices include laptops, smartphones and tablets, used for gaming, online shopping, social media, emails, calls, work and even Dr Google!

With more devices and communication platforms comes more information, updates and messages requiring a response. In reaction to this technological complexity, many people yearn for simplicity. Australian Bureau of Statistics data shows that over a third of men and nearly half of women state that they are always or often rushed or pressed for time.[101] In a world of screen saturation, the office in our pocket, 24/7 expectations and always-on technologies, people are now not so much turning technology off, but turning on apps to make their life function more efficiently.

This is certainly the case for our younger generations, who use integrated apps and devices to plan and execute much of their life. From scheduling appointments to setting alarm clocks, tracking exercise, purchasing groceries, shopping online, playing games online, organising events and making bookings, this is the tech-enabled world native to the youth of today. This is also true of our older generations, who may not be adopting the technologies as quickly but are still turning to them for accessibility and ease – and as a result, are sometimes referred to as the 'digital migrants'. People are increasingly happy to spend money to gain time. We see this with predictive playlists on Spotify and viewing recommendations on Netflix. Another example is smart watches that connect to an app to track health metrics like heart rate, sleep and steps, as well as containing workout tips and the ability to track nutrition.

Technology and child development

Technology affects us all, but Generation Alpha's exposure to it during their formative years has a greater impact on them than any other generation. While we all use apps, access digital playlists and ask Siri and Google to find information, we didn't all have access to it from our youngest years. For Generation Alpha, however, it is seamlessly integrated into their lives, and they can't imagine a world without it. It's all they've ever known. Take, for instance, Christina, a mum of two Generation Alphas, who described taking away her daughter's iPad as being like 'you're literally ripping her heart out. That's her most prized possession'. When we asked some Generation Alphas themselves whether they could imagine the world without the internet, nine-year-old Bianca replied, 'I would be bored and angry. I would have to read a book instead!'

Generation Alpha have been using technological devices from before they could talk, so we are yet to see the full impacts of their interaction with screens. There will certainly be some positives, but it will also provide Generation Alpha with some unique challenges.

Social development challenges

When children are young, especially between birth and three years old, rapid learning and development occurs. As many parents and caregivers can attest, children observe adult behaviour and imitate it. With screens so embedded into adult lives, it is no wonder that children are observing this behaviour and imitating it from a young age. Additionally, if the kids are always looking at screens they miss opportunities to observe and learn about the physical world around them. This not only impacts their ability to learn new things, but also how they interact with others and how language develops.

It can also have an impact on their communication skills, which are developed through observing and participating in conversations. It is here they learn to read facial expressions, develop language skills and interpret and respond to their surroundings. This is something that is lost when children spend too much time on screen-based devices.[102] For a generation who are growing up with screen-based devices more than ever before, developing the necessary interpersonal skills away from screens is going to be a key area of focus for them, and their parents. In order to equip children with the skills to not only listen actively but to show attentiveness, we need to be attentive listeners and model this behaviour for them.

The five actions of active listening: SOLER

Squarely face the listener. By facing the speaker squarely, we can demonstrate full attention and interest.

Open body language. Putting screens down and uncrossing arms communicates interest and attention.

Lean forward. Leaning towards the speaker as opposed to leaning back helps hold the attention and demonstrates this.

Eye contact. If we are focused on the speaker and we look them in the eyes, our attention will also follow.

Responsive gestures. From nods to 'a-ha's and other affirming feedback, the speaker will share more and we as the listener will display our empathy and ability to engage.

Brain development challenges

A potential lack of social development is not the only concern around children's use of and interaction with screens. Another concern is their brain development. A child's brain develops quickly between birth and the toddler stage and they are extremely sensitive to the environment around them. These early years are the most foundational in brain development; all brain function is built upon them.

Spending too much time on screens wires the brain in a certain way. A study conducted by the National Institutes of Health in 2018 reported that children spending more than two hours on screen per day demonstrated lower language and thinking test results, and children spending in excess of seven hours per day on screens were found to experience thinning in the brain's cortex.[103]

One of the biggest tensions parents face is striking the balance between screen time and non-screen time. Many parents want their child to be tech-savvy for the future they will inherit. But they are also aware of the developmental challenges associated with technology, the need for free play and time away from screens to engage in a tactile world. 'Our children earn screen time on weekends for doing homework and chores during the week,' said mum of three, Elena. 'We implemented that rule because the kids were turning into zombies and not helping out in the home. It [screen time] was beginning to rule their day and become a bit of an obsession. We needed to strike a balance. I have to say – the kids are lot more engaged in family life and talk more. We got a lot of attitude from them at first, but they've come around and we all still like each other, maybe a bit more!'

Another challenge is that a child's use of screens can prevent them from being bored, and therefore from being creative. 'It's not how long we're using screens that really matters; it's how we're using them and what's happening in our brains in response,' says Michael Rich, director of the Center on Media and Child Health at Boston Children's Hospital. 'Boredom is the space in which creativity and imagination happen.'[104] In a world of robotics, automation and computerisation, creativity is becoming the key attribute that children will need. Computers are excellent at repetitive tasks and linear processes. Any functions that are structured, sequential and systematic are at risk of being outsourced to machines. However, computers are completely ill-equipped to generate ideas, function creatively and innovate. This is the domain of humans and essential to the future of humanity.

> 'There is a lot of unknowns around technology and what the repercussions are. If you look at the history of play, unprescribed play is important. This is play not determined by an activity, not confined by "now you have to do this or that" but just letting kids play. Instead of telling them what they are going to do, when they are going to do it and who they will do it with, it's saying "you're going to have the afternoon". I do think boredom creates creativity. Even in the car, on the go, we as parents aim to entertain kids all the time and it leaves them without being able to gauge the world and figure out "what do I do when I don't have things", which is part of developing resilience. We don't see that as much – children having the opportunity to be bored. There is this huge surge again of parents understanding that creativity is important.' – *Monica Dreger, Mattel*

Instant gratification

The amount of stimuli at children's fingertips and their instant response to it is another concern for their brain development. Using technology too early or too frequently in the early years can mean processes which the developing brain needs to go through in order to grow are skipped or covered too quickly, affecting normal brain development. The devices we all have in our homes are ultimate shortcut tools and there is a danger that use of them will influence young minds to believe that all stimuli lead to instant results and gratification. A finger swipe on a tablet results in action on the screen, and with that, the child's brain responds with dopamine, which is the chemical messenger for happiness – it's how we feel pleasure. And from that, over time, a child will start to internalise deeper in their brain that all actions should have immediate effect and bring immediate joy.[105]

'All the information is at their fingertips,' Angela, a mum of three, told us. 'We didn't have Google and the internet when we were in school. Whereas anything they want to know, they can Google.' Rommy, another mother of Generation Alpha, agrees. 'I find them [Generation Alpha] very demanding and impatient. Everything has to be now. You don't have to wait for anything anymore. If you want to search for something right now, it will be up on your phone in five seconds.'

This instant gratification brought about by technology poses a challenge to many educators, too. Marilyn Cox, a teacher, told us how this is 'a difference today because kids are being entertained and used to having everything presented in such a way that it's exciting. Not knowing anything else but technology, they are looking for that quick answer. I find children today have their own laptop, but oftentimes when I'm asking them to do research, they don't really read, they're looking for things that stand out quickly. It comes from them always swiping. But dense text or anything that requires effort and thinking is a challenge for them. There is also the addiction that comes with that.'

It is easy to identify with, even as adults. We've all sat at a red light in traffic, waiting for what feels like much longer than two minutes for the light to turn green and felt frustrated, so imagine how a child feels having grown up being able to instantly access practically anything with a few clicks. But it's not just our ability to be patient that's at stake here. There are layers of cognition too. If a child listens to a story being read to them, they have to take time to process the storyteller's voice into words, imagine in complete pictures the world or situation that is being described and use effort to follow the storyline. If our children watch a story on their device, they lose that opportunity to develop their creativity and imagination. They are entertained, but no mental effort is required. A device does the thinking for the child and their cognitive muscles remain under-stimulated and weak.

This is why unstructured play and blank-canvas creativity is so essential. When given an open space or a simple piece of sports or play equipment, children are compelled to create or shape an activity. When given just the blank page and pencils, the brain is forced to impose meaning on the space and imagination is triggered. While creativity can't be taught, it can be developed and stimulated when children are given regular opportunities like these.

Addiction

More research is coming to light about both the positive and negative impacts of our relationship with devices. One of these negative impacts is addiction, which psychologists link to the dopamine release triggered by screen interaction. As psychologist Dr Liraz Margalit describes it, 'When a child gets too used to an immediate stimuli response, she will learn to always prefer smartphone-style interaction – that is, immediate gratification and response – over real-world connection.' She likens this pattern to 'the dangerous cycle psychologists and physicians regularly see in patients with drug and alcohol addictions'.[106] Things that are addictive often lead to us feeling:

- a constant urge to use it
- difficulty self-managing our use of it
- changes in our mood
- a loss of time awareness while using it
- less focused on priorities like relationships, study or work.

Screen and social media usage certainly fits this description for many people.

In 2020, Netflix released a documentary called *The Social Dilemma*. In it, tech insiders and former employees of companies like Facebook, Instagram, Google, Twitter and Pinterest shared their experience working for these tech giants and the unintended downsides of social media. This compelling documentary shows how easy it can be for people of all ages, but especially our emerging generations, to become addicted to the use of social media.

The documentary also explores issues around the role social media plays in sharing and shaping opinions, and concerns about surveillance. It serves as a good reminder for us all to exercise caution about how much time we spend on these devices and how much agency we exert when it comes to our interaction with them. For parents, these questions are even more important as we consider both our children's and our own use of screens and social media platforms. This is particularly the case with younger children, who don't have the same level of impulse control as adults or older children.

How parents can help create a healthy relationship with screens

Since a child's brain is still developing, the onus is on parents to manage their child's use of devices and the amount of time they spend on screens. Here are some tips for how parents can help their children to have a healthy relationship with screen-based devices.

1. **Share digital experiences.** If we expect children to be interested in the sports activities and pastimes we enjoyed, we need to show an interest in exploring their world and interests too. Show interest in your children's viewing choices and take the opportunity to share and discuss it together. This type of shared viewing or experience can create a sense of belonging and connection. Essentially, utilise screens to build family relationships. This also allows us to assess the appropriateness of the programs, games and apps they use so that we can direct them towards healthy media consumption.

2. **Put children to bed like our grandparents did.** Utilise the power of stories and books, and have a screen-free bedtime pattern to connect with your children.

3. **Practise what we preach.** Just because our screen use involves emails and checking work texts doesn't change the fact that it disrupts family interactions and creates distractions. Model screen discipline and screen-free family time to encourage your children to do the same.

4. **If needed, implement a reset.** In families where screen use is out of control, we encourage parents to collect up all the devices and remotes, and call a 24-hour – or even better, weekend technology fast. Plan some alternative family activities: head out for a picnic, day trip or walk. Make it fun and, importantly, use the break to decide on a healthy screen use strategy.

Using devices as a reward that children earn can also help them build a healthy relationship with technology. Ben, a dad of three boys under ten, shared how his kids earn their time on the iPad by going for a run outdoors. 'When we implemented this, they never bugged me so much to exercise!' This initiative combines exercise and technology, and frames time on technology as a treat and not an every-day entitlement. Plus, it reduces the potential for a child to become addicted to their device at a young age. Of course, as children get older, it is a little harder to manage. ViacomCBS researched over eight thousand families and found that two thirds of them use technology as a reward.[107] So, as Ben has demonstrated, device management seems to be a growing reality in family homes as parents navigate the tension between restricting screen time and offering it as a reward.

The benefits and challenges of the great screen age

Generation Alpha have grown up as 'digital natives', and as the oldest begin to hit their teens, they will become 'screenagers'. Not only are they interacting with technological devices regularly, but they are also being shaped by them. 'My four-year-old, he's got an American accent,' Amy, a mother of Generation Alpha, told us. 'We reflected on how he learnt to talk, and it was the influence of YouTube, *Dora the Explorer*, and any of those sorts of shows that were teaching him how to speak. They are American or English based, there are no Australian accents, so he has a mixture of accents. I find it influences the way they act and talk and everything. So, we had to rethink how we do screen time.'

Our research discussions with Generation Alpha Australians confirms this. For many, the footpath has become a *sidewalk*, tomato sauce is *ketchup*, lollies are now *candy*, soft drinks have become *soda* and rubbish is *trash*. The Americanization of Australian English is seen not just in the more liberal use of **z** (organization and analyze), but in the pronunciation of it ('zee' rather than 'zed').

Generation Alpha, having grown up with digital technology from the youngest age, are confident and intuitive users of it. Often, they are even teaching the adults in their life how to use it. As a teacher and a mum, Kara told us, 'Every kid has to have an iPad, and because I'm working at school as a teacher, I thought I was pretty good at using one. But since working here, I'm the one learning from my kids who are in year four. They're showing me how to do all these shortcuts and how to speak into it to bring up the word, and I thought, wow, I was good, but now I feel like an amateur.'

Benefits of screens

One of the benefits of technology and this great screen age is access to information. Consider generations X and Y (the most likely parents of Generation Alpha) who were taught how to find library books and information in encyclopaedias. Now, any piece of information is accessible to Generation Alpha through the internet, and computers, laptops and learning portals are used for in-class learning. 'I think it's better for kids today because there is so much more information at your fingertips,' a parent in a focus group told us. 'I help my son with school projects, and just the amount of information available, especially educationally, means you can really educate yourself on anything very quickly – it's amazing. We didn't have that at our fingertips when I was a kid.'

The benefits of technology were also clearly demonstrated during the COVID-19 pandemic when, like everything else, education had to move online. Suddenly parents needed to facilitate their children's learning from home – while many parents also worked from home themselves. Although the quick adoption of this new learning style was a challenge for many, when we asked those who had participated in online education how they had found the experience, 71 per cent said it was a positive one for their household.[108]

Saving time

One of the direct benefits of technology is the time savings, especially for students. Online searching provides direct, efficient access compared with the physical and alphabetical searching for information in libraries and encyclopaedias. 'The time to go to the library is lost time, but that time becomes your quality time with your child looking up on the computer versus them going to the library,' said a Generation Alpha parent in one of our focus groups. This was also expressed, quite aptly, by Trinity, a nine-year-old Generation Alpha, who said, 'If my parents were looking for a definition, they had to find it in the dictionary. But now I find it on Google or something. But like, the dictionaries are so big. I don't want to go looking through every single letter in the alphabet to find my word! You can search your word or meaning on the internet, and it will tell you what your word is. With a dictionary, you have to look through every single page!'

Bringing people together

Screens can also bring people and families together. While streaming and services have changed screen viewing, for many the family television is still the digital fireplace around which people gather for a shared experience. 'Television shows such as *LEGO Masters* have brought our family together because we all wanted to see what they were creating, and *MasterChef* brings our family together as well because we love to cook and have tried to make a few of the dishes together,' said a Generation Alpha parent. Increasingly the content being watched on the household TV is not broadcast television but streamed content from Netflix or YouTube. However, the main screen still provides the gathering point and shared experience. One parent told us, 'Our fifteen-year-old introduced us to online multi-player games where you use your own screen to answer a quiz question or draw a picture that everyone can then see on a main screen. Now when we catch up with extended family both the Baby Boomer grandparents and our Gen Alpha five-year-old are keen to stream the game in the lounge room as it brings everyone together.' These multi-player games like Kahoot! or Quiplash allow people to participate using their mobile phones while gathering around a central screen. And it's not just for families but for other social gatherings. Our team at work even play them at lunchtime on occasion!

Screen challenges

While the increased use of screens in daily life provides positive opportunities, it also presents unique challenges. Many parents of Generation Alpha expressed to us how impossible it can be to pry Generation Alpha away from their screen-based devices. One parent told us her six-year-old was 'hiding underneath the computer desk at 11.30 pm because he wanted to wait until we had all gone to sleep so he could go on the computer. He knows he's not allowed to, so he waited until 11.30pm to go on it, until my husband found him. We were like, "Where's Jackson?" My husband searched everywhere – even outside. Then we heard this tiny little noise underneath the computer table and there he was. Technology can bring your family together, but it can also tear you apart.'

Generation Alpha are sometimes also called Generation Glass because screens and glass are the primary medium they learn and engage on. You might remember being instructed as a child to keep your hands off the glass. How different it is for children today whose life revolves around them putting their hands *on* the glass.

Connecting to others

Technology affords us some great benefits for connecting with family and friends who live overseas or are distant, but it can be a barrier to real emotional intimacy, distracting us from solid human and one-on-one interaction.[109]

Even though online learning was a blessing for many during COVID-19, and 52 per cent believe education will be delivered more online in the future,[110] the sentiment of many students and teachers while learning from home was that they looked forward to going back to school. While Zoom helped connect us during the pandemic, many suffered from 'Zoom fatigue' and missed interacting with friends and colleagues in person. This highlights that technology does have some limitations with regards to connecting and relationships, and that workplaces and places of education are more than just somewhere we go to work and learn – they are key pathways to social interaction, connection and belonging.

Our most important relationships occur at home with our partners and family and it's here where our lives can benefit from focusing on connecting. Creating a meaningful depth of emotional intimacy comes down to the *quality* of interaction. So, when you sit beside your partner or your children, scrolling on your phone, writing and responding to emails, though you have spent time sitting next to each other it isn't considered meaningful connection. As parents, our example influences the behaviour of Generation Alpha, so it's up to us to model meaningful relationships by giving our full attention to one another, listening, talking and looking at each other.

Though people are busy, with intention, ingenuity and a bit of discipline there can still be quality interactions and meaningful connection in the digital age. 'My husband found an app that locks our internet off at five pm every day, until the next morning,' a mum of three told us. 'That's become our norm and it means we spend time hearing about one another's days – the highs, lows and the things we're grateful for. The app has served us really well and I guess it goes to show that we are in charge of our quality time. We have come to prioritise the wellbeing of our kids and each other over whatever is happening online.' It's imperative for us all to balance the use of screen time, and for each family to cultivate a culture where there is time to turn off devices and time to build and nurture relationships with our children and with each other. This is an important foundation to establish so that, in turn, Generation Alpha will be able to build solid relationships as they mature.

Up-ageing

As we have seen, the entrenched use of screens and the internet in Generation Alpha's lives also means they are up-ageing – growing up faster, and at a younger age. 'I feel like kids are growing up earlier because they're exposed to a lot more than we were exposed to through social media,' Jen, a mother of Generation Alphas, said. 'I just feel like they're becoming mini adults before they actually need to. They should be playing with dolls or with trucks, and I think the internet does have a lot to do with it.' Parents are finding up-ageing challenging. Danielle, a mother of Generation Alphas, shared with us that she doesn't like screens and wants to 'chuck them in the bin. I can't monitor it. They've all got homework on the computer and who knows what they are doing on there. I just feel like I lose control and I think they lose a few skills that they could have, too.' Parents feel the tension of raising children in the great screenage, where their children need devices for school and to know how to use them, but they also need boundaries to ensure they remain safe.

Though the increased access to information afforded by technology is causing many Generation Alphas to experience up-ageing, it's important to remember that they are still children. Play and innocence are rites of passage for children, and should be preserved for their development and growth. As Trinity (aged nine) said in our Generation Alpha focus group, 'Everyone says they want to be older, and I've said that sometimes too. But my mum's like, "No, you don't want to be older because then you have to pay fees and bills, pay for food, pay for petrol," and she lists all this stuff, and that makes me glad that I'm a kid.'

Teaching Generation Alpha the necessary digital and critical-thinking skills required for them to thrive in the great screenage is a key responsibility of adults who lead, parent and educate them. It is also our responsibility, as adults, to allow them to just be kids.

Sitting still
There is also growing concern for the health implications of increased screen time – in particular, a more sedentary lifestyle, and the impacts screens have on sleep and social skills. Over recent years, workplaces have responded strongly

to the health implications of prolonged sitting with the introduction of standing desks, stretch breaks and the oft-repeated mantra 'sitting is the new smoking'. Yet even with improved ergonomics and protection against screen-omitted blue light, the broader issue remains: children are spending longer in front of screens from a younger age than has ever occurred before.

Online bullying

Our research shows that parents and their children are increasingly tuned in to the dangers and impacts of the online world from a mental health perspective. Parents want their children's social media experience to enhance their wellbeing and relational health. When considering the negatives, parents are most focused on the bullying, trolling and inappropriate content their children might encounter through screen use rather than the privacy and internet security aspects.

As we saw in Chapter 3, bullying is a key issue for young people and in some ways it has been accelerated by technology. Bullying used to be confined to the school yard, but technology means it can extend into the home. The Australian government's eSafety Commissioner outlines cyberbullying as '... behaviour [that] takes many forms, such as sending abusive messages, hurtful images or videos, nasty online gossip, excluding or humiliating others, or creating fake accounts in someone's name to trick or humiliate them.' They state that 'Online bullying can have a devastating impact on young people, whose online life is a key part of their identity and how they interact socially.'[111]

Three in five students have experienced bullying, and shockingly one in five experience it weekly. In fact, more students have experienced it than haven't, with 2.3 million students having experienced bullying and one in five experiencing it weekly.[112]

Children developing with technology

'Hey Alexa, play *Bluey*.' These are the kinds of words commonly uttered by kids as young as two. Although it can be a bit of a shock to hear the phrase spoken so confidently by a two-year-old, it is reflective of the world in which their generation is being shaped, where artificial intelligence is found in many homes and is being used by people of all ages.

A team of researchers at the MIT Media Lab recently ran a pilot study to explore how children interact with artificial intelligence devices.[113] They observed how a group of children aged three to ten interacted with four artificial intelligence 'agents': Google Home; an Amazon Echo Dot, with its 'Alexa' assistant; a chatbot tablet app called Julie; and Cozmo, a small autonomous robot made by toy company Anki. Most of the children found the artificial intelligence agents to be friendly and trustworthy, and the older children often asserted that the artificial intelligences – especially Alexa – were smarter than themselves.

Voice recognition technology has become more widely accessible in the last few years, to the point that Generation Alpha are confident users of it. Jen, a mum of some Generation Alphas, confirmed this in one of our focus groups when she told us that 'the kids use Siri for everything, and I'm like, "Who are you talking to?" and they're like, "Oh, Siri."' Another mother shared how, even though 'we have a clock in the kitchen, my son Aiden is like, "Hey Google, what time is it?" He's talking to the Google Home.' It's great to see that parents can also see the lighter side of their children's interaction with voice technology, with a dad named Alvin sharing with us that he's had to remind his kids, 'My name is not Google, Siri or Alexa!'

As technology develops alongside Generation Alpha, these user-friendly trends of artificial intelligence and voice recognition will become increasingly common methods of communication between human and machine. This will lead to keyboards and screens giving way to controller-free gestural interfaces and two-way conversations between device and human.

An Ofcom report[114] on children's media use has shown that smartphone and tablet ownership among kids aged five to fifteen is increasing, with 41 per cent of children owning a smartphone and 44 per cent owning a tablet. Until age ten, children are more likely to own a tablet device, yet between the ages of nine and ten, smartphone ownership more than doubles from 23 per cent to 50 per cent. By age fifteen, almost all children own their own smartphone.

A majority of children aged three to four (55 per cent) are reported to use a tablet.[115] There has also been an increase in the use of YouTube among Generation Alpha, with YouTube increasingly seen as the viewing platform of choice, particularly among those aged eight to eleven. Those who become successful on YouTube and develop a large following, 'YouTubers', are different to celebrities, actors or pop-stars in that their success is not created through big marketing budgets, movie studies or music labels, but rather through growing the views, likes and recommendations of their audience. Their success is achieved organically and so they have a relatability to their fans. This has resulted in Generation Alpha observing that they too could become like this, with many we spoke to saying that when they grow up they want to be 'a YouTuber'. Generation Alpha feel a connection with the YouTubers that they follow because through their votes, likes and shares, they feel key to creating the YouTubers' success. Further, through the interactivity of commenting, buying merchandise (or 'merch' as they call it) and being one of the first to view each new video, they feel a connection with the YouTuber.

From our interaction with Generation Alpha, here are the five most mentioned YouTube channels, each of which has accumulated hundreds of millions of views.

- PewDiePie
- Dude Perfect
- MrBeast
- Ryan's World
- TheOdd1sOut

In addition to these, are the plethora of YouTubers whose videos are comprised entirely of them playing popular games such as Fortnite and Minecraft, of which LazarBeam and Lachy are popular examples.

Newer platforms such as TikTok have also gained immense popularity. TikTok is not just a social media platform, it is an entertainment platform that provides short-form visual content. It also intuitively adapts to the users' interests.

TikTok is a popular platform among kids, especially tweens and teenagers. In November 2018, TikTok reported 680 million monthly active users and this increased to beyond one billion by early 2021,[116] with a surge during COVID-19 lockdowns. It's certainly alleviated a lot of boredom in some homes with kids sharing videos with friends. Even if Generation Alpha are too young to use TikTok now, they know the dances and the trends of the platform.

Keeping kids safe

Social media platforms like TikTok often raise concerns for parents about privacy – specifically, what data is being collected about their child, and how it is stored. But kids today don't think that way. It takes twentieth-century thinking applied to the twenty-first century world of devices to worry about such things. Parents think, 'We didn't have all of that because we could access a book or encyclopedia from the library for our information.' Yet Generation Alpha's whole existence has been about leaving digital fingerprints. It's the only world they have ever known. Kids think about the now; they aren't worried about the future. They have a different time perspective and are pragmatic: if tech platforms can serve up more relevant content or useful ads by gathering their information, then the kids tend to think that's all the better for them, because it makes their experience customised and relevant. They also don't differentiate as much between advertising and content. In fact, advertising is harder to distinguish, because it is part of the social media world, and they are not trying to screen it out as previous generations did; nor are they sceptical about it. In a world of social media, the advertisers are often the social media influencers and content creators themselves. They are the ones placing the products, endorsing the brands and starring in the ads that Generation Alpha consume. If it is promoting a brand or endorsing a product it is an ad – but for Generation Alpha it is just content.

Parents have an important, nurturing role to play in their children's lives. Kids do not care about what they eat, but parents have to. Kids do not think about wearing a hat in the sun, but it is the parent who reminds them. Just as parents are prioritising the long-term health of their children when they encourage nutritious eating and sun-safe behaviour, so too do they need to think about their children's employment and social future when they intentionally manage what their kids share online.

As we become more aware of how platforms like Facebook, Google, Instagram and TikTok gather and retain user data, it will become more important for parents to teach Generation Alpha about the permanency of their posts and the ramifications (such as identity theft, data scraping and facial recognition) of giving these platforms information.

What concerns parents about their child's internet use?

The main concerns parents have about their child's internet use, according to parents of children aged five to fifteen who go online, are:[117]

- Companies collecting information about what they are doing online (50 per cent)
- Damaging their reputation either now or in the future (42 per cent)
- Giving out personal details to inappropriate people (41 per cent)
- Pressure to spend money online (41 per cent)
- Cyberbullying (40 per cent)
- Content which encourages them to hurt or harm themselves (39 per cent)
- How much time they spend online (37 per cent)
- Online content (32 per cent)
- Possibility of them being radicalised (29 per cent)

These concerns about isolated screen time and safety were also expressed in the focus groups we conducted of Generation Alpha parents, with one parent saying, 'The difference between YouTube or social media is what kids are taking in. When everyone was watching a TV show, we all had a shared experience that we could bond over – there is something kind of social about that. But with YouTube, kids are watching these things all by themselves. It's isolated and really hard to keep track of.' From graphic content to inappropriate ads for children, parents are concerned about the rabbit hole of the internet, and in particular that children will stumble across content that is inappropriate for them, such as content containing violence, pornography, gambling, swearing, cruelty, sexism, racism, drug use or unmoderated chat rooms. One mum, Kristel, acknowledged that kids 'are very smart these days, they're very switched on', but she also spoke about the privacy and safety of content online and how easy it is to accidentally click through to something inappropriate. 'If you press the wrong button on YouTube, a pop-up comes up for porn.' Parents can prevent kids from viewing inappropriate content by using parental controls and ensuring you have visibility over what your children view. It is also good to openly talk about the content your children view online as much as possible – this way you can respond quickly to any incidents that happen.

Encouraging digital intelligence

As we lead and parent Generation Alpha, it's important to note that their online social life is just as important as their in-person social life. The eSafety Commissioner has some excellent tips on building intelligence from a young age[118] and we have expanded this into the following five habits:

Habit	How to do it and why	Example
Give respect	Encourage children to respect everyone they meet online, using the manners they would use in person.	Highlight, for example, that if you weren't comfortable to say something to someone in person then it's probably best to not say it at all.
Look for ways to exercise and teach about empathy	Encourage children to consider different points of view before responding to something. Discuss why people have different points of view – opening their eyes to see that people's different life experiences affect how they see things. And explain that just because it's different, it doesn't mean it's bad or wrong.	Share examples or stories with your child from when you learnt about someone's circumstance which made you better understand why they were acting or feeling a certain way.
Encourage scepticism	Teach children to be critical of what they read and see when on the internet. Give them standard questions to help them identify fake news or misleading messages. Explain why they should be suspicious of unsolicited messages and emails and encourage them to have a healthy scepticism of social media, apps and why these platforms are collecting personal data.	Children spend much of their time responding to instructions, answering questions and doing what other people tell them to do. So they can be particularly vulnerable to filling in forms or providing information to dubious sources. Encourage them to have their guard up when online and help them to be aware of the many various online operators.
Promote and model balance	Work on achieving a healthy balance in children's online and offline activities and ensure strong passwords and boundaries are set for digital device use in the home. Try using family passwords, limit time on devices and set operational hours on internet routers to encourage time off screens and promote meaningful connection.	Many parents told us how they have device-free dinners or device-free car trips. These little initiatives can be very effective in showing kids that time away from technology is an important priority. Many parents are now utilising lock boxes for phones and TV remotes that can keep the devices under padlock for screen-free time.

Habit	How to do it and why	Example
Find the moment to teach and foster resilience	Keep calm if your child encounters a negative experience online, and look for ways to teach them about the learning from the situation.[119]	One parent shared that, against their better judgement, they paid for a loop box code to help their son advance levels in an online game. Whether a scam or a fault, the code didn't work. The son's disappointment became a permanent reminder of how easily money can be wasted, and as a consequence he has not shown any desire to spend further money in these online platforms.

How companies can help

We've seen a level of proactivity from app developers and social media platforms such as Facebook, Instagram and Twitter that have made it easy for users to report anti-social behaviour. The ability to report things such as hate speech, violence, sale of illegal goods, bullying or harassment, fraud, false information, self-harm and exploitation are all positive steps. As parents and adults, it is our job to educate ourselves on the apps children use, and to proactively report the content that we don't want them to see. This way we can make online spaces safer for every child.

We are seeing that app developers are playing their part when it comes to protecting young users. In May 2020, TikTok outlined its commitment to digital literacy by providing a Youth Portal. The portal covers things like safe password creation, what a user should keep private and how to spot suspicious behaviour.[120] The launch of Youth Portal followed the release of their Family Pairing feature in April 2020. The increase in app usage during the COVID-19 lockdown led to parents and experts raising concerns about the safety of the app. TikTok now partner with leading online safety organisations, including the Family Online Safety Institute, ConnectSafely and the National Center for Missing and Exploited Children.[121] The Family Pairing initiative has the ability to manage screen time, create a 'restricted mode' which limits content that may not be appropriate for young audiences and allows restrictions to be enabled in the 'direct messages' feature.

In 2017 Facebook introduced a new app called Messenger Kids, which is designed for kids aged between six and twelve. The app allows these children to communicate (using pre-approved GIFs, stickers and other drawing tools) with parent-approved friends and family. Parents have to set up the account, and parents must approve all contacts. There is also no advertising on the app and Facebook says that children's data is not collected for commercial purposes.[122]

Similarly, in 2019 Instagram removed the number of 'likes' in an effort to reduce the digital peer pressure many young users face.

It is positive to see that app creators have taken deliberate steps to help educate parents and users about online safety, and provided them with tools to help manage this. As parents we need to ensure we have an understanding of the apps children use as soon as they start using them, and check what features are in place to ensure our children navigate the digital world safely.

The social in social media

The online social lives of young people are just as important as their in-person social lives, but many people are starting to wonder, 'Will young people be socially inept if they spend too much time on their devices?' Many parents express concern that their children are so absorbed in their devices and on social media that they won't know how to interact with other humans.

> 'The drawback is the loss of physical or social interaction. When you're isolated with technology, you're not spending that time just hanging out with your friends. Growing up, I used to be like, "Oh, you're free. Let's go play!" We'd go ride bikes or play and have that social interaction and be outside. Now I fear that some of that is lost. There is so much value in social interaction and human contact, and if we're losing some of that, I don't know what would replace it.' – *a parent of a Generation Alpha*

For many parents, this social media world is vastly different to the social interaction they are used to, and have concerns about it. While this is a very real concern for parents, many young people themselves don't see their social media use in this way. It's vastly different for their parents, yet it is all Generation Alpha and Generation Z have ever known – plus, they are too busy being on it to worry about it! While we have found that the emerging generations broadly acknowledge there can be challenges with social media use like bullying and sedentary lifestyles, they still see it as a fun and creative way to be connected to their friends and peers.

> 'TikTok is for fun. It's me and my friends dancing and being silly, but we're doing it together. And Instagram – I use that for shout-outs for my friend's birthdays. Or like for posting a nice pic of me and my friends. But we will come up with a nice caption for the pic together. I know adults all think it's super-dangerous online, but that's not how I use it – it's just me and my friends having fun together.' – *Lacy, aged thirteen*

As we can see, the 'social' in social media has a very broad use. It's social in that the reach is wide and can connect with a broad audience. The content also creates social interaction – we share the meme or video and we laugh about it with our friends and family. We then go on to share related memes or personal stories. This builds a sense of connection and community. Younger people like Lacy also collaborate on social media, creating pictures or videos together. Plus, it's social in the way that it connects us one-on-one with people we might not ordinarily meet.

Generation Alpha: a global experiment?

In some ways, Generation Alpha are part of an unintentional global experiment in which screens are placed in front of them from the youngest age. The results so far have been mixed. Even now, after a decade of integrating portable screen-based devices and social media into our lives, lessons have been learnt.

In our research with Generation Z (those born from 1995 to 2009, some of whom would be Generation Alpha's older siblings), many indicated to us that they have self-diagnosed the problem of too much screen time and social media. We are now seeing many from Gen Z partake in a 'social media detox', whereby they remove themselves from social media for a period to reconnect with the tangible world and people around them.

Of course, we need to help young people manage their use of technology and social media – in terms of who they interact with, ensuring they are safe online and how much time they spend on it – but there is certainly a socially beneficial aspect to social media too. As we learn more about the impacts and opportunities of social media in the great screen age, it is encouraging to think Generation Alpha will be better placed to navigate and respond to these technologies and platforms, as they've now had more than a decade of integrating them into everyday life.

Brand value

The ability to access any piece of information on the planet has altered our expectations of the brands and organisations we engage with. As consumers we value trust – whether it be in a brand, person or entity – above price, promise or experience. Brands who can gain and keep trust, through transparency and by offering products that meet this generation's core values, will thrive in the future. This even applies to the types of shows and entertainment Generation Alpha engage with.

One popular new show for this generation is *Bluey*, which follows the adventure of blue heeler puppy Bluey. Bluey lives with her mum, dad and sister. She is an excitable six-year-old who sees everyday life as an exciting adventure, developing her imagination and resilience in the process.[123] When we asked Geoff, a dad of three Generation Alphas, why his children love the show so much, he said, 'It presents childhood perspectives of everyday Australian life scenarios that are relatable in an engaging and humorous way. As a Gen Y dad who grew up in the leafy suburbs, these short episodes quickly connect with many of my childhood memories and reveal new ideas for my current parenting dilemmas!' Bluey is one example of a TV show that parents and their children are engaging with because they trust the positive values it communicates.

Young children don't consider the values of a brand as much as they care about the trends and fads of their friends – although it is something they may care about in the teen and young adult life stage, as their Gen Z counterparts are doing today. However, many parents are keen for the brands they engage with to be founded on ethical and sustainable values. The best way parents can achieve this is by voting with their wallet – or in other words, not buying from brands that don't align with the values important to them and their family.

The future of successful toy brands is also about values-based organisations creating toys that enhance connectivity, facilitate community interaction and develop social and global skills among the next generation. Diversity, inclusion and representation are important issues for brands to communicate with kids today. Monica Dreger from Mattel told us that 'we have a doll with alopecia who is bald, a prosthetic-leg Barbie, and our American girl of the year has hearing aids. This is so that kids from a very young age can see that there are many different types of people. In our research, we showed the dolls to kids and one girl loved it so much because she had cancer, and as her hair grew back, no one knew she was a girl. When she saw the doll, she wished she had had one at the time and she said, "It would have been so special having known someone like me was out there."'

We are also seeing greater expectations placed on organisations' ethos, products and marketing because the emerging generations want to engage with brands that have a cause and ethics. The oversaturation of marketing means there are now many companies to choose from, and the decision to engage with a product is shifting to the good that the overarching company is doing in the world. One such company is Hello Sunshine. Founded by Hollywood actor and Oscar winner Reese Witherspoon, Hello Sunshine is a media company that puts women at the centre of every story they create. 'We really are looking to change the narrative of women's storytelling,' Andrew Tolbert, Senior Director of Kids and Animation at Hello Sunshine, told us. 'We are looking to put the spotlight on content where the female characters have power, ability, make good decisions, and act on them – women with agency.' This is a change, happening now, that will have an impact on the future of movies and television and what Generation Alpha girls will grow up watching and being influenced by. The more characters played by women and the more stories about them, the more Generation Alpha will see examples of women who have agency. After all, we can't be what we can't see.

'I read a lot of pitches, a lot of stories,' Andrew told us. 'And I'm quite picky, but that's because our mission is so very clear. And as I'm reading, I'm asking myself, "What values are we bringing as a company that we can elevate in the story and bring it to the next level?" This is important to us, that we not only stay aligned to our core mission, but we elevate content to increase its impact in the world and on the next generation.'

Hello Sunshine is a clear example of a company that is creating and proactively seeking content that correlates with their values. And this, we believe, will become increasingly commonplace with content creators being more deliberate about addressing and including social issues, but in a nuanced way.

'We're mindful of the need to normalise some things in our programming,' said a television producer we interviewed. 'So we are looking at ways we can include things like a child character recycling a milk carton after drinking from it. It doesn't need to be explicit to send a clear message, but it is important that we have characters that kids can relate to, whose positive behaviours they can emulate.'

Generation Alpha are being defined by technology, screens and their devices; however, we believe they are a generation that will not be dictated to by them.

The well-known African proverb 'It takes a village to raise a child' is still true today. Parents, caregivers, teachers and content producers all need to work together to educate, inform and entertain a child, but we also all need to work together to instil values in the upcoming generation. It's true that Generation Alpha are being defined by technology, screens and their devices. However, we believe they are a generation that will not be dictated to by them. As understanding and awareness grows around technology, Generation Alpha will make empowered decisions based on their personal preferences, not the push of a marketer. Ultimately Generation Alpha will act in a way that shows that they are in control of their personal experience of technology and its impact on them, their peers, their family and their world. It's our responsibility as parents, educators and leaders to help them to that end, which we will explore in the following chapter on parenting.

Key takeaways

In this chapter we have explored the world of technology that Generation Alpha are being shaped in, and the tensions parents face when it comes to children and technology. While there are benefits of greater access to information and connection with others, there are also challenges presented by technology. These can include challenges for social and brain development in children, instant gratification, screen addiction, growing up faster, sedentary lifestyles and online bullying. Although the list of challenges is long, it is encouraging to see that companies are making changes to ensure technology, social media and the content they produce are values-driven. In an increasingly tech-driven world, it is more important than ever for parents of Generation Alpha to have practical strategies in place to equip their children with the skills to thrive in the great screen age.

CHAPTER 5

Parenting Generation Alpha

'Children are not a distraction from more important
work. They are the most important work.'

C. S. Lewis

This chapter is full of experiences and stories from parents raising Generation Alpha. Though it's not a comprehensive 'how to' when it comes to raising children, we wanted to include both the stories and our observations about the challenges and opportunities that parents face today, as well as take a look at how parenting has changed for these emerging generations.

The crucial role of parents

There are many people and groups that play an important role in a person's life – from when they are a child right through to adulthood. These people include friends, teachers, siblings, aunts, uncles, co-workers, partners and spouses. Yet of course, the most significant people are often our parents or guardians.

As Collett Smart says in her book on parenting, *They'll Be Okay*, 'Primary caregivers are the first and most predominant role models in children's lives. Although children make their own choices, carers play a significant role in helping to shape and mould the attitudes, ethical development and resilience of young people as they grow.'[124] Which is why we even have international days of recognition to celebrate and thank our mums and dads for all they do.

Would you apply for this job?

Job title: Operations Director However, it's really a lot more than that.

Responsibilities and requirements: Extensive. The job requires you to work standing up most of the time. You'll constantly be exerting yourself, so it will require a high level of stamina.

Hours: Unlimited. Twenty-four hours a day, seven days a week. No breaks allowed, and your lunch can only be eaten when the associate is finished eating their lunch.

Skills required: Excellent negotiation and interpersonal skills. Tertiary qualifications in medicine, finance and the arts are preferred. A happy, positive outlook is also a prerequisite.

Job description: It's all about the associate. They will need constant attention. Sometimes you will have to stay up with the associate during the night. You will need to be able to work effectively in chaotic situations. If you had a life, you would pretty much need to give that life up. No holidays are permitted. In fact, the workload is going to go up during Christmas and other holiday periods.

Salary: $0. That's right, it's an unpaid role.

As you might be able to tell, this is a fake job ad, and is adapted from a YouTube video by the greeting card company, American Greetings. They created this ad, posted it online and in newspapers and recorded the reactions of online applicants. Suffice to say, all the applicants were shocked when they were told that billions of people already held the position described in the ad.[125] 'Who?' respondents eagerly asked. 'Mums,' said the interviewer. As the penny dropped, the interviewees all smiled, laughed and some even got teary as they thought about their own mums. If you haven't seen the video, it is well worth a watch, as it creatively shows the important role that mums, dads, parents and caregivers play in the lives of their children.

> 'I love being a parent (most of the time). It's crazy and challenging but also a lot of fun. Our one-year-old son is cheeky and hilarious, and I wake up every morning excited to see his face. The entire first year has been an ebb and flow of hard and frustrating phases, followed by very sweet and easy phases, then back again. The first few months in particular were a huge learning curve, but the more we have gotten to know our son and learnt to trust our instincts and relax, the easier it's been. The most joyful times have been when we've just let go (of cooking, cleaning, sleep schedules, etc.) and enjoyed him, because it goes so fast.' – Emma, a mum of a Generation Alpha (with another on the way)

Parenting in the new century

One of the biggest mistakes parents can make is to parent in the identical way they were parented. While there are some aspects of parenting that are timeless (changing nappies, for example), parents today cannot apply all of the same principles that were used when they were growing up, because it was simply a different time. A different century, in fact! Parents of Gen Y didn't have to deal with social media like parents do today, for example. And so, parenting in a different era warrants a review of what worked well in the past and is timeless, while also incorporating strategies that are appropriate for the changed times. This could look like setting structures in place for screen time or deciding how to care for children when both parents are working – issues that parents in the past didn't have to consider as much as parents do today.

Parents today look and act differently to how their parents did a generation ago. Demographically, parents today are older than parents were in the past. Like other developed nations, Australians have been pushing back traditional life markers like having children and getting married. A first-time parent in the 1980s was typically in their mid to late twenties. Today, the average age of first-time parents is the early thirties.[126] The main reason for this is a social one – more women are now able to access education and enter the workforce than used to be the case, and they are delaying moving out of home, getting married and having children. The cost of 'nesting' – buying and fitting out a family home is higher and saving for this takes longer. Additionally, medical advancements have enabled women's child-bearing years to be extended. While this means there are a greater number of years between the age of children and their parents (for most it will be more than three decades), it also means that more children today get to observe both parents working. As one mother to Generation Alpha children, told us, 'It means, especially for girls, that they can see their mothers and fathers both working, and it can be quite positive. They can see that they can have a career as well as a family.'

The role of mothers

There has been a significant increase in female workforce participation over the last fifty years, which has given rise to growth in 'dual-earner' couples – that is, couples in which both members are employed and contributing to the household finances. Since 2001 there has been a 10 per cent increase in the number of families where both spouses are employed.[127]

While there are many parents who love their career and work because they want to, for others it is not a decision as much as a necessity. The increasing cost of living, and the dream of home ownership (or the reality of mortgage repayments) means that many don't have a choice when it comes to work.

Striking a balance between paid work and raising children is something every parent strives for, yet this can be challenging for full-time workers. The Household, Income and Labour Dynamics in Australia Survey (also known as the HILDA survey) reveals a clear connection between longer working hours and greater work–family conflict. And it shows that mothers seem to feel the effects the most. Not only have mothers' working hours increased since 2001, full-time working mothers, on average, also express a significantly higher degree of difficulty in balancing work and family life than is the case for all parents. Being able to achieve a work–family life balance also depends on the person's family situation, including the age of their youngest child, number of children and marital status. Mothers with young children (from birth to three years) report relatively low levels of work–family conflict, which is partly explained by their concentration in part-time jobs.[128]

While we have come a long way in supporting mothers as they balance the competing demands of work and family, many in our research expressed that 'mum guilt' is still something they experience.

'Mum guilt'

'As mums, we put the pressure on ourselves. If we don't send them to a good school, put them in a sport, do an after-school activity or put them in tutoring because they're struggling, then we're not good parents. You're just constantly wondering, am I doing a good job?'

'I feel like there's more pressure on me as a parent to put the effort in. My son goes to tutoring, is on a tennis team, does computer coding, and the time it takes to organise all that is a lot – and I work full-time.'

– *comments from two mums of Generation Alpha children*

Raising children is extremely rewarding, but also tough. In order for parents to be the best they can be, we need to alleviate 'mum or dad guilt'. As hard as it can be, it starts with having compassion for yourself and for those around you, to encourage and uplift each other in the parenting journey. As a mum of a one-year-old, told us, 'I feel very thankful to have a great group of friends and a close family who have given my husband and I a lot of support every step of the way. Sharing the burdens and stresses of parenthood with other people makes a huge difference and helps keep the difficult times in perspective.'

Life today is busier and more complex than it was just a few decades ago. As one mum phrased it, 'I'm like an octopus playing netball. I'm constantly doing something.' Generation Alpha mum, Jen, also shared with us a similar experience. 'I think women have it harder than ever because before they could stay home and look after the kids, whereas now they have to work full-time, look after the kids, do the washing, do all the housework. So now it's like they've got two or three jobs. There's more stress because it is hard work juggling all those things.'

The data backs up Jen's experience. The latest HILDA survey showed that women are increasing their paid work participation but men are not picking up more of the unpaid domestic hours. Females continue to work longer hours doing housework and childcare tasks than males, regardless of the earnings arrangement of the household.

In couple households who have dependent children where the male is the breadwinner, the female on average spends fifty-five hours per week on housework and childcare, compared to the male contribution of twenty-six hours. When the paid and unpaid work hours are totalled, there is little difference between males and females in these households, with females working 76.5 hours compared to 76.8 hours for males.

In female breadwinner households, not only do females work longer in paid work but they also work longer in unpaid work. In these female breadwinner households, women on average spend forty-three hours on housework and childcare, compared to thirty hours of unpaid work for males. Females with dependent children in households where they are the breadwinner are the busiest people in Australia, working on average eighty-one hours per week (total of paid and unpaid work), compared to their male counterparts (sixty-eight hours).

In couple households with children where the earnings are approximately even, here again females (when including paid and unpaid work) work longer hours (eighty-one hours) compared to males (seventy-six hours).[129] Again, in this category while the hours invested in paid work are similar for males and females, it is the hours spent on housework and childcare that differentiates females from males.

While women have increased their participation rate in paid work, males, although they have increased the hours spent in active childcare tasks, have not made significant inroads into closing the gap on unpaid domestic work. This shows an area of improvement for households across Australia, and the need to show our appreciation for busy mums by helping lighten their load and distributing the housework and childcare responsibilities more evenly.

The role of fathers

The concept of fatherhood has shifted over time. Historically, fathers were the primary authority in the family, whose decisions were final and unquestioned. As the 'second caregiver', a father's impact on his children used to be viewed as less significant than a mother. If a mother was the nurturer then the father was the provider.

The twentieth century brought about social and economic shifts which have changed this perspective of fathers and the value they bring to their children's lives. With both parents often working, the role of the father has moved from the distant breadwinner to a more involved co-parent.

'I spent most of my life growing up being taken care of by my stay-at-home mum. My dad worked long hours and even the weekend, so I didn't really see much of him. I appreciate all the work my parents have done in raising me in their respective ways, but today as a father of a two-year-old (and one more on the way), I share equal responsibility raising our daughter with my wife. We're also both in the workforce to reach our goal of owning a home one day, but also because it allows my wife to continue her career that she is passionate about.' – *Peter, father of a Generation Alpha (with another one on the way)*

Not only has a shift in family structures provided fathers with more of an opportunity to be involved in their children's lives but the benefits of this involvement have been significant. There is a vast amount of research which suggests that involved fathers play a crucial role in various aspects of a child's life – from their cognitive development to their behaviour, mannerisms and overall wellbeing. It is often said that having a positive male role model is especially important for daughters, as it helps them to form positive associations with men in the broader sense, but it is equally important for growing boys to have involved fathers and positive male role models in their life. As the role of fathers has become more of a focus over time, it has become more widely acknowledged that fathers play an equally important role in the lives of their children as mothers do, and for many fathers, this encourages a greater desire to involved in their children's lives.[130]

'If my husband Andrew is away, I really notice it when the kids haven't seen him for a couple of days. They get a little bit agitated and fussy. Our youngest daughter, Chloe, who is three, demands that he says goodbye to her every morning, even if she is still asleep.' – *Monique, a mother of three Generation Alpha children*

Supportive and active fathers strengthen families by making their children feel loved and cared for. Because men and women are different, involved fathers bring a different perspective to various matters. They also bring a different parenting style, one that is often expressed in how fathers play

—

While *quality* time is a worthy aspiration, it is *quantity* time that matters more to children. Bonding moments can't be curated – they just happen, but they require presence and time.

—

with their children. Play that is stimulating and challenging helps children's social and emotional development, helps to regulate their feelings and develop their resilience. Not only can fathers bring active play, fathers today are also able to be caring and nurturing as we move away from the stereotypes of mothers as the only parent able to nurture. It has also been shown that children, adolescents and young adults have better educational outcomes when they have caring and involved fathers. Research indicates that fathers who are both active and nurturing have an impact on their child's verbal skills, academic achievement and intellectual functioning.[131]

What this shows us is that being a good parent is less about gender, and more about the time and effort invested. In order for fathers to continue to be involved and active parents in Generation Alpha's life, they need to spend significant time with their children, be available for them and take responsibility for organising aspects of their life, like childcare and other appointments. While *quality* time is a worthy aspiration, it is *quantity* time that matters more to children. Bonding moments can't be curated – they just happen, but they require presence and time.

> 'I think dads need to do a lot more in affirming their sons and daughters. That's an important role for dads, to set their kids up well.' – *Marilyn Cox, primary school teacher*

More broadly, it is also important that fathers are trusted and seen to be as capable as mothers in caring for their children. It's important to acknowledge that fathers also need to be given the time and space to develop their parenting, which may call for adjustments to parental leave and what father-friendly work environments look like.

In June 2018, New Zealand's Prime Minister Jacinda Ardern gave birth to her baby girl, Neve Te Aroha, making her the first elected world leader to take maternity leave and the second to have a child while in office. Ardern's partner, Clarke Gayford, stayed home to look after baby Neve. While of course this isn't the first instance of a man being a stay-at-home dad, these two parents are setting the example on a global, political stage. In an article in *The Telegraph*, the comment is made that 'Gayford is making a seismic statement. If there's one thing the world needs, it's positive role models for fathers to look up to. And here we have a guy with a successful media career who is cutting right back on his workload in order to do the heavy lifting at home.'[132]

Changes to the 'nuclear family'

Another way that parenting looks different today is with a change to the traditional 'nuclear family' structure, which is becoming more diversified. For the first time in Australia's history, the nuclear family (couple with children) will no longer be the most common household. Today they make up 30 per cent of all households, but within a few years the couple-only household (currently 25 per cent) will be the most common type of household.[133] There are a number of factors influencing this transition, including Generation Y couples having children later, and Baby Boomer households becoming empty-nesters in record numbers.

The median age of mothers and fathers at new births is now thirty-two and thirty-four respectively.[134] The increasing of the median age at new births means that households are remaining couple-only for longer.

Besides couple-only households, other household types are becoming more prevalent. Multi-generational households are on the increase with Gen X being sandwiched between taking care of their parents (Baby Boomers) and their children (Gen-Z), many of whom are either studying while living at home or choosing to stay or return home after moving out, to combat the increasing costs of living out of home. While all families with dependent children by their nature are multi-generational, there are another one in five Australians who live in multi-generational households where all residents are aged over eighteen and related.[135] The fastest growing age group for multi-generational household members are those aged over sixty-five.[136] This shows the trend of Australians looking for alternatives to institutional aged care and retirement living, moving in with their adult children for social reasons and financial savings and to assist with childcare.

In addition to multi-generational homes, single-person households are also on the increase. Such is the impact of the ageing population that by 2036, single-person households will also be more numerous than nuclear families.

'The nuclear family was always the mum and dad and the kids, and dad went to work and mum stayed home. That's completely different now,' Danielle, mum of three, told us. 'There's many, many combinations. There's grandparents raising kids, there's single mums, there's mixed families and it's all acceptable. You don't just rely on the parents to teach the kids. There's input coming from all over the place.' As Kara, another mum, put it, 'the family dynamics and therefore the parenting is different. I think back then it was more structured. The father was the breadwinner and the mother looked after the kids, but then these days, it could be any kind of combination really, it's whatever works best for the family.'

The modern family is more than a TV show, it is the reality of diverse households and families that are shaping

Generation Alpha. Of all couple families (this includes couples with and without children), 1.4 per cent are same sex.[137] Additionally, almost one in twenty marriages currently are of same-sex couples.[138] Australia is one of the world's most culturally diverse nations with more than one in four Australians born overseas.[139] The top five countries of overseas-born Australians are England, China, India, New Zealand and the Philippines.[140] Nationally, one in five people speak a language other than English at home, and in the inner-city areas of Melbourne and Sydney it is more than one in three.[141]

Shout-out to solo parents

As this chapter has highlighted, parenting amid juggling the other responsibilities of adult life is a tough job, but there is one job that is tougher, and that is doing this alone. We want to take a moment here to acknowledge the one million families (one in seven families nationally)[142] that are being led by either a single mum or dad who are doing the role of both parents. And although there is much research on the pivotal role of both mums and dads in a child's life, one of the best predictors for how well kids turn out is that they have a secure attachment with at least one person. This is a concept explored in *The Power of Showing Up*, written by Daniel J. Siegel and Tina Payne Bryson. In the book they talk about how, in a busy world, the most important thing a parent can do is show up and be present for their children. How? By helping them to build secure attachments – ensuring they feel safe, seen, soothed and secure. So here's a shout-out to the single parents. We see you, and we appreciate all you are doing for our Generation Alphas.

When it comes to parenting Generation Alpha, some of the biggest changes have been in emotional belonging and play with children.

'Different generations have different ways of doing things,' one mum of Generation Alphas shared with us. 'Growing up, we didn't talk about emotions. Whereas today, it's very different. I have been working with my kids so they know they can talk about their emotions and for me that is important. Whereas I found when I was growing up that it was very much that you were there, but you weren't heard.'

The Victorian saying that 'Children should be seen and not heard' seems outdated in our current world. We're actually living in days where it's considered that children should be seen *and* children should be heard. As one mum of three told us, 'Today it's the opposite of the old saying "Children should be seen and not heard". Kids are more outspoken and are happy to talk. Whereas before they would have been hiding behind our backs or under the table, now they're more engaged and want to be involved. They want to know what's going on.' Children being 'seen' leads to a growth in confidence because it creates a forum for a child to think through an idea from differing perspectives and help make decisions with guidance.

'It had been a long time since we, as a family, had been into the city. As we were walking around the shops, my ten-year-old stopped suddenly in the middle of the pavement and began to cry. He was standing in front of a homeless man. I put my arm around him, assuming he was frightened, and simply reassured him. But his tears weren't fear based. "Why has this happened to him?" my son said to me. "I feel sad that he lives on the street." My son got me in the heart with that! He's always had a high level of empathy, but seeing such an emotional response when he was confronted with homelessness helped my wife and I to see what matters to him. From this, we talked with him about how we can help as a family – by giving to a charity, and, when we next encounter a homeless person, offering to buy them some food or a blanket. This was one of those pivotal moments for us, where not only did my son see a social issue that he wanted to bring solution to, but it gave me and my wife the opportunity to truly see the heart and the concerns of our son. And to be honest, it's been a huge pleasure taking time to see what affects my boy and positively influence him to engage with a social issue that matters to him.' – *Ben, a father of three boys under eleven*

In recent years we've seen significant shifts within the home. There used to be a clear separation between parents and children, but today children are being included in decisions that affect the whole family, from choosing a school to purchasing a holiday or introducing some tech for the home. In fact, kids under twelve are playing an increasingly active role in household decisions. Involving a child provides tremendous opportunities for teaching moments, and for parents to build a community, togetherness and belonging in the home. Early Childhood Australia (ECA) recently spoke about this: 'Having a thorough understanding of how to engage children in genuine opportunities to participate will allow children to build confidence into the future and can only be supported through shared understanding with children and viewing the child as a valued citizen and social actor. The confidence of children to be involved does not occur instantly or overnight but takes time – gradually acquired through practice.'[143]

Parents have never had more access to information on child development, parenting advice and a greater understanding of emotional intelligence than they do today. All of this information can be overwhelming, but it provides a tremendous opportunity to truly 'see' children and help them to become the best they can be in a rapidly changing world. And, among all the information, it can be easy to forget that parents and caregivers remain the number one influencers of kids.

We've seen through various parenting blogs, websites and our research that parents are backing their own methods of training and raising their children. The one-size-fits-all approach isn't quite the way anymore. As a parent, the one thing you have over and above any expert with any number of qualifications is the daily interaction with and your personal knowledge of your child.

The cost of childcare

As many parents can attest, childcare is an expensive part of raising a family and has become a major concern for parents and caregivers as they seek to balance caring for children with paid work. Due to the increased uptake of childcare over the last few decades, the increased staff ratio requirements and the costs of delivering quality care, the affordability of childcare has been eroding. The HILDA survey data shows sustained and substantial rises in median weekly expenditure on childcare for children not yet in school over the 2002 to 2017 period – by around 145 per cent.[144]

Australian parents pay almost four times as much as their international counterparts for childcare. By international standards, Australia has one of the highest out-of-pocket childcare costs in the world, behind New Zealand, the United

Kingdom and the United States.[145] The high cost of childcare is forcing many parents to arrange informal care, or to decrease participation in paid work because the amount of money they earn relative to the cost of childcare is marginal. This leaves many children without a head start in their learning.

COVID-19 brought this issue to the forefront when childcare was made free during the pandemic to continue this essential service and keep providers afloat. A few months later, the Federal government announced its plan to wind back the free childcare scheme, leaving many parents in the difficult position of weighing up childcare and career.

Part of the reason childcare is so expensive in Australia is because it is of high quality. But this quality comes at a cost to working parents. Affordable childcare is needed so that parents can continue the juggle of looking after children while engaging in paid employment. This not only benefits the children, who can socialise and begin learning in a formal environment, but it also benefits parents who want to re-enter the workforce.

In our conversations with parents, it was clear that childcare is a challenging part of parenting Generation Alpha.

'I don't work. I'm a single parent. Childcare costs $100 a day, per child. It's not viable for me to work right now. I'm bored, and I want to work, but I'd actually end up losing money if I worked.' – *Angela, a mum of three Generation Alphas*

'I can't wait until my little one goes to school next year because childcare costs me an arm and a leg right now, because she's four.' – *Rommy, a mum of two Generation Alphas*

The value of parental instinct

Gone are the days when the doctor was always right simply because they were the professional. In fact, doctors are now taught, as medical students, to listen to and heed the instinct of parents. Queensland has introduced Ryan's Rule, and most Australian jurisdictions, as well as many overseas, have an equivalent policy. It is named after Ryan Saunders who tragically died in 2007 after being misdiagnosed with mumps. His parents took him to hospital, but they felt that their concerns were not being acted upon. Despite their pleas for action, Ryan died thirty hours after being admitted, from an undiagnosed bacterial infection that developed into toxic shock. Ryan's Rule empowers patients and their parents to raise their concerns and if not satisfied, talk to the clinicians in charge and if still not satisfied, request a clinical review.[146] If a parent says that something is not right with their child, or during their pregnancy, doctors now have a duty of care to listen. The instincts of the parent are an important piece of perspective when it comes to diagnosis, especially for younger children who aren't able to articulate their symptoms. Parental instinct was less considered in the past, but in recent years there has been an empowerment of parents and their voice amplified in the doctor's consulting room.

We now have access to professionals who can help us with any issues, our child concerning, from psychologists to physiotherapists, nutritionists and, of course, Dr Google. As one mum put it, 'Once upon a time, if we didn't know what to do as a parent or the baby was crying, you'd just ring your mum and she'd tell you one, two, three. Now there's social media or Dr Google.'

Disciplining Generation Alpha

The 'wooden spoon' may be well and truly out of the picture today, but the reinforcement of core values to a family and a child's safety remain central to helping children to grow into well-adjusted adults. The American Academy of Pediatrics[147] have put together some guidelines on discipline for today's parents which include teaching children right from wrong with calm words and calm actions – essentially modelling the behaviour you want to see and not neglecting to outline consequences to choices they make that aren't in line with the behaviour expectations. Consistent rules that are easy to understand and age appropriate can also help.

The Latin origins of the word discipline mean 'instruction and knowledge', and the word disciple means 'learner'. As Daniel J. Siegel and Tina Payne write in *The Whole Brain Child*, 'Too often we forget that *discipline* really means to teach, not to punish. A *disciple* is a student, not a recipient of behavioural consequences. Take moments of conflict and transform them into opportunities for learning, skill building and brain development.'[148]

'As a parent, you have to be self-disciplined and follow through on the consequences, and when you've had a big day or week at work, that's really tough to do. I often remind myself that the consqeuences, the small corrections aren't just about our children being well-behaved to make our lives easier, but we are training them to be good, well-adjusted and respectful adults and contributors to society. That matters to me, because, let's be honest, we are adults far longer than we are kids.' – *one mother's approach to discipline*

The American Academy of Pediatrics also emphasises the importance of listening to your child before intervening and giving them your full attention. Hearing the full story, before helping or disciplining, gives you an opportunity to talk through their experiences conversationally instead of simply telling them what to do. As parents it's easy for us to quickly come down on our child's misdemeanours, but we need to 'catch them being good' – praising good choices and successes and affirming good behaviour. We do have to develop our own savviness, determining when not to respond. This is a challenging one when we want to protect our children from harm.[149]

> 'We have a fire pit in our garden and, like lots of boys, my five-year-old son is fascinated by fire. This freaks my wife out, but I let my son help me light the fire with matches. He can feel the heat when he's too close to the fire and I can teach into that as he flirts with danger, so to speak. I'd rather he uses matches in front of me than play with them behind my back. That's something I try to cultivate in all my kids, as few secrets as possible, and to be with my kids as they face the consequences of their actions' – *a father of Generation Alpha children*

A part of 'seeing' the children under our care is also being mindful of why they are misbehaving – are they bored or under-stimulated? Perhaps their bad behaviour needs redirecting. 'Time out' is a common and useful tool to use when a rule is broken. Start with a warning, explain what the child did wrong in a few words and with little emotion, outline the consequences and then follow through if the child steps over the boundary. This strategy, which can help young children learn and practice self-management skills, also works well for older children and teens.

Who are my child's friends?

Remember when you had a landline phone at home? Home phones may seem redundant now, but it's worth recalling the part they played when it came to gaining an understanding of who your children's friends were. The landline often acted as a central control or bottleneck for communication between children and their friends. It gave parents the opportunity to get to know their kids' friends and boyfriends or girlfriends, and to screen calls. With the decline of the landline and the rise in personal mobile phone usage and social media, that connection has been lost. Now it requires greater effort for parents to get to know their children's friends, or even to know when they are communicating with them. And with social activities taking place outside of the home more often than not, there is less in-person interaction too.

'Being visible is the easiest way to get to know their friends. I make the effort to talk with their friends, and my husband and I make it a priority to attend as many of the events our kids are involved in as we can. Then at those events I'm deliberate in asking my kids to point out their friends. Kids aren't necessarily going to make the first move, so it is up to us as parents to do that. As my daughter entered tweendom, I started to drive her and her friends to dance competitions so that I had a chance to get to know them. And, boy, being the taxi driver to tweens is hugely insightful!' – *a mum of two*

'My wife manages our daughter's netball team and I coach our son's soccer team. This provides us plenty of opportunity to not only get to know our kids' friends, but also to initiate barbeques and social gatherings to get to know their parents.' – *Richard, a father of two*

Ways to be an active part of your child's school and social life:

- **Volunteer** in whatever capacity you are able. You could consider joining the school council, volunteering as a class representative, helping out in your child's classroom, or putting your hand up to help when volunteers are requested.
- **Attend** your child's sporting events, musical performances, assemblies and other interests of your child.
- **Offer** to drop your children off at parties or social gatherings and make a point of meeting the parents of their friends.
- **Ask questions** about your child's friends and encourage them to open up about their friendships. But remember, stay cool! The quickest way to ensure they don't open up to you is by overreacting to something they tell you.
- **Stay neutral** about conflicts your child tells you they may be having with friends, and resist the urge to jump in and take action yourself. Give them the resources and advice to resolve it.
- **Get to know** the parents of your child's friends and initiate social gatherings if you feel comfortable to do so.
- **Look for opportunities** to get involved with aspects of your child's social life, like coaching their sporting team.

Parents can get to know their child's friends by interacting with them at a school or local event, or being the one to host the social gatherings. Ask your child what they all do when they hang out and what they talk about. Be informed, absolutely, but keep a low profile – none of us want to be a pestering or interfering parent! Get to know the parents of your child's friends – on the phone or by meeting them at an event. One great way to do this is when the parent drops the child off or picks them up from your house – invite them in.

As you can see, communication with your child, their friends and their friends' parents is key. It takes deliberate effort, but it's worthwhile to get a sense of your child's development and their safety. It's also good to encourage boundaries in terms of what behaviour is and isn't acceptable and how to handle challenging situations.[150]

As children get older, friendships take on new meaning and importance. With the development of these meaningful relationships come lessons in trust, honesty and upholding values outside of the family unit. Friendships matter – and the ones you make as a child are formative because they take place during significant developmental changes. With our busy lives, it has become common for children to make friends by association – through sports involvement or after-school activities – but psychologists encourage unstructured time for children to discover and develop their friendships. When it comes to teens, the friendships can shape one's romantic bonds in the future.[151]

As Generation Alpha move into tweendom and teenage-hood, their friendships and relationships are a training ground for long-term bonds. One way to connect with your child and their friends is by encouraging your kids to invite their friends over to your house.[152] This idea was expressed to us by many parents in our research, with one parent sharing that 'I want our house to be a comfortable, open space for our kids to bring their friends. It's important to us that our kids feel safe here, and feel safe to bring their friends here.'

The ABCDE of training children

We have developed a simple five-step approach to guiding children's behaviour and setting them up to thrive. It is sequential, easy to remember and follows the letters ABCDE.

- **Acceptance:** Make it clear in words and actions that your child is loved and accepted and that you are able to separate who they are from poor behaviours they may manifest.
- **Boundaries:** Communicate clearly the rules and expectations that you have, and the values and reasons behind them.
- **Consequences:** Children need to learn that overstepping agreed and reasoned boundaries comes with consequences. A key goal of parenting is to help children over time set and manage their own behavioural standards, and an important part of this is recognising that, in life, poor choices will result in poor outcomes.
- **Development:** Help children grow their social skills so that they can understand the impacts of their actions on others. This also helps to develop their communication skills so that they can use words rather than actions to resolve conflict, deal with frustration and mitigate the negative actions of others.
- **Encouragement:** Mistakes are a consistent part of the journey of life. Encourage children, when they make mistakes, to learn from them. This ABCDE process ends where it began: offering encouragement through showing and communicating love and acceptance.

Parenting through the COVID-19 experience

The COVID-19 pandemic proved to be a uniquely global, yet personal, experience which people all over the world will remember as a defining part of history. As we have seen, children experienced a significant shift in their lives as a result, including conducting school from home and not being able to visit family, play sport or simply go to the park.

For Generation Alpha and other school-aged children, time is relative to the years they have lived. Everything is zoomed in (figuratively as well as literally!) and every day can feel like a long period of time. Consider an eight-year-old's experience of COVID-19. Memories of life (our episotic memory) usually begins by the age of four – now think about them experiencing one year of COVID-19, that makes for a quarter of their lifetime memory, which is very significant.

In 2020, many school celebrations or rites of passage were cancelled due to the pandemic. School formals and graduations, athletics carnivals and concerts, prize-giving ceremonies and camps, excursions and fairs – all were either cancelled or conducted in more limited ways. In a child's world, these moments of importance, these rites of passage in some instances, were completely lost. And the loss of these events is greater than we, as parents and caregivers, might think. While to an adult it's simply another school event that we don't have to attend, these events are often both defining and rewarding in a child's school experience. Just think about it from a child's perspective: 'I'll only be in year six once. This is the only time we'll have a year six graduation.' As parents and caregivers, it's important to be empathetic and sensitive to that. It was a loss for the child (and for parents, a mix of disappointment and relief to have escaped some events!).

Time is of the essence, but patience is still a virtue

You'll probably never catch today's Generation Alpha child watching a full football game. Instead they watch a condensed, three-minute highlights video with all the goals, tackles and near-misses. They just want to know who won, who scored, when and what people were commenting most on.

This tells the story of the experience of a child's digital life. It's intense, and involves quick hits, instant access and shortcuts. But this isn't reflective of the seasons of life and this is something that parents are going to need to work hard at helping Generation Alpha understand. It's like always consuming protein bars – they are dense and highly nutritious, but you can't live off them alone. In life, there are rhythms like in nature: a time for sowing, for watering, for sunlight, for weeding, for growth and for harvest. There are similar rhythms within education – it can't be education as concentrated consumption, there needs to be time for reflection and learning.

It's up to parents to cultivate the practice of patience and the ability to be present – which can certainly be a challenge in a world of 24/7 technologies and the office in our pocket.

> 'There is a lot to keep up with – emails, school things, text messages and social media is all on our phones as adults, but now the kids have got stuff on their phone too. I find there is pressure to respond to everything straight away. It makes it hard to unwind. I feel guilty for putting my phone down, moving away from it all and having a break. And then I've got double the amount of stuff to keep up with.' – *a mother of three*

While it can be difficult to cultivate, patience is a necessary virtue. Like learning, life can't be crammed. Yet there are many apps that fast-track connections, to the point that they can make our friendships more transactional than relational. Social media has allowed us to mass-manage relationships and with a few clicks share life updates, photos of holidays, food and selfies with friends and followers alike. In essence, it has become a form of personal public relations and surface-level relationships. Whereas in reality, it takes time and care to build friendships and relationships. This is an important distinction and lesson for Generation Alpha to learn.

So how can we cultivate patience in our children? 'We have to model it first,' shared a mother of two. 'With our kids, when we see them showing signs of impatience, we tell them to stop what they are doing, take a breath and think about what they are trying to achieve. Often the impatience comes about because they are looking for a quick solution. It seems to be about teaching them to slow down, think and then act, and to have realistic expectations for what can be achieved in terms of time, quality and quantity. When they ask us to help them with something, we often ask the kids to wait a moment until we have finished something else before we rush to help. They have to understand the world doesn't rotate around them, and that other people's issues can be just as important. Patience is about learning to wait well, and we often encourage our children to be more considerate of others' needs, opinions or approaches to life.'

A key reason that experienced parents insist that their children ask politely and use the words 'please' and 'thank you' is not just because it's respectful and good manners, but because it provides a moment of gratitude and a brief relational interaction before the child reaches for the treat on offer. Patience is the antidote to the regular moments in households with children, where there is a squabble or an intense moment of frustration or anger. At such times, a circuit-breaker is needed and a wise parent can push the pause button amid the chaos with the words, 'Can I ask you a question?' or, 'Let me tell you a story.' These interjections and the sentences that follow are often enough to momentarily break the spiral of retaliation to produce some self-reflection, or redirect the situation. Then parents can share moments from their own life where they have made mistakes or reacted poorly and use their own tale as the teachable lesson.

The art of responsibility

Home dynamics have changed over the years. With both parents commonly working, and kids' extracurricular activities increasing, simply managing everyone's schedules can feel like a full-time job.

> 'When things started to open up after the first wave of COVID-19, my husband and I decided that we were going to put our kids in sports teams in the same locale. We'd been spending one to two hours doing drop-offs and pick-ups on top of our school and work commutes. COVID-19 afforded us the time to rethink how we could manage family without being exhausted all the time. Life is full on and we need all the help we can get!' – *Carly, mum of three Generation Alphas*

Busy schedules mean that Generation Alpha siblings will have fewer opportunities to interact with each other. As each member of the household has their own schedule, we've observed that older siblings won't necessarily be the back-up babysitter or caregiver to Generation Alpha. And since many external activities are age-based, older siblings will also have fewer opportunities to look out for their younger siblings in group settings, like sports camps or holiday activities. Unless parents and caregivers actively encourage it, older siblings won't carry the more traditional role of the big brother or big sister. As such, the stereotype of the eldest sibling being a role model, a protector, a leader and a companion is steadily waning among Generation Alpha.

The rise of technology in the home is also contributing to Generation Alpha having less opportunity to develop responsibility. Now, many homes are equipped with dishwashers, washing machines, dryers, cleaners, dog-walkers and gardeners that take the edge off the housework, or 'chores', that we used to assign to children. Of course, it's a welcome relief to those of us who are leading busy lives, but what meaningful jobs are there today to help develop responsibility and leadership in our children? As parents, it's important to proactively look for opportunities to develop a sense of responsibility and leadership in our children. Activities that involve making decisions, learning to take ownership of our actions and being trusted are good for teaching responsibility. Although many modern household tasks can be outsourced or completed by machines, it's still important to equip Generation Alpha with a sense of agency over household tasks – like putting washing away, keeping a tidy room, packing and unpacking the dishwasher or doing the dishes – to instil a sense of responsibility in this generation.

Today's tensions

ViacomCBS did some extensive research into the current worries of parents.[153] The top five concerns across sixteen countries were: the child's future, their mental health and wellbeing, bullying in person, screen time/social media and the state of the world. Each of these worries leads to tensions which parents are navigating in today's world.

Giving children independence vs. keeping them safe

While many parents want their children to have freedom and independence, at the same time, most parents (91 per cent) have a desire to know what their child is doing. Although these notions may seem in competition with each other, it indicates that parents are trying to build their child's resilience by not putting them at risk while also not shielding them from opportunities to learn and grow.

Exposing children to the real world vs. sheltering them

According to the research, 92 per cent of parents think children need to gain an understanding of the world and can't be shielded from everything. However, most parents (60 per cent) also want children to enjoy this life stage and believe they shouldn't be sheltered. While parents want their children to see and experience the world, they have to balance this with what is too much exposure.

Formal learning vs. play

When it comes to how children learn, parents see value in both formal learning and less structured play. Of the survey group, 77 per cent think structured classes are best and 88 per cent think kids learn best through play. While these two approaches may seem in competition with each other, children actually need a mixture of both types.

Traditional education vs. 'school of life'

While more than seven in ten parents (73 per cent) would sacrifice much to get their child into the best school or university, 80 per cent feel it's more important that their child learn practical life skills than to do well academically.

Restricting screen time vs. using it as a reward

Perhaps one of the most relevant issues for parents of Generation Alpha is the tension that exists around screen time. On the one hand, four in five parents (80 per cent) say they limit screen time as much as possible, yet many also use it as an incentive for their kids. Close to three in five parents (58 per cent) reward good behaviour with TV or screen time. What it comes down to is each parent's attitudes. Many see the benefits, with 84 per cent agreeing that TV is great for family bonding and 65 per cent believing that video games can be good for a child's development.

'When our kids were toddlers we lived in a very small house and when they played with the toys, we would get one or two boxes out and they would play with those. Then before they could play with any more toys, the kids had to pack up the first lot. The kids were always encouraged to help, in a capacity obviously in line with their age. As they entered primary school, my part-time job became full-time and my partner and I involved them in the decision-making process. We gave the kids a choice – I could stay home and do all the jobs, and be available to pick them up, etc., or I could work full-time but they could contribute and then we could afford to have a really great family holiday each year. The kids wanted the holidays and so have always pulled their weight around the house – cleaning, doing laundry and so on. We also decided to buy some chickens and they've helped by cleaning the coops, feeding them and checking for eggs. We reward the kids with a small allowance which they can spend on anything. And we've found that, as they've got older and busier, we're flexible with the timing of when chores are done – we just do our best to keep lines of communication open.' – a *mother of two Generation Alphas*

Nature Deficit Disorder

The term 'Nature Deficit Disorder' was introduced in 2005 with the publication of Richard Louv's book *Last Child in*

the Woods: Saving our children from nature-deficit disorder.[154]
It's a phrase that Richard Louv formed to describe the latest
generations' lack of interaction with nature.

According to Louv, 'although human beings have been
urbanizing, and then moving indoors, since the introduction
of agriculture, social and technological changes in the past
three decades have accelerated our disconnect from the natural
world.'[155] Our children's lack of interaction with nature is
contributing to the 'epidemic of inactivity' and to 'a devaluing
of independent play'. As one parent shared with us, 'It's an
issue of whether it's safe for our kids to play outside. It's also an
economic issue. You might not be able to afford a yard, but you
can give them Fortnite.' In speaking with parents of Generation
Alpha, one mum told us how she was 'sick of everyone having
screens in their faces. Everyone, everywhere you go – people
are walking into you because they're on the phone. When my
daughter's friends come over, they all sit there on their phone,
and there's no conversation happening. And I have to tell them
to play some music or go outside. So I've started taking them
on hikes to help them get off the screens.'

Studies on nature deficit disorder don't only focus on what
is lost when nature experience fades, but on what is gained
through more exposure to natural settings, including nature
in urban places. Spending more time in nature can help kids
to build confidence, promote creativity and imagination,
teach responsibility, provide different stimulation, get kids
moving, make them think and reduce stress and fatigue.[156]
Time in nature also teaches children about wonder, and the
ability to engage with the natural world. 'One of my greatest
joys is taking my kids to the wild places of this world, and
to explore the natural beauty of Australia,' Andrew, a father
of three Generation Alphas, told us. 'I'm really intentional

about using weekends to get out in nature and explore with them. And every time, they want to go further. I'm trying to teach my kids that adventures are what we do, and how we learn.'

Ways to get your family in touch with nature

- Plant a garden bed or a pot
- Visit a park
- Plan weekend walks in nature
- Consider taking family trips or holidays based in nature
- Try camping
- Visit lookouts that inspire wonder and awe
- Swap out a restaurant lunch or brunch for a picnic
- Gather around a campfire, or do some backyard stargazing
- Play a game or sport outside
- Move indoor tasks (like homework or reading) outdoors

Richard Louv's book *The Nature Principle: Reconnecting with Life in a Virtual Age*[157] explored the key question of 'What could our lives and our children's lives be like if our days and nights were as immersed in nature as they are in technology?' His follow-up book, *Vitamin N*,[158] offered five hundred ways that individuals, families and communities could incorporate more nature connection into their daily lives. In 2019, Louv's newest book, *Our Wild Calling*,[159] explored how connecting with animals can transform our lives – and save theirs.

Connection to animals is an important topic. Regardless of when you were a child or what generation you belong to, a love of animals seems to be a timeless characteristic of children. If you are a parent then we're sure you've been asked, perhaps one hundred times, for a puppy or kitten. Pets are not only cute and cuddly but they encourage childhood responsibility, empathy, self-esteem and social skills. Sharing with other family members in the love and care of a pet also forges additional bonds, can help to reduce stress, anxiety and loneliness, and generally increases time outside and in nature in an increasingly sedentary and screen-based world. As Ian, a parent, told us, 'when we got our dog Roxy, it really changed our family dynamics. Roxy brought us together more. We went for more family walks and spent more time together as she became a part of our family.'

With new housing developments comprising smaller backyards and an increasing proportion of children being raised in apartments where strata laws don't always allow pet ownership, having a pet is no longer the widespread rite of passage it once was.

Parents' role in schooling

A big part of a child's life is school, which has evolved over time. While Chapter 6 is focused on education, we want to briefly explore here how parents are coping with the complexity of schooling and the integration of technology.

According to our research, more than half (55 per cent) of Australian parents feel somewhat, slightly or not at all equipped to assist their child/ren with assignments, school learning and learning technologies.[160] The cause is twofold. First, parents believe the school curriculum is elevated beyond their experience. Second, it is being delivered on unfamiliar platforms, like app-based programs Moodle and school intranet.

We're sure many parents can identify with what one parent told us, when she said, 'Some of the stuff that both my girls are learning, I'm like, wow! Mind you, we didn't even have computers when I was growing up, so I think that was always going to be the case.' Another mum has found that her children 'are doing all sorts of stuff at school that I don't understand. My son (aged eight) summed up the situation when he said, "It must have been really hard because my mum was around before we got the internet!"'

In an increasingly complex and technologically integrated world, it is positive that the education sector is responding with a more complex curriculum delivered through online platforms, even though parents may find it challenging to keep up with and help their children with their schoolwork.

Getting the best outcome from your child's school

1. **Think of your child's education as a partnership** with your school rather than a function you outsource to the school. As much as you can, keep across the communications from the school and make it two-way communication – where possible interact with the school and your child's teachers.
2. **Ask your children about their learning.** Find out what subjects and areas they are most confident in and where they are needing support. Where you discover areas of low interest or low achievement, intervene early with extra support and conversations with relevant teachers.
3. **Communicate with the school**, participate in scheduled parent–teacher opportunities, but if you can't, arrange phone or video calls with teachers to get feedback from them about your child's education.

Parental expectations of schools are also more complex than in the past. Parents today expect schools to aid in not just academic development, but to also contribute to their child's social skills and development of life skills. In the last five years, almost half of parents (48 per cent) have increased their expectations of their child's school to support wellbeing. More than one in four (27 per cent) have significantly or somewhat increased their expectations. Although expectations are increasing, parents still value the educational partnership. They see an equal responsibility between themselves and the school in the areas of academic development (46 per cent), developing social skills (41 per cent) and discussing social issues (39 per cent).[161] The reality is that both parties – parents and educators – play a crucial role in a child's development across these areas.

Out with the old, in with the new	
WHAT'S OUT?	WHAT'S IN?
Sleepovers	Pyjama parties (that end at 10pm)
Lolly bags	Food allergies
Riding or walking to school	School drop-offs
Calling	Texting
Sports team: Player of the Season Award	Sports team: Player of the Week Award
School-wide swimming carnivals	Competitor-only events

Enjoy it!

Being a parent can be tough, but also immensely rewarding. As Geoff, a dad of three Generation Alphas, shared with us, 'My six-year-old daughter Olivia came home from school today with a Father's Day card for me, which had an iteration of the latest slang BFRN (Best Friend Right Now) on it. Instead, the card said BDRN – which she informed me stands for Best Dad Right Now. It made me laugh. Parenting Generation Alpha is the best.' While you might have moments like Geoff's, if you're currently experiencing a lack of sleep, competing demands and feeling the responsibility of raising the next generation, you may be feeling (justifiably!) overwhelmed but remember, you are making impacts that will live into the twenty-second century!

How to be a reflective parent

In our research and experience, one of the sentiments parents express most often is the marvel of how quickly children grow up and the parenting years pass. By being a reflective parent, embracing the small moments and consciously building relational bonds, the positive impacts will be lasting.

1. **Don't just take photos or videos, every so often look back through them with your children** and reflect on the journey. Also, use your phone or app to voice-record little interviews with them at times while they are young. When they are a older you will all enjoy listening to them.

2. **Have a readily accessible quote book** where cute expressions or funny mispronunciations can be recorded and shared as your children grow.

3. **When you are together, share stories of family experiences.** The reliving of these fun and funny times creates great family traditions and reinforces the memories. Also, share with your children stories from their baby and infant years of which they will have no memory. It will remind your growing children of your role in their life and your love and care for them from day one. These are, after all, stories on their favourite subject (themselves!).

4. **Recognise and celebrate the changes.** In the midst of the chaos of parenting, we work hard to shape habits and develop them, but often don't recognise that the learning has been applied and that the frustrating behaviour has changed. Reflect on the changes you are seeing and celebrate these wins.

---

5. **Say yes.** Try to embrace the moments, when they arise, by saying yes to the request for a quick ball game or activity. Such requests for attention and involvement from children rarely come at convenient times and even though there is always something else vying for your time, take advantage of these fleeting opportunities. After all, all we've got is moments.

Key takeaways

In this chapter we have explored the crucial role that parents play, how parenting looks different in the twenty-first century, and how the role of mothers and fathers, changes to the nuclear family, the value of parental instinct, discipline, rites of passage, responsibility and nature deficit disorder will impact Generation Alpha.

Parenting is one of life's greatest challenges, but also one of its greatest privileges. If children experience relationships where they feel nurtured, connected and protected, it will set them up well for any future relationships they might have – maybe even, one day, with their own children. By investing into how we parent Generation Alpha, we are making an investment in them, their future and the generations to follow.

As Generation Alpha grow up they will be empowered to take action, improve the world around them, stand up for what they believe in and live a life of contribution. They will continue to be exposed to the real world and be surrounded by information. And they will expect the truth and value authenticity. Generation Alpha are an empowered generation, and parents and caregivers play an important role in equipping them with the right tools to live their best life and thrive.

CHAPTER 6

Educating Generation Alpha

'Education is the most powerful weapon which you can use to change the world.'

Nelson Mandela

Education plays a fundamental role in children's lives – not only to prepare them for the world of work, but to develop them as a person. In this chapter we explore what education and the school years will look like for Generation Alpha. We investigate how classrooms are changing, from the integration of technology to the different learning styles, teaching techniques and the impact of COVID-19. We also delve into how education is equipping Generation Alpha for an unknown future, and how schools can best provide them with a successful education.

Education has evolved since the Education Acts of the colonies of Victoria and New South Wales, legislated nearly 150 years ago, introduced free, public and compulsory education. In the early days of education there was heavy weight put on moral conduct and religion in addition to numeracy and literacy. Since then, the emphasis in education has shifted from moral conduct to societal contribution. Today over 3.9 million children are in school[162] and they make up approximately 15 per cent of Australia's current population.[163]

Education today

The school years are a significant life stage for each generation. School helps prepare children for their working life, but it also helps them learn social skills, as this is where friendships are formed and negotiated, and other important life skills and characteristics are learnt. School also gives children an opportunity to think critically and creatively about the world around them, explore their own interests and develop a love of learning – the most important gift education can give to a student.

Literacy and numeracy

'The impact of technology on language has been massive. As teachers, we don't even know some of the words kids use, which they get from watching YouTube.' – *Jonathan, a primary school teacher*

Beyond the three Rs

While parents are placing greater emphasis on a holistic education, according to our 2019 Future of Education report,[164] four out of five parents see a school's greatest priority as equipping students with basic literacy and numeracy skills. Other key priorities include developing transferable skills, which students can apply to all situations, and future-proofing students by equipping them with the necessary skills to enter the workforce.

When parents compare students' capabilities in literacy and numeracy to ten years ago, a third believe students are performing worse.[165] This is also reflected in the latest NAPLAN results, with the writing skills of year seven and nine students going backwards over the past decade. Australia's PISA (Program for International Student Assessment) results in maths, reading and science have also been declining over recent decades. While just above the OECD average, Australia is not in the top fifteen countries in any of these three categories.[166] It is laudable that school curricula have broadened from the three R's (reading, writing and arithmetic) to provide more holistic education for today's students ('curriculum creep', as it has been labelled). Teaching methods have also shifted from rote learning and instructional delivery to the less efficient (but for many students more effective) collaborative approach. However, declining basic education outcomes should not be the cost of a more engaged and well-rounded school experience, and as the federal education minister said when these results were released, 'These results should have alarm bells ringing.'[167]

The education sector is growing in Australia, with almost 10,000 schools across the nation. Most students are enrolled in government schools. One in five are enrolled in Catholic schools and over one in seven students are enrolled in independent schools[168] – a sector which has been growing over the last few decades as many parents seek out schools they believe will not only help their child achieve academic success but will help develop their character and leadership skills.

Amid these new teaching and learning challenges arrives this new generation, wholly shaped in the twenty-first century. Educators are aware that this generation is highly connected through digital devices and engaged through social media.

When they finish their school years, most of Generation Alpha will pursue further education and training, with more than half predicted to go on to university.[169]

Due to advances in technology, growing workforce demand for technical competencies, and the decline in students studying higher level maths and science, there has been an increased focus on STEM in Generation Alpha's lifetime.

What is STEM?

STEM stands for Science, Technology, Engineering and Mathematics, and is an approach to learning across these areas. Recent advances in robotics, artificial intelligence and automation has led to teaching these subjects in a way that relates them to the real world and this has gained traction over the last decade. A key part of the STEM approach is to not view these subjects on their own but in relation to one another and how they are connected in the real world. According to the WA Department of Education, 'Through STEM, students develop key skills including problem solving, creativity, critical analysis, teamwork, independent thinking, initiative, communication and digital literacy.'[170]

'We are focusing a lot more on twenty-first century technology and STEM subjects. We are looking at what jobs will be in the future and what will benefit students. There's new subjects and we're doing a lot more integration of subjects, so it's not just stand-alone English and music, it's cross-curriculum lessons.' – a primary school teacher

Technology and the classroom

Those of us who went to school in the 1980s and 1990s might remember special rooms or buildings where we went for 'computer lessons'. Perhaps, as we progressed through high school, computers became more integrated into our lives as students, but they were still relatively separate from day-to-day classes. Only some classrooms had them, or there were a handful in the library. Now most students in kindy to year two have class sets of iPads and the upper primary years have school devices, and students in high school have personal devices. While we remember the introduction of technology into the learning landscape, for Generation Alpha it will always have been there as an integral part. At home, we want our children to turn technology off and engage in their lives off screen, but schools are (understandably) increasingly introducing technology into the learning processes of the next generation.

While technology is more integrated into Generation Alpha's lives than any other generation, it's interesting to hear what they like most about school. They value a mix of technology and IRL (a common Gen Z slang term which stands for 'in real life').

> 'I like writing the best because I have neat writing. And I like maths.' – *George, aged eight*

> 'I like recess at school. I use laptops and Mathletics has helped me know, like, maths and stuff. I use laptops in the afternoon and the morning sometimes.' – *Bianca, aged nine*

> 'My number one hobby is homework. My last hobby is video games.' – *Byron, aged eight*

Benefits

The education sector is facing the task of managing technology to make the best use of its benefits and minimise its drawbacks. As we explored in Chapter 4, technology presents numerous benefits, and this is also true within the classroom. Benefits of technology within the classroom include greater opportunities for efficient and collaborative learning, the ability to engage students through the use of video and interactivity, independent learning and task extension, as well as training them for online and remote learning, which as we saw through COVID-19 can happen with little warning and will likely be be a big part of their future. To future-proof their careers, students will need to develop technological literacy, the ability to adapt to new digital platforms, and technology competencies, which will be required for many of the emerging jobs.

Drawbacks

Technology in the classroom can create significant challenges, such as safety issues, online bullying and distraction. As one teacher shared with us, technology 'is like a mountain you have to climb. It provides constant distraction. When you are a teenager the most important thing in your life is your peers, not a population pyramid. Nothing I can say is more important than that, so I need to bring my lesson to the next level to even be able to compete with that. Spreadsheets aren't very exciting compared to what's happening on Snapchat and Instagram.'

Educators and parents both agree that technology devices inhibit the development of handwriting skills, which will still be an important skill in the future. Research has shown that the benefits of writing are superior to typing for memory retention, creativity, critical thinking and problem-solving.[171] The strength of devices is that they create 'lean forward' experiences that are multi-modal, video-rich and interactive. This is also a drawback, because it can impair the ability to focus, reduce attention spans and as many teachers we interviewed have said, reduce their overall concentration abilities.

Have teaching methods adapted to accommodate today's students? Almost half of educators and a slightly higher proportion of parents agree that the main teaching methods have kept up with today's students. Around half of educators and parents are satisfied with their classroom management procedures which integrate technology into the classroom.[172]

How much screen time at school?

Given the increased integration of technology in the classroom, it is interesting to consider how much time children should spend on a device at school. Educators are more likely to lean towards a 'less is more' approach. Nearly seven in ten educators think that screen time should be limited to 40 per cent or less of a regular school day, and more than half of all parents (51 per cent) feel the same way.[173]

You may be wondering why parents and educators differ about what amount of screen time at school is best. Parents are more likely to think children should spend a greater amount of time using screens for learning and productivity purposes, because they want their child to be equipped for future jobs, which they believe will be characterised by technology. Educators, on the other hand, see first-hand how technology can add learning efficiency but often increases distractions, and they are faced with the challenge of managing this behaviour at school.

So, when should tablets and laptops be introduced into the classroom? Even though educators advocate a less-is-more approach to technology at school overall, most educators support some learning on devices in the junior years, with laptops being introduced in years seven to eight.[174] Parents largely agree, but are caught in the tension of embracing the integration of technology as a way of life, while wanting to provide healthy boundaries for their child around technology.

The reality is that Generation Alpha will need to know how to use screen-based devices for their future employment. But, as a parent, you can be comforted that these devices are very intuitive to use, and easy to pick up. This means that the age at which your child learns to use them doesn't really matter. As a parent, the context of your child's school and when they introduce screens into the classroom, as well as your own child's preferences, will guide you as to when and how to introduce screens as a more regular part of their education. Remember, there is no perfect time, so do what works for your family and your child, and take advice from your child's teacher.

Also, remember that as screens become more integrated into education, off-screen activities outside of school become more important. By setting aside time to unplug, encouraging outdoor activities, prioritising free play away from screens and making a child's bedroom a screen-free zone, parents can help Generation Alpha to strike a healthy balance with screens and time off screens (which are often compulsory at school – whatever the year) and time off screens.

Striking a balance

As we explored in Chapter 4, there can be concerns around the type of future Generation Alpha will inherit, and their interaction with technology such as artificial intelligence (AI). While it's good to exercise a level of scepticism, there will also be benefits, like improved efficiency and ease of tasks in the future.

The Australian government is investing $1.5 million to develop a range of curriculum resources to assist with the delivery of AI and other emerging technologies in the Australian curriculum. This means that there will be significant advancements in the type of work and content Generation Alpha will partake in. Classrooms may change and incorporate new technologies to adapt, teachers may need to upskill and learn new content and ways of teaching so that Generation Alpha are equipped for jobs of the future.

> 'This group of kids will probably be doing jobs that we
> don't even know about yet. So, they need to learn how
> to use technology at home or at school and keep up
> with everyone else. If the person next to them knows
> how to do computer programming and my child doesn't,
> then they're the one that's behind. I think it's expected
> that they should know how to use it, and that the school
> should keep up with that.' – *Christina, a mum of two*

Jobs of the future recruiting now

Cybersecurity specialist, UX manager, drone pilot, blockchain developer, data designer, virtual reality engineer, robotics technician, AI specialist, medical nanotechnologist, app developer

---

Technology assisting teaching

Many people are often concerned that AI will make their roles and jobs obsolete. But it's important to remember that technology and AI exist to serve humans, not the other way around. There will be moves into AI in the future of learning, and these will have direct benefits for teachers. If AI carries the load of administration, such as standard testing and marking, and can free up teachers to focus on the human side of teaching, then it will be welcomed with open arms.

Google's Jonathan Rochelle says the current education system, which involves a lot of standardised testing, an ever-expanding curriculum and engagement with bureaucracy, can overburden teachers. While the current system often asks teachers to do more, technology and teaching innovations will help solve this in the decades ahead.[175]

Teachers will need training in order to allow AI to operate most effectively, and schools will require additional tech support staff. In our interview with education consultant Dr Anne Knock, she said, 'AI shouldn't simply be implemented for the sake of keeping up with technology. It needs to serve the teacher and the classroom and needs to enhance and potentially improve the way teachers are teaching. Ultimately it should improve the outcomes and results of the students.'

AI won't remove the necessity of a human teacher who, through empathy, can guide and educate a child. In fact, it will likely increase the opportunity for teachers to interact with students one on one and give them more space to collaborate and innovate.

The impact of COVID-19

During the COVID-19 lockdowns, schools were forced to rapidly adopt flexible learning arrangements. Overall, our research during the pandemic showed people are very positive about a shift towards online learning. In fact, nine in ten said they were positive about an increased use of online learning in vocational training (90 per cent), university (89 per cent), workplaces (90 per cent) and in school (86 per cent).[176]

Some positive outcomes

While education online was an exhausting process for many educators, it was certainly not done in vain, and educators should be commended for how they responded. When we asked those parents whose children had participated in online education how they had found the experience, 71 per cent said it was a positive one.[177] This was largely due to the support provided by the school and the opportunity for parents to spend more time with their child. The greater engagement in their child's learning also allowed families and parents to develop deeper understanding of their child's skills, abilities and challenges with learning.

'The school has been very supportive, and my children enjoyed the level of online education provided by their teachers and school.' – *a parent of a primary school student*

'We have more understanding now of what they are learning in school.' – *a parent of a secondary school student*

Another positive to come out of COVID-19 was the respect and appreciation teachers were shown during the pandemic. The speed at which teachers and the education sector adapted to COVID-19 taught us all that we live in uncertain times, and it is important that, when required, we can be flexible and adapt to our changing circumstances. During this national and international pressure test for the education sector, teachers responded well to the technological infrastructure and different skills required to deliver quality education online. This, unsurprisingly, gave rise to lots of memes highlighting the esteem in which teachers were held in 2020, including one that said, 'Gifts for teachers in 2019: mugs, apples, cards, candy and flowers. Gifts for teachers in 2020: diamonds, gold Rolex, spa day and vacation'.

The challenges

Schooling from home posed challenges, however, with many parents finding it difficult to motivate their children, keep them focused and juggle their own workload. Even teachers admitted it was challenging at times.

'Teaching remotely brought some challenges,' Gaby, a high school teacher, told us. 'Namely, being able to check in regularly with students as you would during a normal lesson. The lesson had to be narrowed down enough so that you would teach one skill and be able to check in on that skill by the end of the lesson. This meant that my students who needed further clarification were often the kids that needed more pastoral support, so they really struggled in this online environment.'

Although they are extremely tech-savvy, interestingly the emerging generations themselves were slightly less positive about online learning than the older generations. Six in ten students said they found learning from home more difficult, and two thirds found it more productive to study at school rather than at home. The majority of young Australians understood that this remote learning arrangement was necessary; however, 37 per cent didn't believe it could be something they could live with on a permanent basis.[178] As these generations are in the formal education life stage and most likely to be participating in these online learning environments, it is important to take note of these differences in attitude. Educators agree that students are highly engaged in classroom learning (90 per cent), more so than during online classes (69 per cent).[179]

Traditional, in situ learning is considered to yield greater results among students because teachers can guide the learning process and interact with students more easily. While the online learning environment provides accessibility and flexibility, it can also be less productive.

Even though online learning was a blessing for many during COVID-19 and 52 per cent of students and teachers believe education will be delivered online to a greater extent in the future,[180] the sentiment of many students and teachers was that they looked forward to going back to school where they could interact with friends and colleagues in person.

More than just places of learning

It is clear that schools are about more than just learning. They also play an important role in developing a child's interpersonal skills, leadership skills and friendships, as well as providing opportunities for participation in sport and other fun initiatives. Many parents believe the greatest strength of their child's school is the community. Almost nine in ten parents (88 per cent) agree that the school community has a positive impact on their child's education, and that the school community provides good role models for their children (87 per cent).[181]

Not only do children's social lives benefit from school, it turns out that parents' do, too. One parent said, 'My children have made many friends, as have we, with other parents.' Positively, most parents agree that the school community they are a part of provides them with the opportunity to make good friends (75 per cent), they feel known by the school community (71 per cent) and can count on their school community to be supportive in times of need (82 per cent).[182] Amid busyness and more frequently moving house, people are less likely to know their neighbours, less likely to volunteer in their local community, or be members of sporting clubs, service organisations or faith communities. In such an era, schools provide places of connection and belonging for students, parents and staff.

As a senior school teacher, Chris, told us, 'Our school has a lovely culture between students and staff and I think parents sense that too. It's about healthy competition, having fun and working hard. Whole-school events are great, too. School always feels extremely busy but every aspect of that is exciting and enriching.'

New classrooms for new teaching styles

Classroom teaching styles are adapting to a changing world by incorporating new teaching methods and styles of learning. More than four in five educators (83 per cent) and seven in ten parents (71 per cent) believe schools are much better today at engaging with students and their varied learning styles.[183] This is a great development as schools that foster an experiential, hands-on approach to learning will help students cultivate the skills they need to be workplace-ready. Yet there is still more to be done – a similar proportion of parents and teachers believe schools should continue to work harder to make learning more interesting (81 per cent of educators and 88 per cent of parents).[184]

Yet the change in schooling in the span of a generation, has been dramatic. Today's educators and parents, when they were students themselves, mostly experienced a teacher delivering content with little or no interaction, and classroom layouts reflected this. Traditional classroom layouts were ones with rows and columns of chairs. This style reflected an individual learning approach and a teacher-centric model.

Today's students, however, are experiencing a teacher-facilitated, interactive, learner-centric environment, and classroom layouts are designed to reflect this. When we spoke with Melanie Karaca, an architect at NBRS Architecture, she told us that when she is working with schools she designs spaces that are flexible and reflect the current movement towards collaborative teaching and integrated technology. 'We create spaces that make it easy for teachers to supervise children, who make their own decision about whether they want to be in a sheltered corner or a quiet space. These are environments where students are empowered and encouraged to learn and explore themselves, rather than be fed information from the authority figure. Rather than it being so controlled, the space encourages children to take responsibility for their own learning and socialising as they navigate their environment.'

These environments aid teaching styles that focus on developing Generation Alpha as learners, and encourage them to take responsibility for their own learning. As Jono, a primary school teacher, shared with us, 'I think we need to figure out what we want for these kids. For me, it's all about making quality learners. The best thing you can teach a kid is learning how to learn, but they need to learn how to find it out themselves. For Generation Alpha, we need to teach them about the process of learning, and I think teachers are starting to teach a little more strategically.'

This combination of student interaction and collaboration is the most preferred teaching style among educators and parents today.[185] Educators believe the teaching styles and techniques that most effectively engage with today's learners are project- and inquiry-based learning, collaborative group work, and teacher-facilitated and student-centred learning.

Practical, hands-on activities are thought to be the most engaging form of delivery with over nine in ten educators and parents.[186] This is followed by case studies and demonstrations where real-world examples are presented, then facilitated interactive discussions and, finally, group work. Educators strongly believe, along with parents, that the most engaging forms of delivery tend to be based on interactive learning styles.[187]

Nine in ten educators believe schools are effectively educating students today.[188] As one primary school teacher shared with us, 'we do focus more on inquiry and collaboration, and I think the difference that I have seen is that kids get that line of inquiry and are able to collaborate a little bit more. Sometimes they do need technology to do that. I had a student where whenever we had a group task he would hide under the table, and then we used Google Docs and worked collaboratively on the same document and then he was like, "I love group work".'

Yet all of these educational innovations and improvements need to be better communicated to parents, because two in five say that student behaviour, a proxy for engagement, is not as good as it was ten years ago. Principals acknowledge that this sentiment exists, despite the fact that teachers are more qualified, and learning is more engaging and interactive than before.[189]

'It is just a perception. Students today are much better prepared and much more well behaved and smarter than we all were ...' says Graeme Irwin, Executive Principal, St Philip's group of schools. 'The way of teaching students now is a whole lot better from the relationship the teachers build, to the style of teaching we use, engaging students not just delivering. We use a lot of project-based learning which is very effective, and they rise to the challenge.'

Individualised, self-directed learning

Self-directed and individualised learning is a common approach currently used in the education sector. Self-directed learning is an approach where the teacher is the facilitator, and the student takes ownership of their own learning by searching for resources, strategies and techniques to apply. For example, a teacher may give a general learning goal of understanding the topic of climate change. In self-directed learning, students will then decide what specific area of climate change they will focus on, the time frames and the result. While one student might deliver a video presentation on melting polar ice caps, another might decide to write a report on climate change agreements. This enables students to work to their own strengths, exercise creativity and take greater responsibility over the decision-making process and management of their work.

The personalised and individualised approach allows for higher levels of interaction, where teachers are the architects of the learning. The teacher is still the teacher, but the student takes on more responsibility for their learning outcomes and this has its place in an era of more online and remote learning. The teacher tracks each student's progress in the knowledge and skills that the national curriculum requires. This approach, however, puts tremendous pressure on teachers to form individualised plans and consistently assess students and update the plan. As Jess, a primary school teacher, told us, 'It's sad because as teachers, we are passionate and do care and want to take on more, but the load that comes with that desire and that willingness is just enormous. It gets to a point where you lose the joy of it. You're constantly being pulled in all these different directions and not being able to do any of them to a level you are satisfied with.'

Collaboration

To produce well-rounded individuals, schools are committed to developing social and relational skills in addition to education and learning outcomes. Every area of Generation Alpha's future, from family and household living to thriving in their community and flourishing in their workplace, will require the ability to get along well with others and get the best from them. Group work and team-based learning is being increasingly implemented in schools with the goal of not just learning by collaboration but learning about collaboration. In their future, Generation Alpha will work with more diverse generations of more varied cultures and with more gender and social diversity than any previous generation.

Inquiry-based learning

Quite the opposite to rote learning and memorisation, inquiry-based learning is an active way of learning, incorporating personalisation in the education system. It means a move away from teacher instruction and note-taking, to being able to find the information and then use it. Instead of teachers presenting information up front, they encourage students to ask questions to find the answer. Imagine that students were learning about photosynthesis and their teacher took them out into the school grounds to observe different types of leaves. Then the students were asked to draw the leaf shapes and discuss how leaves make energy for the rest of the plant or tree.

Traditional methods of learning	Modern methods of learning
Verbal	Visual
Sit and listen	Try and see
Authoritarian	Participative
Curriculum-centred	Learner-centric
Closed-book exams	Open-book world
Books and paper	Glass and devices
Theoretical thinking	Practical skills
Direct instruction	Inquiry-based learning

Inquiry-based learning is a method that has been well regarded and supported by educators and education systems around the world over the past decade.[190] It's proving to be successful. Instead of a teacher regurgitating information and teaching *at* students, this method *involves* the student from the outset, as they pose questions as an active form of learning. The process involves the teacher asking 'how', 'what' or 'why' guiding questions. Then through analysis, reflection, collaboration and communication, the student explores and responds to the questions. This requires an element of curiosity and puts the student at the centre of this learning process, commonly referred to as 'student-led learning'. The teacher facilitates the process and can introduce concepts, research and facts around a topic that's on the curriculum and cultivates students' inquiring minds by using practical elements.

> Imagine a teacher at the front of the classroom talking to a year three class of nine-year-olds about the animal kingdom. To combine art and science, the teacher could ask the students to draw a cheetah, but before doing so they could spend some time researching the cheetah's habitat, its role in the ecosystem, its diet, skeletal and muscular system and how that affects the shape of the animal that the student draws. This is an example of inquiry-based learning as opposed to factual, textbook regurgitation, providing the opportunity for a holistic approach and understanding.

The aim with this approach is to create an environment where students develop and pose their own questions. The role of the teacher is to encourage questions, aid the students in going through the processes of research during class, and then ask them to present their findings. In order to embed this process for the student, it is important to make space for reflection. A teacher might do this by asking questions about the student's findings and the process they took to reach those findings.

With the internet enabling so much of students' learning to take place outside the classroom, this learning style reflects a shift from teachers being all-involving to being facilitators. This is why the inquiry model is proving to be successful, because it involves the student in seeking out information and knowledge.

These are valuable skills that can be utilised in all areas of life. Inquiry-based teaching is a way of future-proofing students as it encourages and equips them to be lifelong learners. Defining the scope of an issue, exploring the factors, analysing the facts, workshopping ideas and communicating proposed solutions – these are some of the many skills they will use throughout their careers.

Equipping students for an unknown future

'In a societal sense we are on the cusp of a lot of change and it's hard to predict how to best equip students for whatever is to come.' – *a senior school teacher*

Undoubtedly, the world around us is changing. Many jobs that exist today didn't exist the year Generation Alpha was born (2010), like blockchain developers and certified UAV (drone) pilots. The rate and speed of change means that it is very likely that the world of work Generation Alpha will enter into will look vastly different than what it does today.

More than three in five educators agree that many current jobs will be at high risk of digital disruption in the future and, in response, schools should embrace the use of technology to future-proof both students' careers and their learning.[191]

Digital disruption

A change to existing products, services and business models caused by emerging digital technology is known as digital disruption. One of the most famous examples of a company that did not respond to digital disruption is Kodak. A leader in handheld cameras, Kodak was convinced that analogue cameras and film would continue to appeal to the masses and downplayed the introduction of digital cameras and camera phones. In 1996 when digital cameras were just a ripple on the consumer landscape, Kodak was valued at US$30 billion, but just 16 years later, in 2012, the ripple had become a tsunami and Kodak filed for bankruptcy.

Companies which have disrupted the marketplace due to their digital solutions are companies like Facebook (connecting people online through social media), Amazon (an online marketplace) and Netflix (an online video service).

Transferrable skills

While the future is uncertain, we do know a fair bit about what students will need to thrive in life. To equip them for a life of many jobs (eighteen on average) across many careers (six on average) we need to be focusing on equipping students with what is known as 'transferrable' or 'enterprising' skills.[192] As the term suggests, this refers to skills that can be transferred across different jobs and industries. It signifies a move away from a 'career for life' approach to a 'skills for life' approach.

If you had asked a high school student fifteen or twenty years ago what they wanted to be when they grew up, they likely would have said something like nurse, doctor, pilot, firefighter or teacher. Today, many students have no idea what they want to be because technology and the knowledge economy have opened up so many more career pathways.

'My goals are to travel and become a founder of an organisation to help people.' – *a fourteen-year-old girl*[193]

The transferrable skills Generation Alpha will need for life:

- Teamwork
- Empathy
- Leadership
- Communication skills
- Personal motivation
- Time management
- Adaptability

- Technology literacy
- Problem solving
- Work ethic
- The ability to learn
- Creativity
- Critical thinking
- Resilience

Children of the twenty-first century are growing up in a vastly different world than those of the twentieth century. The changing landscape of business, workplaces, consumer products, technology and education highlight the need for skills that are transferrable across disciplines and industries. This has shifted the focus on to what the World Economic Forum have called twenty-first century skills for lifelong learning in their New Vision for Education[194] adapted below.

Twenty-first century skills

Foundational literacies (how students apply core skills to everyday tasks)	Competencies (how students approach complex tasks)	Character qualities (how students approach their changing environment)
Literacy	Critical thinking/problem solving	Curiosity
Numeracy	Creativity	Initiative
Scientific literacy	Communication	Persistence/grit
ICT literacy	Collaboration	Adaptability
Financial literacy	Concentration	Leadership
Cultural/civic literacy	Celebration	Social/cultural awareness

___

The best teachers have always been focused on students. The emphasis is not on what they're learning but who they're becoming. As the world of work changes, it is the qualities of adaptability, initiative and personal resolve that help to future-proof the students of today.

___

When we asked about these twenty-first century skills, parents believe students are most equipped with ICT literacy (digital skills) (60 per cent) and creativity (57 per cent). The area with the greatest room for improvement is critical thinking, with just over two in five parents (43 per cent) believing students are equipped in this area.[195]

In an age of digital disruption and rapid automation, employers are looking for workers who possess a broad range of transferable, twenty-first century skills. These adaptive skills require creativity, problem solving and critical thinking. While technology and automation continue to disrupt the labour landscape, there are some occupations that carry a lower risk of being replaced by technology. These irreplaceable jobs require a high level of human interaction, empathy and individuality. It is expected that by 2030, workers will spend 30 per cent more time learning on the job, 100 per cent more time at work solving problems, 41 per cent more time thinking critically, 77 per cent more time using science and maths skills and 17 per cent more time using verbal communication and interpersonal skills.[196] Nearly four in five educators agree that creative, people-focused, leadership-oriented or high-level communication roles are most future-proofed as technology cannot effectively replace them.[197]

Positively, three in five parents believe students are extremely or very well equipped with curiosity, while half believe students are equipped with adaptability to the same extent. Leadership is an area requiring growth for today's students, with just over two in five parents believing students are extremely or very well equipped in this area.[198]

Future-proofing students

Teachers are experiencing first hand the changing approach of how to best educate their students for the future. 'It's difficult to predict what will happen, but we can say students need to be flexible, able to think critically, understand information in new dimensions and in multiple ways,' one teacher told us. 'Regardless of what subject you are working in, if the students can do that, we have achieved our key role.'

In this complex environment there are concerns that with such a strong focus on future-proofing, students are missing the basics and are expected to perform beyond their years. 'There's this whole "prepare them for the future",' the teacher added, 'whereas I feel like when I was at school it was "you need to know this because you are seven and this is where you are developmentally at." Now, I feel like there is this whole expectation where in year three for example, they need to know how to problem-solve like adults and think of alternative uses.'

In order to meet the changing demands of employers and future-proof the next generations, Australia's education sector must continue to invest in and develop students by:

- **Engaging** students with participative methods and styles of learning
- **Equipping** students with transferable skills and character qualities that can be applied to ever-changing work practices and roles
- **Empowering** students, schools, industry and parents in co-designing opportunities in and outside the classroom

---

More than seven in ten educators (71 per cent) believe that the most important function of high school is to provide students with lifelong skills they can apply in all situations. Parents are more likely than educators to believe that the most important function is to equip students with skills for the workforce

(21 per cent of parents compared to 5 per cent of educators).[199] Both are an important function of schools today.

As a teacher and a mum, Jasmine sees both sides. She told us how this sort of tension 'leads to a bigger question of what we want for our kids. I feel like having a baby myself has totally changed my perspective, because, yes, those twenty-first century skills are important, but I'm seeing a lot more value in empathy and tolerance for people – that sort of stuff is way more important in my mind. There is less of a focus on that because we are focusing on the push with coding. I see the core being problem-solving and collaboration, not just cooperating, but actually working together.'

While technology is driving job creation, and STEM skills are important, it is the uniquely human and context-dependent skills like creativity and empathy that will be most important for Generation Alpha to establish now for the future – because they are the ones a computer cannot replicate. We explore this further in Chapter 7, which has a focus on the future of work.

Parents, teachers and leaders of Generation Alpha will do well to prioritise the development of problem-solving, communication, creativity and critical-thinking skills in students, as this will teach valuable lifelong skills and equip them for the changing workforce.

Which subjects to study?

A student who commences kindergarten today will graduate from university in the late 2030s with their retirement occurring in the 2080s or beyond.[200] Although there's no formula or computer coding that can predict the future needs of the workforce of 2080, it is undeniable that technological advancement will continue apace. With that in mind, one of the most important questions we should be asking ourselves is: What are we doing today to prepare future generations to flourish beyond school?

> 'Before, you might have been doing home economics, but now you might be doing robotics. It's still a subject, it's just a different type of subject. But I think Generation Alpha are very lucky because, unlike us who had to basically sit there in a row and learn whatever we needed to learn, they've actually created it. It's a better climate to learn in, so I think they're actually a lot better off than we were.' – *a mother of three Generation Alphas*

As shown earlier, this generation require us to pursue excellence in educational outcomes on foundational literacy and numeracy while also preparing them for their transformative technological future. One of the most mentioned laments to us in focus groups by the older generation about the youngest is that they 'can't do any calculations in their head and can't write legibly to save themselves'. The rise in this sentiment coincides with the arrival of ubiquitous smartphones. We absolutely need our children to have the confidence to perform basic mental calculations and to develop their handwriting skills. But does it require the level of emphasis and concern, considering how much we as adults reach for the calculator app, type at our computers, tap into our phones and increasingly talk to our devices.

The National STEM School Education Strategy report states that, 'International research shows that building STEM capacity across the population is critical in helping to support innovation and productivity regardless of occupation or industry. Consistent with this research, industry surveys show that STEM literacy is increasingly becoming part of the core capabilities that Australian employers need.[201]

If this is to be done well, then a key component is ensuring that schools, teachers and students understand the value of STEM subjects in their curriculum and make it a desirable option. But it can't just be left to schools. Parents can help their children cultivate an interest in STEM by introducing them to some of the very engaging YouTube channels or other video content where science is brought to life through practical examples and real-world experiments. There are many coding camps and robotics activities that children can enrol in. There are also many low-cost technology toys that work by children coding in apps or platforms to bring functionality to these devices. And if it's been a while since you've been to a museum, gallery or science centre, it's worth planning a visit. The interactivity, child-friendly fun and engagement around STEM that many of these institutions now bring is remarkable.

Creating learners for life

Although subject choice is important to a child's schooling experience and their future, what is even more important is instilling a love of learning in Generation Alpha. Most educators believe that lifelong learners are needed to succeed in life after school. As we have seen, educators are almost twice as likely as parents to believe that providing students with lifelong learning skills they can apply to all situations is the most important function of high school.[202] As one teacher told us, 'For me it's all about making quality learners. The best thing you can teach kids is learning how to learn, but they need to learn how to find it out themselves. For Generation Alpha, we need to teach these kids about the process of learning.'

Parents, however, say the most important function of high school is to equip students with skills for the workforce.[203] The reality is that both are important, but as we live longer, retire later, change jobs more frequently, and perform more work with the assistance of machines, learning throughout life becomes more important.

Today, more than 80 per cent of the time we spend in education and training occurs before the age of twenty-one. But the idea that education completed in the first twenty years of life will sustain us for work over the next fifty is no longer tenable. To remain employable, workers will increasingly need to 'make a habit of refreshing existing skills and adding new ones'.[204]

As one teacher shared with us, the best teaching style is one 'where students are encouraged to become thinkers and embrace the changing environment, and have the ability to explore, especially in relation to the changing needs for future jobs.'

Rising parent engagement

'Parents are getting a lot more information about their child. For instance, we have data released to the parents every single Friday about every infringement, about every merit that their child has received in a week. So, because there has been so much communication, I think expectations are higher ... and at times there can be more pressure on the whole situation.' – *a secondary school teacher*

As life gets busier, it's easy for those of us who are parents to simply leave our children to the 'system' of education. But in order for our children to get the best out of their education, caregivers need to be deliberate about engagement with our children, their teachers and the school at large. According to our Future of Education report, parent engagement is rising.

In the last two years, two in five parents agree that they have become more engaged with their child's school.[205]

This increased engagement is reflective of a shift in priorities, with almost half of parents making it more of a priority to be engaged with their child's schooling by knowing what's happening in the school and in the classroom and engaging with teachers regularly. A third of those surveyed have more time to engage or have taken on greater responsibility for their child's schooling. For three in ten parents their engagement has increased because the school provides more opportunities to engage than before.[206]

The engagement isn't just about educational achievement but also social interaction and personal wellbeing. Almost three in five parents are extremely or very aware of what is going on in their child's school.[207] Parents are typically engaged through regularly speaking with their child about what is going on at school, attending parent–teacher interviews and doing school pick-ups and drop-offs.

With the increase in school communication to parents, we have seen that three in five parents expect weekly communication from their child's school, with one in every fourteen parents expecting daily communication. School type and parents' age can affect the amount of communication they expect. Non-government school parents are looking for more frequent communication (daily/weekly) than government school parents, as are Gen Y parents compared to Gen X parents.[208]

While parents appreciate and desire communication from their child's school, three in ten feel overwhelmed by the amount of information they receive. Interestingly, while Gen Y parents desire more frequent communication, they are also more likely to feel overwhelmed by the amount of information, as are non-government school parents.[209]

'My kids have got a Google classroom, a Dodo app –
they've got about four, five, or six different logins for
things and it does my head in. I've actually refused to join
most of them except for the school one and, even then, I
forget to go to things cause there's just so many things.'
– *a mum of three Generation Alphas*

'It has been good to be involved in what my son is
learning, but I think there could be a single source of
information / online portal that would relieve a lot of my
frustrations.' – *a dad of a Generation Alpha*

A challenge for schools, when it comes to communication, is that parents' expectations are often informed by their previous experience with early-learning centres. One in five parents whose child was enrolled in childcare prior to attending school received daily updates on their child.[210]

There's no doubt about it, parents play a key role in the education of their children, but it's important to consider the fact that, as parents, we are entrusting our child to an experienced professional. The classroom experience we had is not the experience of today. Innovation and personalisation of education is going to develop our children in a very different way to what we experienced at school. It's not only going to set up our children for successful further education but is preparing them for the complexities of the future workplace.

Building positive schools

Being united in vision and direction as an entire school community is one of the ways to develop a positive school culture. School communities thrive when there are shared values that unite the school. These values also create boundaries for what is accepted and expected.

Positive schools are places where students feel safe to make mistakes and where resilience is intentionally taught through overcoming challenges. In a society where failure is largely avoided, schools have an opportunity to create an environment for Generation Alpha to take risks and innovate, which will help them to thrive in their future beyond school.

> 'I will regularly talk to staff about how I want them to fail. I want them to be taking risks, I want them to be sharing with me their colossal failures, and we'll celebrate them and what we learned from it. It is creating that culture, that we will do things differently, that it's okay to take risks. And I model it myself all the time.' – *Dr Scott Marsh, Headmaster, William Clarke College*

> 'Every school has students but not every school deserves them. We need to build community, so every student says they belong to their school and don't just attend.' – *Graeme Irwin, Executive Principal, St Philip's group of schools*

Looking to the future, principals are expecting significant change on the horizon. They believe standardised testing has a limited life and there may be shifts away from it in Australia. This trend may already be in motion with the shelving of the school certificate in 2012, and many universities using more than just the Australian Tertiary Admission Rank (ATAR) for their selection criteria. The National Assessment Program – Literacy and Numeracy (NAPLAN) was put on hold for 2020 and the commitment to it has waned among some groups. The MySchools website, which reports the results, is not the only focus parents have as they look for holistic educational outcomes.

Great school leaders have a vision for their school, which is, in particular, a vision for their students. As one principal told us, 'I think over the next ten years, with the changing nature of the university sector and the ATAR and the review of the HSC, schooling has the potential to look very different. And I think that's an exciting thing. I see a much greater potential for schools to increase their focus on developing great learners as opposed to great exam-sitters; to reclaim the greater, more holistic purposes of schooling.'

Some principals are concerned about current focus on examinations being the pinnacle of student achievement, as an holistic education of students is more than just rote learning for tests.

> 'I think the biggest issue that will affect things in the next ten years is that there is a perfect storm of change. I would call it a recognition that the existing models are missing the boat in terms of what is needed in learning. And as long as we continue placing an examination as the endpoint of schooling, then that's going to continue to dominate the process negatively.' – *Dr Stephen Harris, LearnLife*

Schools need to not only teach innovation, creativity and flexibility but practise these so that students can best transition to a changing workforce, via emerging pathways.

> 'How our senior students transition through the senior years and into the workplace is going to become a huge issue for schools ... The landscapes are opening up. Not all students have to do a traditional HSC ... If someone wants to go into childcare, maybe they should be doing a childcare certificate at TAFE ... we have to be clever and

find different ways to enable students to move through to the workplace.' – *Graeme Irwin, Executive Principal, St Philip's group of schools*

Positively, our research showed that nine in ten parents are satisfied with their child's schooling experience. The Net Promoter Score (NPS) for the education sector is 14,[211] which is a strong score. Sentiment towards the education sector is positive, with a two in five parents (39 per cent) believing the education sector will be better in five years' time than it is today with only 16 per cent expecting to see a decline.

Successful education

When asked what successful education looks like, education consultant Dr Anne Knock posed the question, 'Is the child happy?' Anne believes that if students are happy, they'll be excited to go to school. 'Why are they happy? One of the key contributing factors is that the student's learning has been given purpose and meaning. Think about work. People aren't happy at work because of the pay. They are happy when they feel like they are contributing to something – a purpose, a common goal. It's the same with schools and education, they need to have meaning and purpose attached to them, otherwise the students will check out. Their social interactions with others are also a contributing factor to their happiness. School may be compulsory in Australia, but it doesn't have to feel like it.'

The more positive the experience a student has at school, the better it sets them up for success in further education, and in their life more broadly. Australia provides plenty of opportunities for students to grow as individuals and into a career path that will best enable them to thrive.

Although education will play an important role in helping Generation Alpha to thrive in their future careers, a successful education is about more than just achieving academic success and preparing them for the workforce. It is about instilling a love of learning in this generation, opening their eyes to new ways of thinking, building lifelong friendships and connections, and developing skills like critical thinking and leadership, all of which they can take with them into life beyond school.

Key takeaways

In this chapter we have explored how education today looks different to how it did in the past, through the introduction of technology in the classroom. We examined the benefits and drawbacks this presents. We've also looked at both the positive outcomes and challenges presented by COVID-19, and how education styles are changing for the teachers of Generation Alpha. While basic literacy and numeracy are still key priorities, we have also explored how schools can equip Generation Alpha for an unknown future by focusing on transferrable skills.

As education continues to adapt to our rapidly changing times, rising parent engagement is helping schools deliver a positive contribution to the community and to Generation Alpha's lives. A successful education is one that helps set Generation Alpha up to not only partake in meaningful work throughout their life, but to thrive as active and global citizens in a changing world.

CHAPTER 7

The Future of Work

What do you want to do for work when you grow up?

'The same job that Daddy does. I don't know what his main job is.' – *George, aged eight*

'When I finish school, I'm going to travel and go to university. And then when I finish university, I'll get a job as a cook and a doctor.' – *Olivia, aged eight*

'I'll go to university, travel, find someone to marry and have kids and then get a job. I want to be a race car driver. And I wanted to be Spiderman, but I can't.'
– *Jaden, aged eight*

'When I finish school I will travel.'
– *Bianca, aged nine*

'I will be a vet or a teacher.' – *Claire, aged nine*

When it comes to the future of work, often what people really want to know is, 'Will a robot take my job?' For Gen Y, not only is this a concern for themselves but also for their Generation Alpha children. While work seems like it is a long way off in the future for Generation Alpha, it will be here before we know it – especially for the oldest Generation Alphas, who will

221

commence their first experience of work, even while students, over the next decade.

In this chapter, we use the trends of today to analyse and predict what is likely to occur in the future, and affect Generation Alpha. We explore what the post-school pathway landscape is like, including the university versus vocational education and training (VET) debate, and the role parents play in this decision for their child. We take a look at how post-school pathways prepare Generation Alpha for the changing nature of work in the future, and explore what sort of jobs Generation Alpha will have, as well as how and where they will work.

Generation Alpha will be the most formally educated generation the world has ever seen. With post-school qualifications ranging from university to VET, apprenticeships, traineeships and adult community education, there are a number of choices and educational opportunities for the future school leaver. Students today face a lot of pressure to meet the requirements for entry into these respective study avenues. But with more options and pathways available than ever before, it is also much easier for students to pursue their chosen profession or career.

In 2018 the Australian Bureau of Statistics conducted a national survey, the Survey of Education and Work.[212] It revealed that almost 10 million Australians aged twenty to sixty-four years had attained a post-school qualification (a certificate, diploma or degree). This accounts for two thirds of that population group. Of those without a post-school qualification, more than half had a year twelve or equivalent qualification. Almost three quarters of those who were employed had a post-school qualification, and almost a third had a bachelor's degree or above.

Of Australians aged fifteen to sixty-four years, almost one in five were currently studying. Of those who were currently studying for a post-school qualification, two fifths were completing a bachelor's degree, over one tenth were doing post-graduate degrees and a similar number were studying for a certificate III. The most popular field of study for a post-school qualification was society and culture, followed by management, commerce then health. Of Australians aged fifteen to twenty-four years, four fifths were fully engaged in employment or education. Clearly, education plays an important role in our career and employment journey.

Parents' dreams for their children's future

Understandably, many parents want the best for their children and, often, to afford them opportunities that they themselves never had. Parents today are also working hard to give their children the best life possible, for them to be successful and happy.

Many parents believe these things are heightened by going to university. University develops some great qualities in the students of today and prepares them well for a number of jobs and roles, but it doesn't suit every student and isn't the right pathway for everyone. While some parents are okay with whatever pathway their child chooses, 65 per cent of Australian parents want their child to go to university[213] (although there is a declining trend here; it was 72 per cent the year before).[214] As one parent told us, 'It has to be the case that our society has space for people with degrees and without, but I still struggle because I want my kids to have the [university] education regardless of whether it results in a career.'

Regardless of a parents' expectations and hopes for their children, it is important to note that children look to parents first for advice, guidance and support about their career and life decisions[215] – even if it doesn't always seem that way!

Teachers are another significant source of influence in a child's life. Many are conscious of the pressure being put on students today to go to university. One teacher we spoke with acknowledged that 'there are some kids who probably shouldn't go to uni, yet we put too much emphasis on it. It can negatively impact people far beyond high school and into their career.'

A shift in the labour market to the knowledge economy and a less restricted, demand-driven higher education system has meant that university enrolments have been climbing over the last decade.

Generation Alpha are now being raised in an era where they are getting a few different messages about life post-school. In recent times, the focus at a government level has turned to jobs. This flows into government spending, with increased funding for areas that have a direct and clear pathway to jobs.

In 2020, the federal government changed the funding model of universities to reduce the public funding of courses which don't have a direct pathway to in-demand jobs such as arts, which essentially made them more expensive for the student. They also increased the funding of other courses that were identified as national priorities – such as teaching, nursing, agriculture, psychology and other areas of allied health – to make them less expensive.

Young people are growing up hearing these messages and recognising a benefit in undertaking courses that can make them more employable. They will be guided by financial incentives towards courses that have lower HECS (Higher Education Contribution Scheme) costs, and away from those that require students to pay a higher proportion of the cost.

This is the intent at least, however, as student loans aren't repayable until earnings hit a threshold and early indications are that students are unfazed by the changes in course costs and are still largely being influenced by their interests, not their prospective debt.

The federal government is also stepping into the skills area, which has been receiving a lot more attention and funding. There is now a national skills commissioner, who focuses on clear messaging around where the national skill shortages are and makes efforts to solve those shortages. There is also a national careers institute, which has a focus on vocational education rather than higher education. In addition to the JobSeeker and JobKeeper initiatives introduced in response to COVID-19, there is now also JobTrainer, which seeks to help fast-track students with free and low-fee skills training. There is also a real focus on apprenticeships because, even in the world of digital, we require infrastructure that skilled trades provide.

As well as responding to these economic and government incentives, parents are changing their attitude towards post-school pathways. They don't have the same singular focus or aspiration of seeing their Generation Alpha children go to university as has dominated recent decades. There are now many pathways to university, and with lifelong learning being a pillar for this generation, a degree can fit into any stage of life.[216] Parents are motivated to ensure that their children become employable and be able to earn and save. They are also being more pragmatic, in an era of housing affordability challenges and increasing cost-of-living pressures. Parents are happy to support their children at home while they study, and even as they begin their working lives. They know that the best early jobs are those that will grow their skills, not just their salaries. When starting out, at least until thirty and probably

———

When starting out, at least until thirty and probably for life, what you learn in a role matters more than what you earn.

———

for life, what you learn in a role matters more than what you earn.

Pathways to work

The pathways students pursue after school provide them with a number of broad opportunities – from making lifelong friendships to expanding their knowledge and experience of the world, to preparing them for an evolving world of work. For many students these days, getting some experience in the workforce during their further study is becoming more of a priority. Already a significant proportion of graduates don't end up working in the area of their studies, however the more they can gain practical experience in their field during their study or in their early years post-completion, the higher the likelihood that their career will follow their field of study. So it is important that students maintain momentum and are proactive about work while they study.

Never, in the history of the world, has education been more advanced, more accessible and more flexible. These characteristics of today's education landscape mean that every individual has the opportunity to commit to lifelong learning and can continue to develop their skills, or retrain for a different career altogether.

When it comes to higher education for Generation Alpha, we must remember that whatever path they decide to take, it is the outcome that matters. As long as they are pursuing something they are passionate about and that enables them to begin a career and life of contribution and meaning, then it is a worthy pathway to support.

As Professor Stephen Parker AO of KPMG put it, 'Remember, at the end of the day, a good society is one where people are fulfilled, not just prosperous. Higher levels of education do not of themselves bring greater job satisfaction, possibly the reverse is the case.'[217]

The university pathway

Universities have been a part of the Australian education landscape for more than one hundred and fifty years and over the last few decades, they have become an increasingly popular and accessible choice for school leavers. For Generation X, around one in four people obtained a university degree. For Generation Y, that increased to one in three and for today's school leavers, Generation Z, one in two are choosing to study at university.[218]

The Australian Bureau of Statistics reported an increase in further study among Australians. The headline was that Australians were pursuing higher education in record numbers, with 56 per cent of Australians aged fifteen years and over now holding a post-school qualification, up from 46 per cent in 2006.[219]

Census Program Manager Bindi Kindermann said attaining a university qualification remains an achievement Australians strive for, with close to one quarter (24 per cent) of Australian adults in the 2016 Census having completed a bachelor's degree or above, up from 18 per cent a decade ago.[220] The past five years have also seen significant increases in the number of people with graduate diplomas, graduate certificates, advanced diplomas and certificate-level qualifications.

Getting into university

While the youngest Generation Alphas haven't been born yet, over the next decade the oldest of them will reach their final year of school and, for many, the university placement process will begin. So how different will that process look to how it does today?

Over the last decade or so, placement at university has become far more accessible. For many students, their ATAR score – which ranks students in comparison to one another based on their performance in year twelve – is the cause of much stress. Adults are well placed as they reflect on their post-school years to exhort students that the ATAR does not determine the rest of their lives.

As Anna McGahan, an actor and writer, wrote to the 2020 graduating class, 'Dear year twelve student, I almost didn't complete year twelve. School felt insurmountable. There was so much pressure to make it the year that defined my future, and so many times I felt like I squandered that pivotal time. But I can tell you, fifteen years later, now a professional actor and writer, a loved friend, a leader, partner and mother, that it could not be further from the truth. Trust me. Year twelve only takes you to the edge of Earth's atmosphere, my friend. There's a whole universe out there, waiting to embrace you.'[221]

While there are academic requirements to get accepted into a university course, an increasing number of year twelve students apply for early-entry pathways which are based on extracurricular achievements, school recommendations or other individual circumstances. A recent report by Victoria University's Mitchell Institute found that only one in four students was admitted to university on the basis of their ATAR.[222]

'I was guaranteed a placement at uni; mainly because of my extracurricular activities,' Elizabeth, a Bachelor of Education student, informed us. 'I was getting good grades, but because I had volunteered at a sports club for children with disabilities and had done my gold Duke of Edinburgh Award, I was told that I had a place at uni for my preferred degree, regardless of my final HSC results.'

This shows a shift away from the traditional process of university application. It is no longer only about final grades but also about the character and extracurricular activities of the student.

Some schools have taken things even further and are building relationships with universities to give their students on-campus experiences long before the university application deadline. These programs provide students, particularly those who may be the first in their family to have the opportunity to attend university (such as those from culturally diverse backgrounds, Indigenous students and those from socio-economically disadvantaged areas) to see that the pathway to university is increasingly an accessible one.

So, what will the future of universities and the admission process look like for Generation Alpha? If the trends continue, it's likely even more Generation Alphas won't be admitted just on their academic achievements but due to their skills, work ethic, character and with an intention to account for barriers they may have faced in their education. In what for many is the most stressful year of their life, and with added uncertainties in an era of pandemic-induced lockdowns and the associated remote learning, to have university offers before the stress of final exams is a great support for the mental health of senior students.

Universities of the future will also continue to offer a more flexible learning experience, integrating online and on-campus learning, and eventually, qualifications that can be completed in shorter time frames and fit around existing work roles. The more that universities can allow Generation Alpha to plug back into education easily, in order to keep up with a rapidly changing world and workforce, the better.

There has been some criticism in the past of universities focusing too much on theory and not enough on practice.

Responding to the changing world, future universities will be places where university and industry are co-located and collaborate on projects that solve real-world problems. They'll become precincts of innovation that actively apply research for community impact. And they'll foster relationships between young entrepreneurs and mentors and funders. As industry and universities form deeper partnerships, students will benefit from university-based accelerator programs and incubators, where ideas are stimulated and commercialised faster. Already, there are many courses that encourage or require a business-based internship, business-hosted group project or other work-experience component. This is an exciting characteristic of the future of education where the overlap between school, university and workplaces increases in size and in scope.

The vocational education pathway

Although for the last few decades, university has been the dominant pathway to further education and a career, there is growing appreciation for Technical and Further Education (TAFE). Currently TAFE have over 1200 courses on offer, ranging from a Certificate IV in Floristry to a Diploma in Human Resources Management to a Certificate IV in Plumbing and Services.

There is great debate over whether or not a degree is more valuable than a TAFE qualification. However the pathway into the workforce will essentially come down to what the individual wants to do for work, and how they would like to study. For example, if a student wants to work in a profession like teaching or engineering, they will need to go to university to study. They can, however, work their way up by starting with a TAFE course, such as a Diploma of Nursing, which, in turn, serves as a pathway to further study to a bachelor of nursing. If, however, a student wants to pursue a trade, such as carpentry or mechanics, then the clear pathway is TAFE. TAFE is more accessible than university as you don't need an ATAR or to have finished high school in order to qualify for a course.

What is VET?

Vocational Education and Training (VET), is a set of post-school qualifications which seek to prepare students with skills for the workforce. While there is some overlap with university, VET qualifications provide practical and work-oriented skills, which are evaluated using competency-based assessments. Higher education qualifications, on the other hand, use a grading approach.

By correcting some myths about vocational training, parents will better be able to guide their children to the post-school pathway which will best suit them. The National Centre for Vocational Education Research conducted a survey on the salary of exiting university students and exiting VET students, and their findings go against the belief that VET students earn less. The report found that the median full-time income for a VET graduate is $56,000, whereas a student with a bachelor's degree earns $54,000. The highest average starting salary for a VET qualification is a Certificate in Hazardous Areas (Electrical), which earns an average of $85,400. This is higher than the graduate starting salary of the best-paid degree (which is a Bachelor level degree in Dentistry), which starts at $80,000.[223]

There's also a belief that employability is stronger from university than VET, with three in ten respondents feeling that the main reason Australians choose university over VET is because university graduates find work more easily. Research shows, however, that over 78 per cent of VET graduates are employed within six months of completion, compared to 69 per cent of those with a bachelor's degree. For VET students who trained as part of a trade apprenticeship there was a 92 per cent rate of employment.[224]

Additionally, the VET sector currently provides training courses for nine out of the ten occupations which are predicted to have the greatest growth of new jobs over the next five years.[225] This shows that VET is a relevant option when it comes to preparing Australia to be more globally competitive.

Seventeen-year-old Ellyece sees the value in her own VET experience. 'For me, [university] is a long and expensive road, and may not necessarily lead to employment. I had a passion for real estate and knew I didn't want to spend my time learning things I didn't need to. I just wanted to get into it. I think people should experience careers and jobs for real. It helps you figure out if you like it.'[226]

A distinct feature of the emerging Australian economy is the disruption to the types of jobs people will be undertaking in the future. 'By 2040, 87 per cent of all Australian workers between 21 and 65 will have changed occupations at least once.[227] This means the majority expect they will have to reskill, retrain or face potential unemployment. The standard time to complete a general bachelor's degree is three years, while a growing list of professions require a fourth year, or post-graduate qualification. Many students are opting for double degrees or completing their studies part-time – which further extends the years of study. If careers are expected to change every ten to fifteen years, it is not feasible to spend three or more years out of work retraining each time at university. VET courses, however, range in length between six months and two years. This means VET students can take as little as six months to requalify and reskill.

A different way

By the time Generation Alpha reach this decision-making process, they may actually choose to defer tertiary study, with a number of companies like Google and Apple saying applicants no longer need a post-school qualification.

'When you look at people who don't go to school and make their way in the world, those are exceptional human beings. And we should do everything we can to find those people,' said Google's former Senior Vice President of People Operations, Laszlo Bock. 'Academic qualifications will still be taken into account and indeed remain an important consideration when assessing candidates as a whole, but will no longer act as a barrier to getting a foot in the door,' added Maggie Stilwell, Ernst and Young's managing partner for talent.[228]

Another option for school leavers is to take a gap year – which may involve travel, work or volunteering. One in five students (20 per cent) who complete high school take a gap year.[229] The best gap years are those where their tertiary course is deferred and the year is used to explore other interests, earn some money, learn more about what it means to hold down a job, meet customer needs, volunteer or earn and manage one's own money, knowing that it's just a short season in life and that the next chapter is already prepared. Gap years that don't have a defined pathway and a clear structure and that extend beyond a year can be problematic. Overall, however, a one-year gap can provide valuable work, travel and life experience. Research from National Centre for Vocational Education Research (NCVER) shows that five years after completing school there is no difference between employment rates of those who took gap years from those who didn't.[230]

When it comes to helping Generation Alpha decide on a post-school career pathway, the best thing you can do as a parent is to show your interest and support as they make their study and career choices, give your opinion and perspective when asked for it, and encourage your children to pursue something they are passionate about and which they can use to make a positive impact.

Preparing Australia for the future workforce

Flexibility is the key to Australia's future. In order to ensure the stability of the Australian economy through the anticipated challenges of the future, Australia needs more adaptable workers who are able to engage in learning throughout their lives.

According to the Future Skills Report by AlphaBeta for Google Australia, 'Australians will need new skills to adjust to the future of work. Much of this additional learning will occur later in life as workers reskill in response to job changes and upskill in response to changes in the tasks within their jobs. Today, the average Australian acquires more than 80 per cent of their knowledge and skills before the age of twenty-one. Australians will need to double the share of learning they do after the age of twenty-one from 19 per cent to 41 per cent'.[231] So, what is the answer to this upskilling and retraining? We need to engage in short, bite-sized and flexible courses as well as regular training and upskilling in the workplace, and this will be even truer for Generation Alpha.

To stand out, Generation Alpha workers of the future will need to demonstrate character qualities, real-work experience and other ways of showing why they are the right fit for a role, beyond academics. The Graduate Outcomes Survey, a study of Australian university graduates conducted six months after their course completion, shows that 69 per cent are employed full time with 15 per cent not employed in any capacity.[232] This highlights that degrees won't necessarily guarantee work, especially in generalist areas like computing (81 per cent), humanities (83 per cent) and environmental studies (84 per cent).

Commentators argue that the current rigidity of the higher education system fails to teach graduates how to handle the complexity and ambiguity which they are likely to encounter in the workforce. Generation Alpha will be retraining, upskilling, career changing, or shifting from employment to self-employment and then back again, several times over the course of their working lives, and so ongoing access to formal training will ensure they meet the demands of an ever-changing workforce.

COVID-19 and online study

Online study has been increasing in popularity and scope, but COVID-19 took it to a new level when any provider who wasn't already conducting courses online suddenly had to. With masses of employees working from home during COVID-19, many also took the opportunity to upskill, gaining micro-credentials. As our world became more digital and global during the pandemic, many of these online courses could be completed by people from all over the world – regardless of their physical proximity to the provider.

So, what does this mean for Generation Alpha? As a direct result of COVID-19, online courses and study options will be more readily available than ever before for this generation. And Australians believe they will partake in it more as a result, with 82 per cent of adults agreeing that the COVID-19 experience will mean education will be delivered more online in the future.[233]

What jobs will Generation Alpha do?

No jobs?

We are living in an age of digital disruption. You don't have to look far to see the impact of technology on most areas of our lives, including when, where, how and what we do for work.

The last few decades have shown that any role that can be replaced by technology, will be. From supermarket checkouts to airport check-ins, bank tellers and office secretaries – these are some of the jobs that used to be carried out by humans, but which technology has largely replaced. Positions that require low skills and qualifications are the ones predicted to have the highest probability of replacement by computerisation, which means increased education specialisation and skills will lead to increased job security.

These changes have led to concern among parents of Generation Alpha about the world of work their children will enter into. In a discussion about the future of work and jobs, one parent shared with us, 'The way technology is going, they could totally rule out so many jobs, pretty quickly, with robots.' Even parents who aren't fearful of technology still have concerns about the impact of it on their child's future job prospects.

'I think the concern is that we have no idea what that future will look like. We hope it is wonderful, but there is so much unknown and outside of our control. The rate of change is rapid, kids grow up so fast and the generational differences seem bigger than ever before. How can you prepare your kids for circumstances, issues and jobs that don't currently exist?' – *a mum of a one-year-old Generation Alpha*

New jobs

It's important to remember, though, that technology is not just replacing jobs but it is also creating new ones. As we saw in Chapter 2, the World Economic Forum predicts that 65 per cent of children entering primary school today will end up working in job types that don't yet exist.

While it can be overwhelming to think about what the future of work will be and what jobs that will exist when Generation Alpha begin their careers, there are clear indications of the direction these jobs are heading.

Many of the new jobs will largely come from technology. When today's senior school students were at primary school, there were still people employed as toll collectors on our motorways! Now, many of these students are learning skills in robotics, coding, social media marketing, app development and big data analytics to prepare them for the new jobs and careers they will step into. As they consider their career options, there are jobs available in entirely new industries such as nanotechnology, blockchain, cyber security, autonomous transport and virtual reality.

'Because there are so many opportunities, I have no idea what my son will end up doing. Because there's so much out there, I'm not too sure.' – *a parent of two Generation Alphas*

Human jobs

While the future may seem hard to comprehend, we need to remember that while technology is great for automating systems and replacing repetitive functions, it is not strong at adapting to complex change and engaging with people. Jobs that are highly repetitive, highly administrative and involve low-skill work will be the ones replaced by technology. This means that Generation Alpha will be able to focus on higher-value work instead. Technology will enable them to work in jobs and careers that challenge and grow them and help them to contribute to a flourishing society.

In order to future-proof their careers and skills, Generation Alpha will need to develop skills that are human strengths rather than machine-orientated. This means we need to focus on developing transferable skills such as critical thinking, empathy, leadership and social and cultural awareness. By being collaborative, responsive and innovative, Generation Alpha will be better positioned to thrive in a world of more global and digital careers, now and over the decades ahead.

As one mum profoundly put it in a focus group, 'STEM without self-care, critical thinking and compassion is nothing that any of us wants in the world, right? In any field, if you take out those three components, what you have left is literally the worst of humanity.'

As we explored in Chapter 6, this means that focusing on developing uniquely human characteristics in the next generation is imperative for them to thrive in the future. As one teacher shared with us, 'When we talk about what jobs will be phased out by the time kids in primary school have finished uni, so many of those tech-based roles will likely be replaced by forms of technology. Yet people-based and face-to-face roles that involve hearts, minds, compassion and empathy, they're going to be more likely to last longer in terms of being jobs for people rather than being able to be taken over by technology. And that's where I find so many of them struggle.'

While it seems counterintuitive in a working world increasingly being driven by technology, we need to be focusing on the uniquely human characteristics and skills for the next generation, as well as investing in STEM subjects and skills. This is further enforced in an AlphaBeta report, which explains that 'Many of these uniquely human skills are developed outside of the formal education environment, which means broader society will need to be mobilised. Parents and other family members, community organisations, sports clubs and social media role models should understand and embrace their roles in teaching children skills that make us uniquely human: empathy, ingenuity, cooperation, resilience, ethics and integrity. Having these skills will allow future Australians to succeed in a world where human work will continue to be as indispensable as the machines that enable our society to function.'[234]

Undeniably, technology is going to change and significantly shape the future working landscape. But there are also other megatrends at play that are important for us to understand when thinking about Generation Alpha and the world of work they will inherit.

Demographic change and the future of work

While technology will have a significant impact on the future job landscape, the jobs of the future will also come from demographic change. Australia's ageing population is one demographic trend that is creating new job opportunities, not just in the aged-care sector but also for retirement services, independent living and mobility aids, and health care more broadly. At the same time, Australia's record birth numbers (even though birth rates per woman have declined, with population growth, annual births continue to grow) and more affluent parents are creating new childcare services and career roles. From cultural diversity to changing family structures, population shifts create new demands and industries.

More than most developed nations, Australia's population is growing strongly. Prior to the closure of international borders necessitated by the COVID-19 pandemic, most of Australia's annual population growth came from migration. While it will take some years to get back to the pre-pandemic numbers, the population is still on track to reach 40 million by 2050.[235] The challenges that come with this growth include greater urbanisation, growth of vertical communities and population sprawl. With the working-from-home era that COVID-19 ushered in, it will now be more feasible to work from home, and we expect to see more people making a 'tree or sea change'. These terms describe people moving out of the bustling and busy cities to regional areas for affordability and lifestyle reasons. In the past, employment has been a key barrier to more people leaving the cities, but as remote working increases this will become less of a concern. By the time Generation Alpha arrive to the workforce, we will be even more global, mobile and digital than we are now – and will have even more flexible working options.

Australia, like most developed nations, is also experiencing a rapid ageing of the population. Within a decade, Australia will have more people aged over sixty-five than under eighteen for the first time in history.[236] Nowhere are the implications of this more significant than in employment. An ageing population leads directly to an ageing workforce, which means Generation Alpha as the skilled younger workers will be in greater demand.[237]

Australia is also more culturally diverse than any other developed nation on the planet, with migration a key driver of population. Three in ten Australians (29 per cent) were born overseas. That's twice the proportion of overseas-born residents than the United States (14 per cent) and the United Kingdom (14 per cent).[238]

This diversity is a key characteristic of Australia today, and workers are increasingly expecting their places of employment to reflect the broader society in which they operate. This is particularly true for the emerging generations, who have been shaped in an era of much cultural, gender, sexual and generational diversity. According to our research, for a large proportion of Generation Z, the idea of their leader being born outside of Australia, their leader being a woman and their leader being the same age as them makes no difference (75 per cent, 67 per cent and 66 per cent, respectively). And the majority of those who didn't select 'makes no difference' actually stated that those characteristics in leaders are positives.[239]

The benefits of diversity (from personal characteristics such as age, gender and culture to education, length of tenure and industry experience), enable an organisation to adapt, learn and grow through input from broader perspectives. Additionally, by welcoming different experiences, they are better able to connect with a wider and more global customer or client audience.

In response to a more diverse workforce, we need greater emotional intelligence (EQ), cultural intelligence (CQ) and generational intelligence (GQ). Our survey of workers supports this, with 72 per cent saying EQ is extremely or very important, and 71 per cent saying intellectual intelligence (IQ) is extremely or very important in managers. Additionally, GQ is considered extremely or very important by 67 per cent of workers, as is CQ (62 per cent consider this to be extremely or very important for a manager to possess in the workplace). Leaders need these skills to bridge gaps and create cohesion and a common direction among diverse teams.[240]

By the time Generation Alpha enter the workforce, these different types of intelligences will be increasingly important to facilitate thriving workplaces. For a generation even more

THE FUTURE OF WORK

accustomed to diversity than the current Gen Zs, it will be imperative for workplaces to represent a diverse range of people and perspectives.

Increasing career options

There is an increasing number of options available for the next generation of school leavers, from post-school pathways to gap years, travel options and a vast number of careers to choose from. Generation Alpha will also benefit from their global perspective – they won't just be thinking about their local area, state or nation in terms of where they can work, study and travel.

It's currently the era of the gig economy, contingent work, freelancing and entrepreneurism. Two in five Australians have earnt money through non-traditional work, and three in ten Australian workers are not full-time, they're either part-time, casual, or independent contractors. A 2018 Triple J study found that one in three people aged eighteen to twenty-nine had a 'side hustle',[241] where they pursued a passion piece, started their own venture or worked on the side of a more traditional role. As twenty-four-year-old Anaisha said, 'A few years ago while I was in between study, I created a little side business to sell scrunchies, tote bags and other things I could make. While it was fun to make things I enjoyed, it was also nice to sell them and make a bit of money, plus it taught me some business skills too.'

So, while we may think about the next generation as employees, they may well be employers at the same time. Generation Alpha will most likely experience this work dynamic as well, as highlighted to us by one parent of Generation Alpha: 'they probably won't work full-time, but more part-time or casual contracts, that kind of thing. There's probably more flexibility and more opportunities.'

A key strength Generation Alpha will bring to the workforce will be their ability to apply their skills across multiple roles, as they will bring a range of transferrable skills to the workplace.

Redefined work life

Twenty-first century life is rarely linear and sequential. In the past, we would complete the education stage, move into the working years and perhaps, after a career change or two, head into retirement. These days the lives of the emerging generations are more of a mosaic of different roles, phases and careers. The education phase for Generation Alpha will extend well into adulthood, and throughout their working life. This multi-career generation will very likely need to retrain several times with these careers taking them to other states and countries.

The provision of long service leave after ten years of employment must seem unattainable in this era where the average tenure of a worker is just two years and nine months.[242] This huge decline in tenure comes not from a lack of loyalty, nor a poor work ethic of young employees. It is simply a response to the changed times. They have come of an age in an era where there is little job security, a competitive environment, precarious employment and fast-changing industries and careers. Today's job market has been created by these economic and demographic times and the emerging generation of workers are playing to the new rules of the employment world.

Work as the third place

Historically, the 'third place' refers to social settings that are separate from the two usual social environments: home (first place) and the workplace (second place). Churches, parks, cafés or libraries are traditional examples of third-place environments.

The long-time CEO of Starbucks, Howard Schultz, famously set the vision of making their stores the third place. The Starbucks third-place policy begins: 'We want our stores to be the third place, a warm and welcoming environment where customers can gather and connect.'[243] This vision has become a reality for many thousands of cafés and eateries worldwide that are full of people using laptops and smartphones or reading books – not necessarily connecting with those around them but vicariously experiencing community connection in a busy, fragmented world.

Living in the 'great screen age', in which we spend more time on our devices than in face-to-face interaction, most of us are less likely to be involved with traditional community groups or activities. This will be even more the case for Generation Alpha.

Work now facilitates many of our social needs and plays an important part in developing our sense of purpose, meaning and contribution. As a result, we are seeing the workplace occupy not only the second space but the third place as well.

This idea of work as the 'third place' has given rise to a range of workplace initiatives, from wellbeing programs to volunteer opportunities, breakout rooms, ping pong tables and social events. While social activities used to take place on a Friday night after work, the workplace of today is a combination of work, social and health-related priorities. After-work drinks have morphed into more inclusive social engagement practices, which is important in an era when workers look to have multiple needs met at work.

Sure, work is about achieving task outcomes and receiving financial rewards, but it's also about social connection, training, personal development, greater fulfilment and even environmental sustainability. In this new world of work, employers need to be asking themselves, 'How can we be the employer of choice?', especially as Generation Z and Alpha employees begin to fill our workplaces.

Generation Z and Alpha will want to help achieve profit outcomes, but environmental considerations and socio-economic concerns mean that they are also looking to make a difference with their work. They want to achieve more than just the financial bottom line. As Zoe, a twenty-two-year-old Gen Z, said, 'I think a lot of our generation get mistaken for being rude, but we're just curious. We aren't afraid to speak up if we feel differently about something.'[244]

The world for the emerging generations has also become incentivised. Customer loyalty is bought with frequent buyer programs, points, or discounts. And so is employee loyalty. By understanding and meeting their needs, and motivating through relevant reward and recognition strategies, these generations can be engaged in their roles and be less likely to move jobs as frequently.

Work Wellbeing

The emerging generations of Gen Y and Gen Z (the parents and older siblings of Generation Alpha respectively) expect their workplaces to contribute to their wellbeing and are making decisions about where they will work based on whether that job will help their overall wellbeing.

Although not at this life stage quite yet, work wellbeing will also be an essential consideration for Generation Alpha and their ability to thrive in the future. Already, Australian workers recognise that wellbeing will be a significant factor shaping the future of work. In a survey we conducted of employed Australians, we asked the question: 'How big of an impact do you think the following will have on the future of work?' Of the seven factors we tested, 'mental health and stress of workers' was the factor that workers believed would have the biggest impact, with more than three in five workers (62 per cent) saying it will have a significant or large impact.[245] This was followed by demographic trends, the physical workspace and where work will be done, sectors disappearing, computerisation of robotics, global workforce trends and the gig economy.

A foundational element of work wellbeing is workplace safety. The good news in most developed nations, and in most industries, is that rates of physical injury in the workplace continue to decline. Through better training, technology solutions and heightened employer and worker vigilance, worksites have never been safer. Safe Work Australia data shows that in the latest three-year period, serious workplace incidents have been on the decline.[246] For Generation Alpha, the most dangerous aspect of their job will most likely be their daily commute.

At the same time as we have seen workplaces become safer physically, there has been a growing awareness of the impact of work mentally and emotionally. Workplace health and safety regimens have robustly turned their attention to mental wellbeing, and many organisations have rebranded their workplace health and safety services 'wellbeing services'.

The concept of work wellbeing is about more than just being tokenistic or implementing tick-a-box workplace practices. Work wellbeing is an attitude embedded deep in the culture of an organisation. It is an approach to work, where staff are valued as people rather than as just employees who come to work. Organisations and their leaders need to be careful that their workplace wellbeing practices aren't purely about increasing the productivity and output of the employees.

There are many reasons why work wellbeing needs to be at the top of the agenda of workplace leaders – both today, and when it comes time for Generation Alpha to enter the workforce. Western culture faces significant health concerns from people being overworked, stressed and burnt out, which not only affects people's personal health and ability to thrive but it can also lead to increased absenteeism, relational tension and decreased productivity. All of these issues will affect an organisation's ability to perform well.

Workplaces are also facing a loneliness epidemic. Our research collaboration with Dr Lindsay McMillan shows that almost half (48 per cent) of people in Australia are lonely and that 37 per cent of workers feel lonely at work.[247] In his extensive investigation into the future of workplaces, Dr McMillan's research paper on workplace loneliness sheds light on the growing epidemic of this phenomenon in the workplace. In the report he stated: 'Social connection at work is more than just being happy at work. Humans can easily fake happiness. Instead, it is about contentment and doing good work. The two are not mutually exclusive.'

The report also sheds light on the impact of loneliness on the individual and on the workplace. Of those who feel lonely at work, 40 per cent felt less productive, 38 per cent reported making more mistakes and 36 per cent reported getting sick more often. Additionally, lonely workers are twice as likely to look for a new job in the next twelve months.[248]

Work is important to good mental health and wellbeing in that it brings structure, activity and social interaction to someone's day. In a study we conducted for our book called *Work Wellbeing: Leading Thriving Teams in Rapidly Changing Times*, we learnt that 57 per cent of employees agreed that they found meaning in their work. In turn, the same percentage felt motivated to work hard because they said their job is both interesting and important to them personally.[249]

Amid these trends, a growing number of organisations are seeing the value of implementing and encouraging healthy initiatives for their employees. There has been a significant trend in workplaces towards standing desks, natural light and fruit bowls. Our own organisation tries to prioritise the physical and mental health of our team. We encourage walks at lunch time, we have a communal fruit bowl and we (try to) have regular stretch breaks away from our desks. Organisations have realised that having healthy employees equals having a healthy organisation.

We hope these practices and priorities continue to abound. But wellbeing is more than positive physical and mental health. In its holistic definition, wellbeing is about our ability as humans to thrive and flourish, and we believe that work plays a crucial role in this.

We asked Australian workers this: if they were to win the lottery, would they work again? The results were surprising in that 77 per cent of those surveyed stated they would remain in work, with 27 per cent saying they would quit their current jobs, 33 per cent would reduce the number of days that they work but remain in their current job, and 17 per cent of people would make no changes to their role or employment status. Although this gives a sense that people are feeling fulfilled in their workplace, 30 per cent nevertheless feel that they are overworked and stressed, which blocks their ability to thrive in their role.[250]

Over 25 per cent of workers feel a strong sense of community in their workplace.[251] This is an important insight as it tells us that employers need to do more to cultivate that community and belonging which will in turn have a positive effect on mental health. Another interesting learning was that other than being paid, work contributes to other areas of life.

My work contributes to the following areas of my life	
A sense of purpose	64 per cent
Develops me as a person	59 per cent
Makes a difference in the lives of others	58 per cent
Makes a better society and the world	55 per cent
A sense of community and belonging	54 per cent

Each of these are contributing factors to an individual's mental health and wellbeing, and 72 per cent of respondents rated workplace wellbeing as either extremely or very important to them.[252]

Purposeful work has a positive impact and connects us with others. It is core to our wellbeing and our ability to thrive. If employers and leaders can understand this now and make the necessary workplace changes to prioritise employee wellbeing, then we can create better and more meaningful work and workplaces for Generation Alpha to enter into.

Key takeaways

There are a number of choices and educational opportunities for Generation Alpha's future. In this chapter we explored the post-school pathway options of university, vocational education and training, and side hustles. Not only will Generation Alpha be the most formally educated generation, they will also experience online study in new ways, upskill across multiple careers and see the benefits of a redefined work life. The type of work they will be doing will also be different to previous generations and will require them to develop empathy and interpersonal skills in a more machine-assisted world. Work will comprise a big part of their life, and they will work later in life than any other generation. This makes it a key area for parents to guide Generation Alpha in, helping them to pursue a post-school pathway and line of work that not only helps to pay the bills but is one they are passionate about, contributes to their wellbeing and will be the means through which they make a meaningful contribution.

CHAPTER 8

Leading Generation Alpha

'Everything rises and falls on leadership.'
John C. Maxwell

In life, leaders take many forms. For many of us, the people who have the greatest influence in our lives are our parents. Parents play a crucial role in leading their children, and in doing so shape the type of leaders their children will become. In this chapter we explore the changing styles of leadership, how parents and leaders can best lead Generation Alpha, and how Generation Alpha will lead in the future.

Since the year 2010 – the year Generation Alpha began being born – the world as we know it has seen a vast amount of change. In an effort to describe the extent of change the first decade of Generation Alpha has seen, new terms have entered our lexicon such as 'disruption', 'megatrends' and 'change fatigue', and the unprecedented use of the word 'unprecedented'.

As we entered the 2020s we surveyed Australians to get a measure on how they were feeling about the amount of change they experienced in the last decade. The biggest response was 'concerned' – the feeling of more than one in three. This was much larger than the one in four who were feeling 'positive', and for every person feeling 'empowered' almost twice as many were feeling 'overwhelmed'. Similarly, far more felt 'fatigued' than 'energised'.[253]

In the workplace, while we hope motivated leaders find it an exciting time to be alive, many employees are more subdued. Amid global influences, a volatile economy, emerging (and declining) jobs and accelerating technological change, almost half of Australians say they feel anxious (45 per cent) and uncertain.[254] A stark reality was pointed out by Canadian prime minister Justin Trudeau in his speech at the World Economic Forum when he said: 'The pace of change has never been this fast, yet it will never be this slow again.' An understanding of the trends can give a better vision of where we're headed, and an observation of the emerging generations can give some foresight to prepare us for what's next.

Generation Alpha have never known a world of printed encyclopedias, phone books, street directories, video rental stores or fax machines. It is possible they will never use a desktop computer, analogue watch, physical credit card or car ignition key. In a world of electronic driver's licences and e-payments, most will never own a wallet. As we've observed in the chapters so far, by looking at these changes we gain insight into the future. But what is the role of a leader in all of this?

'Leadership is influence, nothing more, nothing less.' – John C. Maxwell

Leadership author John C. Maxwell gives a helpful definition of his topic of expertise: 'Leadership is influence, nothing more, nothing less.' He notes that as every person on the planet has some level of influence, so everyone is a leader. The challenge is in both how we wield our influence and how we develop our leadership capabilities. Just as we are all leaders, so we are all followers. You may lead your children at home, but have a boss that you follow at work. Your child may captain a netball team, but they are subject to the rules of the game, the calls made by the umpire and the direction given by their coach.

Leaders today need to be responsive to the changing times. We live in a digital economy, where our device playlists are generated by artificial intelligence, online stores use predictive algorithms to make purchasing suggestions for us and primary school students are learning coding and robotics. Those leading Generation Alpha also need to be responsive to the changing cultures, generations, backgrounds and expectations that comprise their teams, communities and families. If we want to be great leaders, we've got to spend more time listening and understanding, not just speaking and directing.

Leading with empathy

The leadership styles of famous leader Alexander the Great could be placed under the banner of 'Great Man Leadership'. Great Man Leadership is about stature, status and power. The archetype is a dominant male, full of charisma, who can use position and power to leverage for leadership purposes. The combined force of a unique personality, dominance of will, high energy and excellent oratory skills compels those around them to get stuff done. These leaders are often seen as iconic, transformative and 'born to lead', but looking more closely, there can be characteristics of egotism or outright narcissism with the associated traits of dominance, arrogance and manipulation.

Today's generations are not as accepting of a autocratic, authoritarian leadership styles as former generations were. Firstly, we are more diverse now – women are recognised as leaders and there's intentionality behind strengthening a platform for female leaders. Personality and presence alone don't cut it today because there is a common thought that leaders are not born, but developed. There are systems and training in place to develop and instil leadership qualities into people, with this starting at school, in sports teams and other extracurricular activities that Generation Alpha partake in.

Ultimately, society has shifted and this will likely continue for Generation Alpha. This shift is away from leadership that is top-down and exerts power, to leadership that seeks to serve the needs of others – a more empathetic style of leadership. We've seen through our research into the workplace, and in particular with generations Y and Z, that there's a big change in what is accepted and what people want when it comes to their leaders. There has been a shift to respecting people, teams and individuals and acknowledging them, which means that leaders need strong people skills. Generation Alpha will be looking for leaders who can enhance the team, develop the community and empower the individuals that they lead. This shift is to team-centric rather than task-centric approaches. In the workplace, this type of leadership leads to better staff engagement and a better company reputation.[255]

Empathetic leadership starts with understanding your team in such a way that you understand their context and can equip, empower, inform and develop them to bring about the greater good. The greater good includes the task goals, but also their own personal goals. There's a focus on the task, but an engagement of the team. This form of leadership is far more engaging. In similar ways that we have recently become savvier to noticing marketing techniques, Generation Z and Alpha will see through inauthentic leadership techniques.

> 'The servant leader is servant first. It begins with a natural feeling that one wants to serve, to serve first, as opposed to wanting power, influence, fame, or wealth. Then conscious choice brings one to aspire to lead. That person is sharply different from one who is leader first.' – *Robert K. Greenleaf*[256]

Leading in times of crisis

In our research during COVID-19, we found that people wanted leadership from our state and federal leaders. They wanted decisions to be made and made quickly, based on the information available, and for the leaders to back themselves and their decisions. During the pandemic there was a sense of urgency from border control policies to public health directions – it was a crisis not unlike wartime. Pre-pandemic, new policies would have taken months or possibly even years to progress, but events forced national leaders to legislate in just days. This ability to pivot, to change and administer quickly may well be one of the characteristics to mark Generation Alpha's leadership.

According to Australians, the two most important aspects of a leader during the pandemic were being completely open and honest with sharing information (50 per cent) and being prepared to make the tough calls, make them early and back themselves (50 per cent). One in three Australians also said it was important for leaders to lead with strength and communicate confidence (36 per cent), and give voice to the experts and follow their lead and advice (33 per cent). While leaders are expected to be strong, confident and open with information, many Australians also said it was important that leaders showed compassion and empathy (27 per cent).[257]

Leading the emerging generations

> Leadership is not a title or role bestowed on just a few, but an opportunity open to all to build positive outcomes. Leadership is responsive to context, not a set of universal techniques. It is more art than science. It creates buy-in, not coercion. As articulated by leaders such as Dwight Eisenhower and Harry Truman, leadership is the art of getting people to want to do what needs to be done.

Leadership will continue to be both a foundational and formative part of our world and our society. We used to think about the future as a place to which we were headed, a place to which our strategies would take us. But these days, such is the speed of change, the future is coming at us – often from unknown directions and at an increasing velocity.

A key issue for leaders is to understand the times and the context in which they are leading. We've learnt throughout this book how society has evolved in recent times. It's amazing to reflect that a mere decade ago we didn't have many of the devices, tablets, apps and programs we now rely on everyday. Therefore, this era requires agility, short response times and digital skills. The emerging generations, therefore, are well placed to lead in this world of global connection and fast change. Generation Alpha expect that information will be delivered visually and processed in shorter time frames to meet their needs. This means that we need to be agile when we lead and communicate with this new generation. In fact, it's fair to say that emerging generations are more equipped to lead and navigate in this world of global connections, of new technology and of fast change. They are globally connected and have been shaped by the digital era.

Here's a little test for you. Read the below sentence a few times and see if you speak the language of the emerging generation:

> 'BAE, my new work gig is legit –
> the hours are defs cray, but YOLO.'

Technology, texting and mobile communications have transformed how the emerging generations speak. So, for us to lead this generation, we've first got to understand them! Influenced by shortened text messages (because speed matters), this sentence shows that a new language has emerged. Texting speak has become mainstream. So what on earth does it mean? *BAE* is an acronym for Before Anyone Else, and could refer to a significant person like a best friend, boyfriend or girlfriend. And the *work gig* in this gig economy. *Legit* is short for legitimate, but in this context means 'great'. This is another example of the shortening of words to quicken communication. Other shortened words include *probs* (probably) and *whatevs* (whatever). *Defs*? Definitely. *Cray*? Crazy. And the popular acronym YOLO stands for you only live once!

In terms of communicating with the emerging generations, we've got to understand the factors that define them. Clearly, our society's recent technological transformations have defined Generation Alpha – how they interact and how they process information.

We once ran a focus group to work out how best to communicate with Generation Z. The focus group was looking at superannuation products but none of the brochures were speaking Gen Z's language. About an hour or so into the focus group, a young fellow spoke up, 'Look, it's not that we don't care on purpose. It's just that we don't care.' And that's a good reminder for all of us. If young people are not listening to what we are saying, we've got to change the way we communicate to cut through and engage. We have to work to engage in more effective ways.

The US has a safety sign around waterways that used to work well, but now its meaning has changed. As you can see, it says, 'If you see someone drowning ...' and in the middle is an image of a stick figure with their arms raised. But in today's world, the stick figure looks like the text speak LOL, which means 'laugh out loud'. Clearly, that's not the right response when someone is struggling in the water! This goes to show the importance of responding to the changes in the use of language and of communication.

Leadership style

Before we can manage and lead, we must be able to understand and connect. This requires awareness between the generations. The emerging generations are not only at a different life stage, but they have been raised and educated in a very different era. Their expectations of a boss, attitudes to the job, and preferred styles of work have all been shaped by their times – not ours.

Our research has shown that more than half (53 per cent) of Generation Z employees said that inspiring and accessible leadership is extremely or very important to them in their place of work.[258] The findings are clear: we need to lead in an inclusive, participative way, and demonstrate people skills as well as technical skills.

The ideal leader for Gen Z and Generation Alpha – whether that be in the classroom, in the home or in the workplace – is one who values communication and creates an environment of transparency and respect. The preferred leadership style of these generations is one that is more focused on consensus than command, is more participative than autocratic, and is more flexible and organic than structured and hierarchical.

Through speaking with the emerging generations, it is clear that their ideal leader gives public affirmation – pats on the back, both figurative and literal. This leader remembers the names and interests of their staff, and creates an emotionally safe, friendly, collegial environment where people feel free to contribute ideas.

The ever-present generation gap is very visible when we attempt to lead using old methods in unadapted ways. Traditional leadership stresses controlling; Gen Z want relating. While the former generation of leaders focused on structure, today's emerging generations are influenced by a collaborative style. We think framework, they think freedom. The answer is to take the time to better understand them, and then we are well on the way to being able to engage, train and lead these emerging generations in more effective ways.

Helping a generation to lead

Leadership in the twenty-first century is about adapting, but it is also about helping the next generation as they move into positions of leadership. One way we can do that today is by helping them to become more resilient. People of this generation are going to be moving across more trends, more careers and more change than any prior generation.

Encourage resilience

Parents today are recognising the importance of building resilience in young people.

> 'One of my favourite qualities of my son is that it doesn't matter how many times he falls down or does it wrong, he's just as happy to do it again. People laugh at him, and he doesn't understand that they're laughing at him. He just laughs too, and then he moves on and keeps trying. His resilience is one of my favourite things about him, and I feel like us as a society could really learn from being more like a duck and letting things slide off our back more, because our feelings are always so hurt about other people's opinions of us. If we could just let go of this more, we would do better as a society as a whole.' – a parent of a Generation Alpha

There is a concern that, due to instant gratification, young people today aren't as resilient as generations past. The word 'resilience' literally means 'bouncing back', which requires an impact from which to rebound. Here is the unexpected upside of the bitter COVID-19 experience. The immediate and longer-term challenges from this pandemic will positively serve this generation – it has presented challenges through which they have developed resilience to overcome them. According to our research with Australians, 78 per cent believe that the COVID-19 experience will mean children of today are more resilient.[259]

———

For leaders, the future
is not an inevitable
destination but something
they are shaping, and
which Generation Alpha
will inherit and themselves
shape anew.

———

Children today need leaders who guide them and encourage them. Rather than protecting or coddling, we need to help them to develop resilience. We need to let them know that it's okay for them to make mistakes, because that's how we all learn and grow.

This points to a key role of leaders today, which is to help the next generation thrive by creating cultures where people can try new things or ideas, and not be afraid of failures. Why is this important? Because being resilient about failure leads to innovation. Great leaders and parents help children to feel comfortable enough to share new ideas and be creative and innovative.

> 'What's the most significant barrier to creativity and innovation? The fear of introducing an idea and being ridiculed, laughed at and belittled. The problem is that often great ideas sound crazy and failure is needed. Learning and creating are inherently vulnerable.' – *Brené Brown in her book on vulnerability*, Daring Greatly[260]

Develop insight

Great leaders also need to have insight – which is gained by looking at where things are headed and what we need to be prepared for. The only reason a leader can lead is because they know which way to go. And that is because they see things not just as they are but as they will be. Generation Alpha will need those insights to face the changes they will encounter in the future. Parents can help to foster this in their children by instilling in them a love of learning, and by sharing stories that illustrate these sorts of qualities – from real-life examples to storybooks where characters have agency and respond to situations to make change.

It was just a little over a decade ago that Netflix made most of their money through sending DVDs by mail. That was their revenue stream in 2008; that was their business model. Wind the clock forward to today and they're one of the largest digital distribution companies of entertainment on the planet, and have swiftly become one of the largest content creators as well. That's the speed of change. That's what can happen in a decade. Generation Alpha will have to adjust to that level of change: the future is coming at them.

Embrace change

Over the span of Generation Alpha's life so far, the world has changed dramatically. As discussed, we have seen technological transformations, but also social trends, global economic shifts, environmental change and demographic transitions. Over a decade ago, the population of Australia had just broken through the 21 million mark; today it is over 26 million. In 1970, our population was half of what it currently is, which means our numbers have doubled in the lifetime of most adult Australians. Even accounting for the greatly slowed population growth rate as a result of the closed international borders due to COVID-19, growth over the next fifty years will greatly exceed that experienced in the last fifty. That is the speed and the scale of the growth that we see currently.

The challenge with all of this is that not many of us like change. We can often feel fatigued or overwhelmed by it – especially when we don't understand it. Take, for example, when the new iPhone was launched all those years ago. There were some who embraced it – the early adopters who lined up and waited outside the Apple store for this brand-new piece of technology. But the majority of us were slower to embrace it, a little sceptical and hesitant, because it meant overhauling the phones we knew how to use, and we had to learn a whole new piece of technology. As parents of Generation Alpha, it's important we help our kids to not fear change by encouraging them to regularly step out of their comfort zone, take on new challenges and use failure as an opportunity to grow. By instilling this in them when they are young, they will be better equipped to deal with change later in life – and more likely to see it as an opportunity to grow and learn rather than something to fear and resist.

Promote emotional and cultural intelligence

Generation Alpha are growing up in a world that is more diverse – culturally, generationally and in terms of gender differences than ever before. Therefore parents need to be teaching Generation Alpha emotional intelligence (EQ) and cultural intelligence (CQ) to create connections. This will currently take place for Generation Alpha at school and in sports teams, and in the future this will increasingly turn to the workplace and other places they will mix in. Parents can help to teach Generation Alpha emotional and cultural intelligence by modelling this themselves, making connections with people who are different from them and ensuring that language and behaviour towards diversity is positive.

It's important for Generation Alpha to be able to see diverse leaders today, whom they can look up to and aspire to be like. For example, we are already seeing more women taking on leadership roles now that the pathways have opened up more, and it's exciting to think about Generation Alpha female leaders and what their experience will be like in a couple of decades' time. Women today can lead by example so the next generation can aspire to and build even further upon their success.

With the election victory of Joe Biden, it was his Vice President Kamala Harris who attracted much of the attention, and more attention than any Vice President of recent times, and it's not hard to see why: the first female Vice President, the first African–American, the first Asian–American Vice President, and a Gen Xer (or at least born on the cusp). The inauguration however saw more barriers broken with a striking poem 'The Hill We Climb', read by a young Gen Z African American poet, Amanda Gorman. Such was the impact of her presence there, she was then called on to recite another poem at the 2021 Super Bowl. Poetry at a football match is definitely an American first, if not a world first and highlights the impact of the emerging generations of female leaders. With global interactions, the examples of diverse leaders and parents resourced to encourage them, Generation Alpha have a great foundation for leadership.

The power of encouragement

'Outstanding leaders go out of their way to boost the self-esteem of their personnel. If people believe in themselves, it's amazing what they can accomplish.' – *Sam Walton, founder of Walmart (the world's largest company by revenue)*

This observation repurposed for parenting:
Outstanding parents go out of their way to boost the self-esteem of their children. If kids believe in themselves, it's amazing what they can accomplish.

Enlarging leadership

As parents, teachers and leaders, we each have the opportunity to lead or influence the emerging generations in positive ways. We have to be deliberate in thinking generationally in our leadership. In order to understand Gen Z and Generation Alpha we have to connect with them and communicate in ways that speak their language. What worked for Baby Boomers didn't necessarily work for Gen Y, and what was an effective leadership style in the twentieth century will be less effective in the twenty-first.

It is desirable that leaders possess intelligence, but it is essential that they exercise empathy. Leaders of the head and heart are best placed to innovate amid disruption and engage across diversity.

The most transformative leadership style and the one the emerging generations respond best to is what we call enlarging leadership. Our research indicates that Generations Y and Z (who are now the majority of the workforce) respond most positively to a leadership style that creates a culture of enlarging not just the competence of those being led, but also their character. It's about helping the people we lead to be the best version of themselves, not just to perform well. And the same is true for children. A key role of parents today is to see qualities in their children and enlarge those qualities. This is often on the hearts and minds of parents, but it also needs to extend to schools, sports teams and workplaces – anywhere that we lead people.

Enlarging leadership is about more than being a great leader; it is about developing great leaders. Collaborative styles of leadership create a culture of leadership development by delegating both tasks and responsibility. These leaders see qualities in those they are leading that they may not see in themselves, and they back people who don't even back themselves. As human beings, we are prone to insecurities, and so when someone believes in us it can be transformative to our life and our career.

Step one: encourage them

The first step to being an enlarging leader is to provide encouragement. This builds people up and gives them the courage and support to try something new or to step outside of their comfort zone. Traditional leadership styles, where leaders barked orders to subordinates, do not help people flourish. Rather, when leaders take the time to encourage their teams and provide constructive feedback, it creates an environment for people to grow both professionally and personally.

This is crucial for leading Generation Alpha, particularly when they are young. In our research for this book, we heard countless stories from parents, teachers and leaders about the power of belief and encouragement.

> 'I try to be intentional about showing love and care for my children – even in the busy times. I always want them to know that I will be there to support and encourage them, no matter what.' – *a mother of Generation Alpha children*

In Brett Murray's 'Make Bullying History' seminars with Gen Z and Generation Alpha students, the core message is that kids are unique. 'We play a word game where they have to use another word for unique in a sentence. And they come out with words like indescribable, awesome, super or GOAT (an acronym for greatest of all time). Then we pause and say, "Okay guys, do you know what you've just described?" We say, "You; you just described yourself. Why? Because you're unique, and I can prove it. Medically, scientifically, physiologically, metaphysically and historically." We say, "There will be no human being before this time, or since, that has these characteristics that are yours uniquely:

your fingerprint, your DNA strand and your retinal scan. Those three attributes are yours and yours alone and no one will ever have them. That's what makes you unique, and you just said that unique is irreplaceable, incomparable, indescribable and awesome." And when these kids get that, it's exciting because many don't have dreams, goals and aspirations, because they're being told that they're not worth it. And so, our common denominator is saying they are of worth, value and positive reinforcement. We have to be, as parents and their primary educators, the most positive, the most consistent and the safest people in their life. And if we can do that, then when the negative forces of the world come against them, they've got some truth to actually hold on to. It's not to get to the point of self-worship, rather it's about helping them understand they are valuable, precious and amazing.'

Step two: equip them

Next, we must *equip* Generation Alpha. In other words, we need to give them the skills and competencies that will enable them to thrive in this era. A primary school teacher we spoke to told us that although being a teacher takes a lot of effort, 'it pays dividends because the children respond and know that the lessons are prepared for them, that there's something interesting and worthwhile for them to learn. We need to make sure that children get plenty of opportunity to demonstrate to themselves, and to others, what they're capable of. It's really important for that to happen.'

How we equip this generation, again, is going to be different to how we did it in the past. Because we're in more collaborative times, they don't need the same authority structures, hierarchies or traditional power approaches of the past. One area we need to equip them with is people skills. Generation Alpha are swiftly becoming the most digitally savvy generation ever, but in the future, if one of them says, 'I'm just not a people person ...', that's going to be a problem, because leaders lead people, not robots or technologies. Of course, we are moving into a world with more robotics, but the robots don't need someone to talk to them and show empathy and concern. People need that. And people do that. So we've got to be proactively equipping this generation with those kinds of people skills. These transferable skills are going to be key traits of future leaders.

These aren't just soft skills, they are critical skills. Technology is well suited to deliver technical outcomes, but it is people with emotional intelligence, cultural understanding and communication skills who are best placed to bring about positive human outcomes.

Anita, a primary school teacher, would like to see schools have more of a focus on this in their culture. She told us that it could help if 'the school has set values that are communicated to staff, parents and students. Not just rewarding when they get great math results, but when they show empathy to a friend. To celebrate and reward other social skills, not just the academic.'

Step three: entrust them

The third way we can develop the emerging leaders in Generation Alpha is to entrust them. Those of us that are training the next generation have to ultimately hand over responsibility, trust them and intentionally give them the opportunities to step up. For example, this may take the form of creating space in family meetings for children's input. It shouldn't necessarily be the older or more experienced people who speak first. Rather, by making room for younger people to speak, we give them an opportunity to grow and learn. By inviting their input, they have an opportunity to contribute and give their take on the situation, or the challenge being faced. Not only does this give them a platform to speak, but it also provides an opportunity to gauge their thinking. Now, not every comment or suggestion will work successfully the first time, but that's how we all grow!

By *engaging*, *equipping* and *entrusting* the emerging generations, we can set them up well for leadership in the future. Take the example of the workplace. When a leader departs and their organisation subsequently wanes, that is not a measure of their success but an indicator of their failure. Great leaders don't just have a succession plan, they have a succession queue – a depth of upcoming leaders they have trained. It is the same with parents. We don't want our children to always be dependent on us, we want them to have the skills, character and leadership to step out on their own into the world (eventually) and thrive. Ultimately, leadership is defined by the culture it creates and the people it develops.

Being an effective leader

'Daring leaders who live their values are never silent about the hard things.' – *Brené Brown*[261]

Trust

One of the foundational characteristics of both a lasting and effective leader is trust. Our research over the last decade highlights an ongoing erosion of trust in institutions. From unions to political parties, religious groups and government institutions, the erosion in trust is widespread. Over this time we have seen three royal commissions, revealing major failings of institutions towards the most vulnerable: the Royal Commission into Institutional Responses to Child Sexual Abuse, the Royal Commission into Aged Care Quality and Safety, and the Royal Commission into Violence, Abuse, Neglect and Exploitation of People with Disability. This has not only highlighted some terrible failings of institutions towards those in their care, but revealed a breach of trust of their leaders.

Today, more than ever, we need leaders and parents who are real. Parents who lead their children and families by walking the talk and being transparent. Parents who are responsive to the needs of their children, and who are family-centric rather than leader-centric. Parents who are relational. If a parent communicates and leads in this manner, their children will trust them more because they will know they are not in it for themselves. They're not in it for their own wins or successes. Rather, they're in it for the sake of the people they are leading, and it's them they put first.

A leader needs to be authentic. In our analysis of Australians we've learnt that they're a gracious bunch. If someone makes an honest mistake, Aussies are likely to give them a break, knowing none of us are perfect. The catch is they have to own up to it, respond and apologise.

When there is systematic, premeditated or repeated wrongs, it is a different situation. But if a leader makes a mistake, is earnest about making amends and moving forward, and if they are, in the vernacular, fair dinkum about the mistake they've made or about the approach that didn't work out, and can admit that, then Aussies will give them another go. And the same is true within families. If parents can apologise when making a mistake, it teaches children to do the same. Building trust is not about perfection. It's about admitting when we get it wrong, owning it, taking the blame and making sure we commit to not making the same mistake again.

Authenticity

In an age defined by connected devices, the online space is near impossible to effectively police. It's rife with opinion, much of which is uninformed or biased, and in the last few years we've seen a surge of what has become known as 'fake news' – news heavy with disinformation and hoaxes. In this era, facts and truth matter more than ever before, as does the need for leaders with authenticity.

Dr Brené Brown closes her book *Dare to Lead* quoting Joseph Campbell, an American Professor of Literature. He says, 'The cave you fear to enter holds the treasure you seek.' Dr Brown encourages the reader to find the cave, own the fear and seek out a new ending. 'Choose courage over comfort. Choose whole hearts over armour. And choose the great adventure of being brave and afraid. At the exact same time.'[262]

Leading Generation Alpha is going to require courage in times of uncertainty and resilience in times of disappointment and trouble. And the most anchoring traits of a successful and effective leader and parent is authenticity. Authenticity is not a word that should be taken lightly or thrown around because it's in vogue. Authenticity demands, by its very meaning, to be taken seriously. A parent who operates with authenticity as a core value, lives up to what they proclaim – they are trustworthy, reliable, honest, credible, dependable and wholeheartedly human.

Writer Simon Sinek puts it well when he says of leadership, 'Leadership is not about being in charge, it's about caring about those who you are in charge of.'[263] And if we truly care about those we are leading, those we are responsible for, we will allow ourselves to be ruled by authenticity.

This is key for us, as the leaders of Generation Alpha, to keep in mind. These children are growing up in a virtual world, where authenticity can be minimised due to the artificial, online world of social media, where someone's highlights reel is portrayed as their reality. If we can lead Generation Alpha with authenticity then it will not only help them to have a more realistic understanding of how life works (that it's not all perfect!) but it will also equip them to be authentic leaders in the future.

Authentic parenting is also beneficial not just for Generation Alpha but for parents as well. In a world of comparison and 'mum guilt', being open and honest about the struggles we face helps us to connect with others who are struggling. It also helps children to see the example of honest and real relationships, rather than pressure to always be perfect. As Dr Katharine Schori put it, 'Perfect parenting does not exist, and it is the imperfections that lead to resilient children.'[264]

Leadership is changing

Positively, we are seeing a shift in what it means to be a great leader. The traditional forms of leadership that have been accepted in the past, such as 'command and control' and 'get you to want to do it' are not serving this generation and this era. These leadership styles are highly structured and all about the end result. The collaborative leadership style is all about the people, the followers and bringing the best out of the team.

The COVID-19 pandemic created a shift from looking to celebrities and influencers, to seeking the advice of the experts. In Australia, Chief Medical Officers (CMOs) were brought front and centre. In fact, these CMOs were given a platform and more airtime than many politicians. Australians followed the CMO's expert medical advice, overwhelmingly complied with government restrictions, and reaped the reward of minimal community transitions. From this historical event, we've seen a shift in leadership with a stronger presence of expertise and rationale over opinion and hype.

The pandemic also brought about collaborative, cross-discipline, multi-jurisdiction and bipartisan leadership to enable a robust and well-rounded approach to disaster. In Australia, a National Cabinet was formed to tackle the challenges of the pandemic which will have a role post-COVID-19. This shift is reflective of the kind of leadership that Generation Alpha requires – leadership that reaches across politics, cultures, backgrounds and generations. Instead of a 'one size fits all' approach, leaders will need to take into account complexities and diversity and lead with more nuanced solutions. Leadership teams will need to embrace and appoint diverse leaders to reflect the global nations and communities that have shaped Generation Alpha.

> 'What our kids have is a global village, and the widening acceptance of "You can be whoever you want to be". They have opportunity and every door is open to them. Whereas, before, things were hidden. It was like, "Oh, everything is nice on the surface", but it was ugly behind closed doors.' – *a mother of two Generation Alphas*

There has always been uncertainty when it comes to the future, but this doesn't mean there has to be fear. Why? Because there is always hope. Hope for better. The future for Generation Alpha is full of hope – not because they are more materially endowed and technologically supplied, but because they have more access to information, more knowledge, wisdom and role models than any previous generation. That is why *how* we lead them matters because, already, they are standing on our shoulders and peering into the future.

Key takeaways

In this chapter we have explored the importance of leadership in helping Generation Alpha to thrive, both now as we lead them as children, and in order to develop them as leaders as they grow up. We have seen how empathetic leadership is required for their future, how to lead in times of crisis, and that we can develop this generation's resilience by leading with insight, empathy, embracing change and promoting cultural and emotional intelligence. If we can lead Generation Alpha with trust, authenticity and the style of enlarging leadership by encouraging, equipping and entrusting them, then we can both lead them effectively and help them to become exceptional future leaders.

CHAPTER 9

Generation Alpha's Lifestyle

'Don't give up. I believe in you all. A person's a person
no matter how small.'

Dr Seuss[265]

The world around Generation Alpha is changing, and if we can observe the trends at play then we can analyse and predict how they might live in the future. In this chapter we explore how household composition, design and affordability today will impact the Great Australian dream of home ownership for Generation Alpha. We delve into how they will likely rent instead of own, and live in vertical communities instead of horizontal ones. We look at how population growth and change will affect the communities they will live in. From transport to the development of regional areas, to the lifestyle changes they can expect to experience, even in their work, this chapter looks at how Generation Alpha will live.

Parents today work hard to give their children the best life and lifestyle they can.

———

Much of what we had pre-COVID-19 we will never see again. We are not moving to the next but the new. It is not a continuation of how things were, but the start of a whole new reality.

———

The economic climate, population shifts, housing affordability and types, smart homes and the definition of community are all different today than what Generation Alpha's parents experienced when they were growing up.

Households, housing and home

The United Nations describes the household as 'A group of persons who make common provision of food, shelter and other essentials for living, and is a fundamental socioeconomic unit in human societies.'[266]

For most people, their family is their household. Increasingly, this includes extended family members, but for those with housemates, in shared accommodation or aged care living, their household is distinct from their family. A home is a necessary base for stability in a person's life, especially a child's life. Some may feel that today, with life's full schedule, smaller families and technology dependents, we have lost a sense of home. Perhaps you're from a generation that refers to and reflects on 'the good old days' where kids played on the streets with their neighbours, climbed trees, made mud pies and rumbled with their siblings. Although Generation Alpha's upbringing and formative experiences will look different, home and its sense of belonging is timeless.

In Australia there around 10 million households. The standard household is made up of 2.6 people, compared to 4.5 people in 1911.[267] Across the nation, a third of houses are owned outright, over a third are owned with the help of a mortgage and the rest are rented. Three-bedroom houses make up the greatest proportion of occupied private dwellings.

Households in the future

By 2041, when the youngest Generation Alphas reach their thirties, there will be more households in Australia than ever – 13 million of them – yet the proportion of households with dependent children will be smaller than it is today.[268] Between now and then, Australia's population will continue to age, and with this longevity, there will be more single-person households, largely of aged Australians, than ever before. There will also be more couple-only households, comprised of empty-nest older couples and couple-only younger people, who will be opting to have children at a later age or not at all. While couples with children will still be the most common household, couple-only households will make up a third of all households and the solo-person household more than a quarter.[269]

Home trends

While styles, technology integration and trends around home design are constantly changing, there are some key aspects to creating a home that are timeless. The primary purpose of a home will always be to have a safe space for people to gather, eat, sleep, rest and connect.

Technology is more integrated in homes today than ever before. 'We work with automation specialists all the time,' Michael, a building site manager, told us. 'In the type of homes we build, which are high-end residential, technology is integrated from the very start. From the home's conception, the client, electrician and automation specialist work together to build a "smart home", whereby everything from climate, lighting, entertainment systems, security and appliances are controlled from a device.'

People are increasingly incorporating this sort of smart wiring into their homes when they build them. It is estimated that one in four Australian homes were considered smart homes in 2020, and by 2025 this will have increased to half of all homes.[270] While it may be a different way of interacting with technology in the home than we grew up with, for many Generation Alphas a smart home will be the only type of home they have ever known.

Australians are moving home more frequently than ever. The average renter moves every 1.8 years and those who have a mortgage stay on average for eight years.[271] The challenge of housing affordability means that families today buy a home they can afford, or in an area they can afford, and, once they pay down their mortgage, they look to upsize the home. This has led to more flexibility in home design and renovations so that a home will have appeal and functionality for quite varied household types. We are also seeing more diverse neighbourhoods where inner urban, high-density areas which were once dominated by single workers, students or budget-conscious older Australians are now popular with young couples and even young families.

Homes are increasingly incorporating separate living features, suited to the multi-generational household or the stay-at-home young adult who is looking for more independence. Indoor/outdoor spaces are increasingly valued in an era where children don't have the same freedom to head out to a park or bushland as they used to, yet still seek a place for some outdoor activity. And after a trend towards smaller homes and apartments, in line with smaller households or families and with an eye on affordability, we are now seeing this trend reverse, with extra rooms and larger spaces being in demand in a work-from-home and study-from-home era.

Housing affordability and the future

Housing affordability is an ongoing challenge in Australia, with the rising property costs most evident in the nation's capital cities, and recently in some regional cities too. Prices are increasing largely because demand for houses is exceeding supply. Population growth, a trend to live with fewer people in smaller households (and so more homes needed, relative to the population), and demand for homes not only from first home buyers but also from downsizers, overseas buyers, local investors and self-managed super funds and trusts, has been driving Australian house price growth for some time. Australia's population is currently growing at around 1.4 per cent per year, and the impact of a growing population on house prices is most evident when prices are compared to average earnings. In twenty years, the average full-time earnings have doubled from $42,000 in 2000 to $89,000 today.[272] Over that time, average Sydney house prices have increased almost four-fold from $233,000 to $1,100,000 today.[273]

Twenty years ago, the average Sydney house price was 6.8 times average annual earnings. Today it is 12.6 times average earnings and in suburbs like Castle Hill, which is located forty minutes' drive from the Sydney CBD (in light traffic!), the average home is now sixteen times annual earnings. While the maxim that house prices double every ten years is not always the case, on average it has been the case for most Australian capital cities over the last half-century. If the same growth metrics play out, by 2040 when the oldest Generation Alphas are in their twenties, their house-hunting years, the average Sydney house price will be almost $4.5 million, with Melbourne expected to be around $3.3 million. Understandably, then, parents have concerns for their Generation Alpha children with regards to housing affordability. 'I've got a couple of older kids and I worry that they won't be able to afford a house,' one mum told us. 'I worry they'll just be living with me forever because the standard of living is so much higher, and it will be harder for them.'

The great Australian dream

'Other than the known challenges financially, those that aspire to own their first home are under social and psychological pressure,' Jay Anderson, a property strategist and buyer's agent, told us. 'First homeowners want their dream home to be their first home. The Baby Boomers had a good run, with a significant percentage staying in the first home they bought, having saved funds to renovate and modernise their property as their family needs grew. These are the homes that Millennials grew up in, and their expectations start where their parents finished.'

To get on the property ladder, young people today are relying heavily on the 'Bank of Mum and Dad', and it is easy to see why. Even in a moderate property market, by delaying the purchase, many are falling further behind. Let's take again the average Sydney house price and average annual earnings, although this time keep in mind that the average after-tax full-time earnings is around $67,000. If the property market increases by 7 per cent in a year, and there have been many years recently where it has risen by much more, then the average property ($1.1 million) has increased by $77,000, which is more than the annual take-home pay.

Rentvesting

If Generation Alpha are unable to utilise the Bank of Mum and Dad when it comes time to buy their first home, they may consider 'rentvesting'. Rentvesting is where you rent the property you want to live in and purchase a property elsewhere. Often, people can rent a nicer property than they can afford to buy, so they get the benefit of living more luxuriously or in a more desirable location, without a hefty mortgage, and at the same time still owning an investment property elsewhere.

Rental market

While the dream of home ownership is still strong among their Gen Y parents, the future of home ownership for Generation Alpha could look quite different to how it does today. As one mum told us, 'I'm not sure that my kids would even be bothered to buy a house. It might be that they just rent a house and then move as needed. And then if they don't like that, they'll just move again.' For a very mobile generation who have grown up using subscription models like Spotify and Netflix, and who are used to seeing their parents rent more, it is likely we will see a shift away from the aspiration of home ownership to renting for Generation Alpha. Currently in Australia the average renter stays for just under two years, and because Generation Alpha will have even fewer links to a suburb, with their services in the cloud, work online and starting families later, we expect this trend of shorter housing tenure to continue.

Such is pull of the Australian Dream of home ownership, even though housing in our largest capitals is amongst the highest in the world, our proportion of rentals is relatively low. The percentage of renters in Switzerland sits at 56 per cent, Hong Kong 49 per cent and Germany 48 per cent, while it sits around 31 per cent in Australia. In New York City, for example, rents are limited to inflation rather than market-based prices, along with a more corporate approach to property management. This provides an element of security in that low-income renters won't be priced out of the market with four weeks' notice.[274]

It's not uncommon in these cities to have rental contracts that start at five years in length. The European Consumer Centre for Germany[275] state that an indefinite rental agreement ('*unbefristeter Mietvertrag*') is the most common type of rental agreement used in Germany. Any rental contract that is agreed upon for a period of more than one year is assumed to be indefinite, giving the right to extend and greater housing stability to the renter. With the increase in the cost of purchasing property in Australia, the decades ahead will see pressure to support more affordable, long-term renting, providing a more secure living arrangement for both the tenant and the landlord.

This will be a positive for Generation Alpha, allowing them to opt for renting over buying as a lifestyle choice. The challenge is that they won't have the benefits that come with home ownership, like the forced savings that paying down a mortgage creates, and a large, appreciating asset.

A rise in vertical communities

The majority of traditional Australian homes are separate, with a garage out the front and a yard out the back. In recent years we have seen a rise of the vertical community (like apartment buildings) as opposed to the more traditional, horizontal communities (detached homes) of the past. Due to affordability and accessibility reasons, many people are choosing apartment living over detached-home living. And it's not hard to see why. Apartments save money and time (see below), and provide an achievable pathway to achieving the Australian dream of home ownership.

People living in apartments save an average of $3713 and 270 hours a year on home maintenance, compared to those in detached houses. Our study also showed that in addition to the financial benefits and low maintenance, the strong sense of security and accessibility to services like public transport and amenities, such as shops and cafés, are benefits for those living in apartments.[276]

Many Generation Alphas won't be growing up in detached homes with big backyards, but in apartment complexes. This isn't a poor alternative. Many of these apartment complexes have cafés, gyms, shops and childcare centres within walking distance of, and sometimes contained within, apartment buildings.

There are many benefits for those living in these vertical communities. As one Gen Y, Jessica, told us, 'My husband and I live in an apartment, and moved here from the detached home we bought in the outer suburbs of Sydney. We decided to move because we spent so much time travelling for work. So, now we rent the house out, and we rent an apartment closer to work. We've really come to love living here, as it's in a lovely suburb and is close to great cafés, the city and Sydney Harbour. We have a lot more time, too, as we don't have any gardening or house upkeep. We'd love to have children in the next few years, but are just trying to work out where we will live when that happens. Our current apartment is too small, so we'd have to move somewhere else. Although, there is a childcare centre at the bottom of our apartment complex, which could come in handy one day!'

During the COVID-19 pandemic, it was heartening to hear of people in vertical communities willing to help out those more vulnerable among their neighbours. People posted notes in lifts in apartment buildings saying things like, 'If you can't go out or are too worried to go and get groceries, feel free to text me what you need and I can get it for you and drop it off.' While the local community might not involve chatting to neighbours over the fence anymore, it's great to see new ways of connecting being achieved in these modern styles of living.

Australia's changing population

Population growth is a matter of national significance that requires coordinated action by all Australian governments. The three main categories of population growth are temporary migration, such as international students and temporary skilled migrants; permanent migration, commonly through the skill stream; and natural increase through reproduction.

At the start of the twentieth century, men outnumbered women (by around 110 to 100) as the population had been significantly shaped by male-dominated migration from overseas. Today, women outnumber men, making up 50.7 per cent of the population at the last census.[277]

One of the biggest changes to the labour force over the last century is the increasing number of women in work. In 2020, two thirds of women participated in the labour force, compared to around 54 per cent twenty years earlier. This has helped to boost living standards for families and drive Australia's economic growth.[278]

Australia also has an ageing population. The ratio between working-age people to people aged over sixty-five has decreased rapidly over the past fifty years.[279] The increase in women participating in the workforce will help to fill emerging gaps as older Australians retire, as will the trend for Australians to work longer. Our research shows that most Australians value the cultural diversity that migration has enriched Australia with, but they also want population growth to be sustainable. With Australia's fertility rate (babies per woman) now down to 1.6 (which is below the replacement rate of 2.0) it is clear that migration is important to help avoid population decline and respond to our ageing population profile.[280] The closed borders from COVID-19 have highlighted how much Australia relies on international tourism, working holidaymakers, visiting seasonal workers, overseas students and skilled migration.

Development and satellite cities

While the majority of the population lives in and near the capital cities, regional areas are also being given attention by the government as it seeks to develop 'satellite cities'. These are smaller stand-alone cities outside of the capital cities and they are seeing much growth as people work locally, reducing the need for people to travel long distances into work, avoiding congestion and long commutes.

Moreton Bay, which is located north of Brisbane's CBD, is an example of a satellite city. Houses are 60 per cent more affordable[281] and salaries approximately 12 per cent less than Sydney.[282] Greater Springfield (to Brisbane's west), Ellenbrook (30 minutes from the centre of Perth) and Werribee (between Melbourne and Geelong) are other examples of Australian satellite cities.

If Generation Alpha can work remotely with ease – which we've seen was possible during COVID-19 – and not worry about losing out on in-demand roles typically located in CBDs, then they may be further motivated to make the move to these newer satellite cities.

The connection between lifestyle and wellbeing

There is more to life than the cold numbers of GDP and economic statistics. The OECD Better Life Index compares wellbeing across countries in the areas of housing, income, jobs, community, education, environment, civic engagement, health, life satisfaction, safety and work–life balance. According to the index, Australia performs very well in many measures of wellbeing relative to most other countries in the Better Life Index. In general, Australians are more satisfied with their lives than the OECD average. When asked to rate their general satisfaction with life on a scale from 0 to 10, Australians gave it a 7.3 grade on average, higher than the OECD average of 6.5.[283]

These findings show us that perhaps we really are the lucky country, and while no country, community or generation is perfect, the future for Generation Alpha is a bright one and we have much to be grateful for.

Lifestyle changes

Generation Alpha's life is going to be aided by technologies and ways of living that make parts of their lifestyle, like manual labour and work, easier. Two decades ago, Australians started outsourcing a lot of household chores, from paying people to mow lawns or clean houses to mobile dog-washers, wheelie bin sanitisers and even oven cleaners. The opportunities will grow as the lifestyle expectations of twenty-first century families change – from meal preparation services to the evolution of childcare services, from professional organisers to personal concierge services, and from professional party organisers to styling and image consultants. These outsourcing services are becoming a regular part of Gen Y's lives, and therefore part of Generation Alpha's upbringing. Additionally, Generation Alpha are not being equipped with the same skills of the past, like knowing how to sew, change the oil in a car or cook a roast dinner. It is understandable why, when technology, online services and outsourcing can do it for them.

These lifestyle changes are also being transferred to the workplace. Corporations are now employing wellbeing managers, and many city buildings have office concierges. Generation Alpha are going to have multiple expectations when it comes to work – it isn't just the job description or salary they are interested in. Their job considerations will also be about the workplace culture, the variety, fun, training, sense of purpose, management style and flexibility that is offered to them.

When we look to Generation Alpha's older siblings (Generation Z), they are more likely to want to work for a medium or smaller-sized organisation than their older counterparts. What this tells us is that size alone doesn't define an employer of choice, with the emerging generations giving consideration to the enjoyment/variety/lifestyle factors that are often offered by small employers and even non-profit organisations.

How work will fit into Generation Alpha's lifestyle

When it comes time for Generation Alpha to enter the workforce, they will be looking for places that prioritise workplace culture, work–life integration, a varied job role, training and opportunities for advancement, and inspiring and accessible leadership styles.

With fewer neighbourhood connections and declining memberships at service clubs, the emerging generations will look for a workplace that they can belong to and that fills social needs as well as the financial need of getting paid. What will be important to this generation of emerging workers is the community in their workplace, a clear vision to which they can contribute to and celebration of their hard work.

Generation Alpha will emerge in a workforce with the gig economy and contingent work, and so will be looking for flexibility in how they work. This flexible style of working was further entrenched during COVID-19, when the global workforce was compelled to work from home, and this looks set to be a big part of how Generation Alpha will work in the future.[284]

Key takeaways

In this chapter we have explored how Generation Alpha will live. Generation Alpha will grow up in more diverse household and family types. They will live in more technologically assisted homes, and their home is likely to be an apartment and not just a traditional detached house. If they live in an apartment then these vertical communities will also provide them with new lifestyle options, like access to modern modes of transport such as driverless trains, and new hubs of community such as shopping centres. A big part of their lifestyle will be work, and like every other aspect of their lives, they will be looking to ensure it contributes to their overall wellbeing.

CHAPTER 10

The Alpha Consumer

'A brand is no longer what we tell consumers it is,
it is what consumers tell each other it is.'
Scott Cook

While it might seem strange to talk about Generation Alpha as consumers, they are already having an impact on household purchasing choices. In this chapter we explore how Generation Alpha are a voice that shapes the future, will be tech-driven consumers and how their consumer behaviour will look different to that of generations past. We look at how companies are using 'hackathons', marketing and science to better understand Generation Alpha and personalise products for them. We also touch on the future of supermarket shopping, the Generation Alpha shopper of the future, the changing nature of consumption and how Generation Alpha are the most empowered generation of consumers.

Technology is developing faster than ever before and is shaping consumption habits in ways previous generations have not experienced. More recently, the COVID-19 environment forced many organisations to adapt and respond to change in mere weeks instead of years.

The last decade has seen the consumer landscape shift from mass market to personalisation and customisation, from a life of bricks-and-mortar shopping to $27.5 billion dollars spent on online goods.[285] Organisations that have thrived in the past decade are those who have understood their consumers and pre-empted the trends.

Today's consumers are increasingly prioritising products and services that are simple and have the ability to be customised to their specific needs. The challenge for organisations is to not just communicate their key brand messages well, but to listen and understand the unique needs of each generation. They then need to respond in a timely manner to set themselves apart from competitors. Although the youngest of them are yet to have been born, Generation Alpha are an important consumer group today and in the future.

The voice that shapes the future

Generation Alpha have brand influence and purchasing power beyond their years. They heavily influence their parents' purchasing decisions, shape the emerging social media landscape, and are the future generation of digital shoppers.

Currently there are three million Generation Alphas in Australia and more than 2.8 million are born globally every week. By 2025, when all of this generation will have been born, they will number more than two billion – making them the largest generation in history. In a decade's time, Generation Alpha will be entering their twenties and will be the most marketed to and message saturated generation ever. If organisations want to not only exist in a decade's time, but continue to thrive and flourish, then understanding Generation Alpha and their world is imperative.

As a generation, the children of today have grown up in environments where they are both seen and heard. As one mum told us, 'My son might be on the other side of the room, but he listens to the conversation we're having and he adds to it. It's like he has to be a part of everything.' Today, children are the focus of the family and influence many household decisions – from what to watch on TV to where to go on holidays.

Monica Dreger told us how, at Mattel, 'we have our own in-house research facilities. We are hands-on with consumer insights, and we talk to kids regularly. We do a lot of foundational research to understand what they are interested in, with regards to products and toys, and also their aspirations, their values, and whether that's going to change, what's going to happen. I think children today are a lot more optimistic and that gives me confidence. As young as seven or eight, we see kids talking about environmental issues and what they personally can do. Which I have never seen in a generation before.'

While this generation has yet to earn any personal income, they have a strong voice in purchasing decisions and are environmentally and sustainability minded. Our research has shown that 80 per cent of parents have had their actions or consumption decisions influenced to be more environmentally aware by their Generation Alpha children.[286] One parent in a focus group told us how 'My kids want to clean up the park when we go. They're like, "Oh, the trash. We've got to clean up the trash."'

Tech-driven consumers

Generation Alpha are part of an unintentional global experiment in which screens and voice assistants are their babysitters, entertainers and educational aids. Two in five Australian children aged between six and twelve own or use a mobile phone, and usage has been steadily increasing since 2013.[287] Throughout their life, technology has existed to serve them, providing instant gratification to everything they seek. Alphas are growing up in households of smart devices, apps delivering food, and personalisation. Algorithms and personalisation are an expected part of their consumer experience. Over the coming years they will transition from being voices of influence in the household to technological trendsetters with the economic power to match.

They've also grown up in a time of digital payments. COVID-19 fast-tracked the path we were on to becoming a cashless society, where payments have shifted from cash and credit cards to digital and contactless. It is very likely that Generation Alpha will never need a physical driver's license or a wallet, with many of these traditional cards accessible on a smartphone, even today.

With services like Afterpay and Zip increasingly marketed to the next generation, they will need guidance to be financially responsible and to avoid unnecessary debt accumulation. While Generation Alpha are a shrewd generation and influence the purchasing power of their household, parents still play an important role in helping and guiding their purchasing behaviour. We were reminded of this when James, a father of two Generation Alphas, told us this story. 'Whenever an ice-cream truck comes to our neighbourhood and it plays music, I've sneakily taught my kids that is means they are out of ice-cream!' We're sure that his kids will catch on soon, but it's a funny story and reminds us that, although kids today are more empowered and speaking up, parents still play an important role in their consumer behaviour.

How consumer behaviour works for Generation Alpha

If we're to take a quick dive into sociology and psychology, we'll see that Generation Alpha's needs have inextricable links with their role as future consumers.

Abraham Maslow, an American psychologist, established a theory of human development psychology known as Maslow's Hierarchy of Needs. Essentially it's a broad classification system of the human needs of society. The theory was first published in his 1954 book *Motivation and Personality*,[288] in which Maslow explored the nature of human fulfilment and outlined a five-stage model that together formed a triangle. The Hierarchy of Needs theorises that an individual's basic needs must be met in order to achieve self-actualisation or their personal potential. As someone finds fulfilment in one level, they will be strongly motivated to pursue the next level of need. As the individual progresses through each level, they experience lower levels of anxiety, ultimately achieving self-actualisation.

When applying this to Generation Alpha it is interesting to observe that they start their focus from the third rung (social) and move up from there as the survival and security needs are generally not something they have to worry about or aspire to. They are starting their decisions at the social level. This means that, when it comes to their behaviour as consumers, the values alignment matters more to them than the price or warranty.

1. Survival

This level of the pyramid includes things that are essential for human survival, like food, air, shelter, warmth and sleep. When talking about the emerging generations, we jokingly add WiFi at the triangle's base, because it is more fundamental for Generation Alpha than many other aspects of their life. Their phone is their alarm clock, watch, timer, camera, contact means and access to information. It's also how they make payments, and it has all the emergency contacts they could need. It's more than just a device – for them it's like the air they breathe and is a key function of their survival.

Consumer considerations: Is it safe? Is it safe for the environment? Will it do what is says? Is it well priced?

2. Security

This originally meant physical security, however for Generation Alpha, while of course that's essential, increasingly there is a focus on their mental wellbeing and safety. Their focus is on security from a relational perspective.

Consumer considerations: What is the warranty? What if it breaks?

3. Social

Traditionally, this level of the hierarchy referred to social needs met through a sense of belonging, love and affection from family and friends. For Generation Alpha, this aspect is very important – partly because they are in the life stage where friends and family are key. We saw during COVID-19 that it was younger people who were most negatively affected by the social distancing and lockdowns. Social considerations matter more to the emerging generations because they are linked to so many other areas of their life.

Consumer considerations: Do I identify with this? Is this brand or product for me? Will this connect me with others?

4. Self-esteem

This is outlined as respect, prestige and admiration, whether it be through achievements, mastery, independence or status. For Generation Alpha, this has changed to encompass public acquiring of self-esteem through social media and documenting their life online. It encompasses motivation to do things that make them feel better about themselves, especially in front of others.

Consumer considerations: How will this make me look? How does this make me feel?

5. Self-actualisation

The top of the triangle, self-actualisation, is the realisation of personal potential that leads to self-fulfilment through seeking personal growth and experiences. It is important to note that self-actualisation is a continual process of *becoming* rather than a perfect state one reaches of a *happy ever after.*[289] For Generation Alpha this is about being a fulfilled individual. It's about reaching their full potential, making a difference, and having purpose and meaning.

This could be through a job where they are able to make a contribution, through social media where they can have a social influence campaign, or through being an advocate about a key cause that they are passionate about. They can leverage their purchasing in a value-based way – sustainably sourced, buying from ethical brands – so they feel like they've made a difference with their shopping.

Consumer considerations: What are the values of this brand? Is this ethical? What about the environment? Will this help me to be the best version of myself? Is it ethical? Is it fair trade?

While the timeless human drivers for social interaction, for belonging, for food, shelter, warmth, security and stability remain the same, the way in which the retail industry provides for and markets to those needs for this generation needs to evolve. Because if they don't, they get left behind.

Agility – surviving into the future

To stay relevant in our global world, marketers, manufacturers and service providers need to maintain open ears to Generation Alpha and design products and services that will be useful for these future consumers. On top of that, businesses today need to learn to effectively communicate with Generation Alpha. How? By connecting with them to find out their wants and needs, and what challenges they face. If businesses fail to understand the world's largest generation of consumers, they will edge towards irrelevancy.

During COVID-19, businesses of all sizes across Australia had to respond and adapt to the widespread changes brought on public health regulations. There were countless examples of businesses within the hospitality industry, one of the most severely impacted by the lockdowns that changed how or what they delivered to customers. Some of Australia's top restaurants turned to serving takeaway during lockdown. And various local gin distilleries turned to making hand sanitiser during the pandemic when supply was low across the country.

If businesses want to not only survive but thrive in the coming years, they need to understand Generation Alpha as the future consumer, listen to them and respond appropriately.

Hackathons

Due to their tech-savviness, Generation Alpha will push for innovation and help make it happen. All we have to do is give them a seat at the table, and before we know it Generation Alpha will help shape ideas and the future.

In recent years, one of the ways in which product developers and marketers have engaged with the emerging generations' perspective is through hackathons. Don't worry, it's not as sinister as it sounds – it has nothing to do with breaching computer security.

Hackathons are events with a little bit of a party atmosphere. A company or product developer sets twenty-four to forty-eight hours aside and invites participants to work in small groups to develop concepts, ideas and prototypes. While hackathons currently most engage with Generation Z, this is a concept well-tuned for a Generation Alpha world because it involves intense but brief engagement, largely to solve social problems or in support of charities. They are team-based ventures that provide the opportunity to celebrate the achievement together. The goal is that by the end of the hackathon a product prototype is built or a business model is developed. Starting with ideation, a team collaborates, designs, builds a prototype, tests it and creates the next iteration until it's ready to pitch. It's highly likely that you have interacted with an item that has been tested in the context of a hackathon – many of which are found on Facebook.

Facebook's Hackathon page tells us, 'Hackathons are a big tradition at Facebook. They serve as the foundation for some great (and not so great) ideas. It gives our employees the opportunity to try out new ideas and collaborate with other people in a fun environment.'[290] Facebook uses hackathons to engage everyone in the company – regardless of their role – to consider how to improve their products.

One of the products that originated at a hackathon is the 'Safety Check'.[291] This feature was built to make it easy for people affected by an earthquake, for example, to mark themselves as 'safe' so that friends and family would know that they weren't caught up in the disaster. An extension of Safety Check was created to give people a space to post and find information about local resources such as shelter, water or first aid.

Universities, governments, NGOs and private companies all use hackathons so they can engage with new or upcoming talent. Although they are also a time- and money-saving way to develop a product, hackathons ultimately invite in fresh and alternative perspectives and create an even playing field for potential employees. Some might say that they help organisations to diversify by opening up the doors to people who they wouldn't ordinarily employ. As we have already seen, more companies are viewing diversity as a strength, and as Generation Alpha grow up, it will be increasingly important to bring their perspective into the conversation.

Marketing and science

Marketing tools have evolved since mobile devices like iPhones were introduced into people's lives. We've all done a Google search for an item and then found an ad (or five or six) related to that product pop up later on our Facebook or Instagram feed. Data matters. And one of the most significant shifts we're seeing with marketing is the integration of data science. This involves using data as a measurement to help marketers build their brand and extend their reach.

This shift is a form of digital transformation beyond the traditional forms of marketing. It is about moving beyond an 'advert' and examining our engagement with the ad and how that informs marketers about their consumers – who they are and what their specific behaviours are. It is a shift from demographics to psychographics, and ultimately from market segments to a market of one.

This has some great benefits for Generation Alpha as they will be delivered more personalised marketing and information, which can make their decisions and purchasing behaviour easier. But, on the other hand, companies will know more about this generation, and from a younger age, than any other generation. There are always ethical discussions involved when marketing to or gathering information about children, so it's important for companies and parents to be aware of this. As we explored in Chapter 3, it's good for parents to be aware of what their children do or buy online, and to teach them how to protect their personal information online.

Supermarket lifestyle

One sector that is proactive when it comes to the future of shopping and the nuances of the future shopper is the supermarket industry.

Australian supermarkets like Coles and Woolworths have shifted from being grocery stores to becoming one-stop stores with butchers, delis, bakeries and even sushi bars. Both have grown exponentially, now managing logistics teams, warehouses and distribution systems, and different-sized stores – for example, large stores in the suburbs and smaller metro stores designed for commuters in the city. While online shopping and delivery has grown, modern supermarkets are working hard to become destinations that offer a sensory experience that gives buyers a reason to shop in-store.

And of course, there has been the steady introduction of self-checkouts. These will affect the expectations of the future Generation Alpha shopper who will look for a quick and easy experience of the supermarket, often avoiding interaction with a staff member altogether. Supermarkets across the world, such as Sainsburys, Walmart, Aldi, Kroger, 7-Eleven and Spar, have all gone through similar evolutions.

The emerging trend is towards no checkouts at all, as modelled by Amazon Go, where AI sensors and integrated cameras add selected items to the shopper's account without the need for scanning. The future will see automated trolleys, store-based technology that integrates with the consumer's device to guide them through their shopping list, scannable shelf labels that provide recipes, ingredients, suggestions and customised specials, and an incentivised retail experience where points are replaced with immediately accessible free products, café items or free parking.

Modern values – local, eco and healthy

Australians are increasingly looking for 'local' in the products they buy and the foods they eat to connect more closely with their local communities. Over half of Australians indicate that buying locally sourced foods is extremely or very important to them. They are looking to maintain a local connection, with two thirds of people being significantly concerned that the next generation of children will not know where their fresh food comes from.[292]

In the store of the future, Generation Alpha will be more likely to purchase local food when stores are visibly active in community engagement and the broader benefits of buying local are made clear. For example, if a local seafood market is known to be sustainable and environmentally friendly, Generation Alpha will be more likely to purchase from there, compared to another store or market that has no eco-credentials. Australians will continue to want to support local farmers and businesses, support the local economy, and minimise environmental impacts.[293]

Shoppers will also want to make sustainable and ethical choices, and retailers will need to meet the demand. We are already seeing Generation Alpha prioritise the environment as young children, and this will stay with them as they grow older and will translate into their consumer behaviour. Greater transparency and traceability of retailers and manufacturers will be required, as shoppers will continue to use social media to share ethical concerns and recommendations, and look to brand rating sites that assess environmental and social responsibility.

A third factor Australians are increasingly considering in regard to their shopping is health, which affects how they see value. Australians are spending more time reading labels, ingredient lists, and scanning for additives than they did in the past. It is not just nutritional health or price bargains that will be driving Generation Alpha's consumer choices in the future, but their social health. Already more than a third of

Australian shoppers are willing to buy sustainable products, with nearly the same proportion willing to avoid purchasing from brands that aren't aligned with their values.[294]

Despite the increase in health bloggers and social media personalities influencing the shopping trends of today's younger generations, Australians as a whole are significantly more influenced by the established health authorities than celebrities in their shopping habits and nutritional choices. Three quarters of Australians report that health organisations and their spokespersons affect their shopping and nutritional choices. Australians will increasingly look for well-researched facts behind the products they buy. In the future, in an age of information saturation, reputable messages from credible sources will be at the forefront in shaping consumer choices.[295]

The online store of the future

The research company IGD in their Online Store of the Future report[296] opens with the words of their CEO Joanne Denney-Finch OBE, who states, 'We track retail innovation around the world and one of the most fascinating areas to follow has been the rapid development of online shopping. However, we think the biggest transformation is still to come, thanks to factors like artificial intelligence, smart homes, 5G and the next wave of young e-shoppers.' These young e-shoppers are Generation Alpha, who are hyper-informed and constantly connected. Only ever knowing a world where smart speakers are connected to other devices, this will play an increasingly important role in making their shopping experience the most convenient and efficient possible.

Artificial intelligence, smart devices and robotics will also have an impact on the online shopping experience.

For example, voice technology and wearable technology – two trends on the rise – may combine to enable Generation Alpha to not only use their smartwatches for a gamified health experience, but also to shop via a smart speaker. This is just one example of how the future of online shopping could evolve to accommodate Generation Alpha's constantly evolving attitudes and consumption behaviour. So will Generation Alphas set foot into a supermarket for their quinoa, kale and tofu? While technology is transforming shopping, the timeless human experience of tactile interaction, the delight of smell, the desire to see items in real life and the experience of taste will keep the instore shop alive. Augmented reality can't replace the age-old tradition of lightly squeezing the avocado to determine if it's ripe enough for their avo on toast.

The personal micro store

Imagine this. Artificial intelligence helps personalise Generation Alpha's future grocery store online homepage. When generally browsing, they will only see the products and pack sizes likely to meet their needs. Many products will only be buyable online, where there is no constraint on shelf space. In high-value categories there will be customisable products, so they can create their own ideal shampoo or cereal. They will see personalised promotions. All the advertising they see will have messages, images and language relevant to them. This way, they will get to see more new products of the kind they are interested in.

The online store of the future will adapt to the individual consumer, learning from experience. For instance, if it's an older shopper the page may adapt its font size and tailor its health-based suggestions. All content will be device-responsive. Another popular way to shop will be by voice control. In and out of the home, Generation Alpha will be able to reorder products this way and ask for product information, with pricing and communications personalised to them as individuals. We all currently experience targeted marketing, often based on our Google searches, but the Alphas will experience this in a more specific fashion.

The personal assistant

Generation Alpha will be growing up with personal assistants ... in the form of Siri, Alexa and other voice-assisted speakers.

If you have Generation Alphas in your life then you know that they regularly engage with voice technology from a young age. While today they are asking Alexa to play their favourite TV show or 'Baby Shark', it won't be long before these young children become tweens and young adults. As they continue to integrate the physical and digital world, we can expect to see a connection of devices used to make their shopping, and their life, easier and more streamlined.

Smarter devices will also make shopping simpler and more relevant. The online store will help to stop Generation Alpha from running out of products, with the ability to subscribe to have their favourite products delivered regularly. Artificial intelligence will predict when they're likely to run out of something and make or suggest a reorder.

You may have heard of the smart refrigerator – the household appliance that lets you use a smartphone to see inside of the fridge. So, what will this look like for Generation Alpha and their household? It will not only let them know when the ice tray is empty and can sense what products are inside of it, but the fridge of the future will also have a built-in display that will let them order groceries, play music and more.[297] And this isn't the only appliance that will order shopping for them – devices such as washing machines will connect to their chosen store and reorder detergent when necessary. This will seek to lock in customer loyalty among Generation Alpha.

Online shopping will make product and meal recommendations and will factor in the weather forecast as well as take into account their social calendar. Shoppers who like to plan will be supported with personalised meal planners. The online store will use sophisticated digital assistants, like chatbots, to help Generation Alpha shop by personalising meal plans based on their current dietary requirements. In fact, there will be apps and programs that will create plans with personalised recipes based on each individual's food preferences and health goals, and will then construct a shopping list which will get sent to their preferred online retailers.

This is already happening for US-based Habit.com, a custom meal site. Their users send them a blood sample, which is analysed, and a bespoke nutritional plan is created based on their findings. Services like this will be linked with Generation Alpha's fitness and wellbeing apps and lifestyle goals. It is foreseeable that in the future, retailers will use data from connected devices to provide more personalised services, and ones that align with people's dietary requirements, for example. With 85 per cent of shoppers surveyed by IGD in 'Shoppers of the Future'[298] actively trying to improve their diet, linked with government legislation and initiatives to combat obesity, investment in healthier products and a growing rate (or perception) of intolerances and allergies, these apps and sites will likely see a jump in popularity among Generation Alpha.

The efficient store

For Generation Alpha shoppers, the online store of the future will be more convenient. It will be quicker and easier to find and buy products. Login and payment will use facial, voice or touch recognition technology. Generation Alpha shoppers will waste less, with more choice of pack sizes and meal planners that help manage quantities and advise on using leftovers, thus limiting food waste. Shoppers will enjoy a better fulfilment service with more deliveries, made on time and with the right quality and freshness. Deliveries will only get faster and more convenient, enabling this generation to free up more time.

Deliveries

Unattended deliveries to homes, cars or even 'straight to the fridge' has been growing in popularity, with COVID-19 making this a regular part of the twenty-first century shopping experience. Drone deliveries from companies like Wing, a Google subsidiary, are already mainstream, making more frequent and smaller deliveries a reality now, let alone for Generation Alpha in the future.

Picture this. In the future, when Generation Alpha reach the workforce, they are on their lunch break at the office – they flick through Instagram, see that their favourite chef has posted an image of a new home recipe, and they click 'buy' on his image. Within a few hours they leave work with all the ingredients in their car, ready for them to cook a fabulous meal that night. This may well be the future of fast food, which people make at home! This efficiency matters, as 71 per cent of shoppers aged eighteen to twenty-four believe their lives will be busier in five to ten years' time.[299]

The frictionless store

The online store of the future will be better integrated with physical stores, creating a frictionless shopping experience. Before visiting a physical store, Generation Alpha will be able to look online to check in-store, real-time availability, access product information, get product usage ideas and read reviews. When they arrive at the physical store they will then benefit from personalised offers and recommendations. An online app will help them find products and pay for their shopping without cash.

The invisible store

While they may choose to do so, Generation Alpha won't need to visit an online store to buy products. Alongside voice ordering, the majority of digital content they see will be shoppable. They could be watching a video or see a still image and just click on it to buy the product. There will be no limits to when they can be shopping. This signifies the merging of media, entertainment and shopping. While it will lead to increased ease for Generation Alpha consumers, we do want to be careful that it doesn't lead to mindless shopping and consumption of goods. Rampant consumerism, impulse buying, comfort shopping, grocery stockpiling and consumer indebtedness are already maladies of our era. So it's important for parents, caregivers and educators to teach Generation Alpha to have a healthy relationship with money, products, toys and debt as they grow up.

The changing nature of consumption

All of these new ways of consuming products and services are being enabled by technology. Namely, our increasing connectivity, artificial intelligence and predictive algorithms.

These technologies are giving consumers a more customised, personalised and immediate consumer experience, enabling greater expectations of services, and greater simplicity. While this gives consumers great benefits, what do we, as consumers, give in return? In exchange for a more streamlined consumer experience, we hand over our consumer data.

While older generations may have some concerns around their data privacy, the emerging generations are increasingly willing to hand over their data for a more personalised experience. According to a WP Engine and The Center for Generational Kinetics study, 'Generation Z expect the internet to connect them, entertain them, sell to them, and build their digital brand. They expect that within five years, everything – clocks, refrigerators, vacuums, dishwashers and other appliances – will be connected online. Over two in five will provide personal data for a more personalized experience. Additionally, 41 per cent would stop visiting a website if it did not anticipate what they needed, liked, or wanted.'[300]

As more of our data becomes available in exchange for personalised services, we need to educate and equip our Generation Alphas with critical-thinking, digital literacy skills and discernment to interact and consume in safe ways. Teaching children today to be sceptical and wary of how much information about themselves they give away is an important first step to helping this generation be safe in a world where their consumer information is much sought after.

Marketing products and services

One of the key characteristics defining the emerging generations is that they are visual. They would much prefer to watch a video summarising a topic than read up on it. The dominant platforms on which these generations spend their time are visual, social media sites like YouTube, Instagram, Snapchat and TikTok. For Generation Alpha, their ideal platforms are social, the content visual and the format is story based. As marketing guru Seth Godin put it, 'Marketing is no longer about the stuff you make but about the stories that you tell.' If our marketing is visual, engaging and tells a story then we have a better chance at cutting through the hyper-connected and message-saturated world Generation Alpha are being formed in.

Empowering the Alphas

Children have long been directly involved in testing toys, but in recent years we've seen a shift in their involvement. Although children are still used to promoted toys in traditional advertisements, there's a huge trend of 'unboxing' videos on YouTube, particularly popular among children aged four to eight. If you have children in your world, it's likely you have seen YouTube accounts like Ryan's World that show videos of kids opening the latest toys, given to them by toy manufacturers. After they have opened or 'unboxed' the toy, they play with and review it. Kids watching the videos get to live the 'unboxing' experience through other kids vicariously. The kids unboxing these toys knows how they should look, how they should feel and what they should do. The fact that they are excited also means their enthusiasm is infectious to others watching at home, who often want to go and buy this toy afterwards.

Unboxing is an example of the future of advertising to children, which will be focused on content as advertising. It plays to their consumer characteristics of being a digital generation, influenced by YouTube vloggers and social media influencers. Not only does it showcase these consumer characteristics but it also empowers Generation Alpha, as they are involved in the process. They are not passively consuming but involved as co-creators. We see this in their behaviour around apps and games like TikTok, Roblox and Minecraft, where they provide, create and build content and solutions.

Generation Alpha's voice matters in the home and in the marketplace. A case in point is that Ryan's exposure through his YouTube channel has led to the development of his own line of toys, now available at Walmart. Generation Alpha are being heard, and are an empowered and involved generation in the consumer and advertising process.

Empowered by a 'new world' mindset

The generations before Alpha have been 'marketed' to so frequently and from so many different angles that there's a savviness to them, which will be emulated by Generation Alpha. This new generation will, in general, make decisions based on peer recommendations, social media influencers and their personal values. As they grow up they will also be looking to companies' social responsibility, because they want the companies they interact with to 'do the right thing'. A company that has eco-friendly credentials can help increase consumer trust by showing they are environmentally and socially responsible.

'Cancel culture'

In 2019, the Macquarie Dictionary's committee chose the word of the year to be 'cancel culture'. Cancel culture refers to the practice of withdrawing support for an individual or organisation because they have said or done something offensive. Often, it takes the form of group shaming on social media.[301] It is often used to describe the actions of younger generations. Celebrity Ellen DeGeneres was recently subject

It is self-evident that every brand, product or company is just one generation away from irrelevancy. Yet such is the demographic size and economic influence of Generation Alpha, any organisation that fails to understand and engage with this global generation will edge towards extinction.

to cancel culture when her TV show was accused of having a toxic workplace culture by current and former employees.[302] But it doesn't just happen to celebrities, it happens to brands as well. Pepsi was recently criticised for a controversial ad that appropriated global protest movements including Black Lives Matter, and after criticism of some of the illustrations and words deemed to be promoting stereotypes, the estate of Dr Seuss recently withdrew several of his books from publication.[303]

In recent times, Facebook has received condemnation over its slow response to hate speech, which resulted in brands like Coca-Cola and BMW pulling their advertising from the platform. The de-platforming of Donald Trump after the US Capitol riots by Facebook and Twitter created controversy and received mixed verdicts. This shows us that Generation Alpha will not only demand that companies act in a socially responsible way but that they will be expecting companies to show how, through bold action, they are standing for the things they profess to be. Yet it also highlights the vexed issue of cancel culture.

This is the 'new world' mindset of the emerging generations: 'If you're selling me something, I want my experience of the product to match what you've sold to me and I want my mind to rest easy that, as a company, you're doing all you can to ensure that the product is made and sold responsibly and you are playing your part in taking responsibility to act on social issues'.

Dove, the well-known personal care brand, is an example of a brand engaging with a social issue. Though their advertising and marketing had perpetuated an ideal of beauty, they got to know their audience through a 'Global Study on Women, Beauty and Well-Being'.[304] The study explored what impacts the portrayals of beauty in pop culture were having on women and 'perpetuating an idea of beauty that was neither authentic nor attainable.' In 2017 they announced their brand pledge to always feature real women, never models; to portray women as they are in real life; and to help girls build body confidence and self-esteem.[305] Dove made a shift to ensure they were a values-driven organisation helping customers see their own beauty, not an industry projection of what they deemed beauty to be.

While cancel culture can call out bad behaviour and hold brands to account, it can also stifle debate and mute some perspectives. In a recent study, we found that 65 per cent of Australians agree with the statement that 'The rise of cancel culture has meant I am increasingly self-censoring when and with whom I share my opinions'. Cancel culture can lead to people feeling like they struggle to be their authentic self for fear of judgement or exclusion (which 52 per cent of Australians agree with), and that they have to hide their perspectives on topical issues because they are afraid of how people will respond (which 54 per cent of Australians agree with).[306]

It's important to teach Generation Alpha that holding brands and people to account is a good and worthy thing, but so too is having open conversations about issues. In 2019, former US President Barack Obama weighed into the debate about cancel culture, saying it was 'not activism. If all you're doing is casting stones, you're probably not going to get that far.' He added that he got the sense some young people felt being as 'judgmental as possible' was the best way to force change and cautioned them that the world was 'messy' and full of 'ambiguities'.[307] Rather than teaching Generation Alpha to constantly criticise someone who makes a mistake, we can teach them to engage in conversation, which leads to learning and progress, rather than expectations of perfection.

An important role of parents is to teach Generation Alpha that there is a difference between holding someone to an account, and public shaming.

If Generation Alpha are to move towards a values-based consumer culture, there's a need to look in the mirror first, before 'cancelling'. And that extends to brands and companies, too. Use of their voice should be encouraged absolutely, but not by 'cancelling', as it removes the opportunity for a person or a company to apologise and engage with conversation that seeks to understand and change.

In this new world, Generation Alpha want to know their brands fully before they invest their time and money into them and thus the response of the retailer is to listen, to engage, to deliver and to be transparent in the process.

Key takeaways

Generation Alpha are growing up as super-informed and constantly connected consumers. This means that their attitudes and consumption behaviour is different to generations past and is constantly evolving. In this chapter, we have defined them as tech-driven consumers, influenced by entertainment media, social media and their peers. The platforms they have grown up using – like TikTok, Minecraft and Roblox – have defined them as active co-creators rather than passive consumers. As they grow up, they will increasingly integrate technology into their consumer behaviour and it will influence how they shop and interact with brands. The online store of the future will be personal and more easily accessible to them than ever before. As empowered consumers, products, advertising and marketing will best reach them when it involves them and meets their expectations, aspirations and values.

CHAPTER 11

The World of Alpha: A Future Forecast

'Young people, when informed and empowered, when they realise that what they do truly makes a difference, can indeed change the world.'

Dr Jane Goodall

The future is shaped by generations who at key points bring forth change that subsequent generations inherit. Take the Baby Boomers, for example. They were instrumental in ushering in social change from racial equality to women's rights, anti-war activism and environmental action that has since gone global.

Gen Y have similarly brought about structural change, from breaking gender glass ceilings to championing diversity and empowering next-generational leadership – impacts that will benefit the generations coming after them.

In this final chapter, we predict what sort of important conversations Generation Alpha will be having, the changes they can expect, how they will manage challenges of the screen age, geopolitical shifts, population change, COVID-19 and how, despite all these challenges, their collective future is still a bright one.

What conversations will Generation Alpha be having?

Like each generation before them, the Alphas will encounter unique challenges that they will have to navigate and lead their generation through. Briefly, we want to explore what kinds of conversations they are likely to be having in the future.

The sanctity of life and dignity while ageing is one such topic. Breakthroughs in and advancement of medicine may see people expecting to experience a better quality of life for longer. Hip replacements, knee replacements, shoulder replacements – each of these surgeries has seen great advances in recent years.[308] With pharmaceutical breakthroughs, emerging medical devices and improved surgical procedures, generations in the future will live longer. This means that there will probably also be more national conversations around the age they plan to retire and their post-work life. Things to discuss might include how we, as a nation, care for our elderly who are living longer, and what the implications are on the economy and on society, as well as how we can offer dignity in people's later years. Australia's recent aged care royal commission report subtitled 'Care, Dignity and Respect' highlighted the challenges of funding quality care amid the growth in demand from our ageing population.

It's not just the advancement of medicine that will lead to national conversations, but also the advancement of technology. In a world where you will be able to give some level of human intelligence to machines, and where there is potential for superintelligence, issues like bioethics and transhumanism are also likely to be on the agenda for the Alphas. In fact,

Every generation creates change, but occasionally the times and trends collide and a generation has enormous impact and shapes the culture beyond all measure. The Boomers experienced it in the 1960s, Gen Y saw it in the early 2000s, and it seems that Generation Alpha are at the forefront of another such time.

Generation Alpha will have to make ethical decisions that we can hardly contemplate at present, particularly when it comes to robots and sentience. Seventeenth-century philosophers used the concept of sentience to distinguish the ability to reason from the ability to feel (sentience). Sentience is attributed to humans and animals, but as robots are further developed to exhibit human-like emotions, Generation Alpha will need strong logic and sensible categories to add clarity to these emerging situations. The ethical dilemmas of the future will require preparing Generation Alpha with a values framework and an abundance of wisdom that can deal with these emerging complexities.

Concern for the Alphas

It is not uncommon for older generations to believe that society's best days are behind them. The past is referred to as 'the good old days' and when speaking about the future for their children or grandchildren, they are dispirited and communicate a sense of concern. You may have heard or even uttered statements like, 'What kind of a world are we leaving them?' 'It was better in my day.' One mum told us, 'I'm old enough to remember when it was safe enough to go and ride my bike to the basketball courts a mile away from my home. Our kids can't play outside the way we did.'

As humans, we have a natural tendency to project doom and gloom on the days ahead, but our view of the future is often influenced by our own worldview, experiences and perhaps even our limited understanding of things like technology. In the late 1700s, a British economist by the name of Thomas Robert Malthus predicted that global population growth would supersede food production, and would lead to international food shortages and starvation. In 2020 we saw a glimpse of this when panic buying arose in grocery stores around the world in response to the COVID-19 pandemic. This led to empty shelves – vacant of toilet paper, pasta and flour – because bread baking had become a national pastime! Although it appeared as though we were a nation on the brink of a food shortage during the pandemic, it was simply a matter of logistics. There was enough food, but the suppliers and drivers couldn't keep up with the demand.

Instead of an increase in population and a shortage of food, Generation Alpha will see the complete opposite – fewer people being born and a dramatic rise in obesity. A United Nations report outlines that only sub-Saharan Africa is projected to double its population by 2050. Far from nutritional shortages, the opposite is the case. The World Health Organization reports that in children ages five to nineteen, obesity has grown from 4 per cent in 1975 to 18 per cent in 2016. That represents 124 million children and adolescents.[309] This is something that we have become increasingly aware of, and as parents and educators we have to lead by example – as challenging as it may be!

Not only was Malthus concerned about the shortage of food but he also became famous for warning about the danger of the rise of horse manure on the streets. Why? Because the mode of transportation in his day was the horse and cart and his logic took him to a place where he saw an increase in population, without the lens of innovation. He didn't have the foresight to predict the development of the car – which is fair enough, but he should have factored in human ingenuity. As social researchers we have learnt that we have to incorporate innovation in our forecasts. Innovation accounts for the challenge of the present day, projects an alternative future state and takes us there.

In a recent survey, ViacomCBS concluded that 'Today's kids are going to be amazing!' – that's a direct quote. They reported that parents believe their kids are, and will be, more tech-savvy, more caring about the environment, more curious about the world, more intelligent and more creative.[310] In a recent conversation we had with a mum, she said, 'I feel like all of the problems that we have with our kids are the same problems that every generation has had with kids.' It's as though, in one sense, nothing changes and, in another sense, everything changes.

The problems that we presume of Generation Alpha's future won't necessarily be their problems. The models of the future are an extrapolation of what we see in the present, but they often don't represent the reality of what will happen, because they are not the real world. In the real world, people adapt. And we have to remember that the future generations will think differently to us. They don't need to be anchored to the problems we project on their future. Generation Alpha will shape their era and we very simply have to set them on course to see the possibilities.

From a young age, Generation Alpha are being taught to co-create and contribute to the conversation. They are an integral part of the solution to building a future in which they can thrive.

Screen time vs green time

One of the great debates of the current era is around screen time and how screens might affect our children's future. Angela, a mother, shared with us, 'When I make my kids put their screens down for dinner, they want to hurry up and eat their dinner so they can get back to their screens. I think screen time affects family life. They would rather be on their screens.

That's the problem. And if you take them out somewhere, like the park, they want to go home. You can't win.'

There are many opinions on the use of screens and how detrimental they might be to children, but a recent study highlights the benefits they bring.[311] It outlined that time in nature was great for mental health, but there was evidence that showed that screen time provides opportunity for young people to stay in touch with their peers, and computer games might help things like brain function and coordination. The authors of this paper reviewed over 186 studies and suggested that 'green time' can offset 'screen time'. This is great in principle, but again, as those leading and influencing the next generation, it's down to us to initiate this and make the cultural shift in our homes and families to help our kids balance time on screens with time outside.

The time is now

A huge part of understanding our children involves taking the time to give them our attention. When we visit schools and speak in classes or assemblies, we often ask the pupils, 'Where else in the world would you like to live?' The most common response is 'Nowhere!' Then when we ask, 'When in history would you rather live than in the twenty-first century?' their response is 'Today!' We've heard adults say things like, 'I'm glad I'm not young today and not trying to get a job in the current climate.' We have found that young people don't think like that, they think, 'These are awesome times!' They have a youthful idealism – which, let's be honest, we have all had at one point in our lives.

Young people see the benefits of their times, and while they don't have the perspective or understanding to necessarily compare their times with the past, they don't think it's the worst time in history, because they see the good and the opportunity. Sure, there are environmental challenges and bouts of youth unemployment, but that's a part of what makes up our lives. The thrill of life on planet Earth is taking steps to address the issues, innovate and bring solutions. And Generation Alpha will do precisely that. They will see with fresh eyes, their different thinking and their generation's unique perspective. Change is about taking one step at a time; it's an evolution, not a revolution.

It has been said that a good leader is one who knows the way and shows the way. We would say that a better leader is one who prepares, resources and inspires a new generation to lead the way and go the way.

Truly global

Think back to the year you were born. Every generation will have their historical events – some that we anticipate, like the moon landing, and some we don't, like the September 11 attacks. Less dramatic are the geopolitical shifts that create a different world to the one our parents inherited. China has grown its influence economically and politically over recent decades. The US has withdrawn somewhat from global interactions as it manages internal tensions. The United Kingdom is navigating life beyond their association with the European Union, and even Australia is forging her own way, becoming increasingly independent from Britain and the US.

Generation Alpha will be the most globally minded generation, the most culturally diverse and the most connected and because of this variety of influences, their alignments aren't as clean cut. In Australia, almost one third of the population were born or has a heritage from overseas.

So while their home is Australia, they may have been born in China, Korea, Lebanon, Italy or England.[312] Generation Alpha are globally invested, connected and influenced. It's not just their DNA that has created this tie, but it's friendships formed through activities like gaming, where they play against similar-aged kids from all over the world. So let's look at this globe they are growing up in.

A growth spurt?

There is genuine concern about the growing population, which we've alluded to, but we recently conducted in-depth research into the matter, and this is what we found. The latest population modelling[313] shows that the dire forecasts of global overpopulation and food shortages are unlikely to eventuate. It is now expected that the global population will peak in 2064 at just under 11 billion people, up from 7.9 billion today. The challenge for many countries will not be managing population growth but trying to attract migration to deal with population contraction.

By 2050 the population of Europe will be in decline, Asia will be nearing its peak, South and Central America will see growth slowing, while Africa's population will continue to grow until 2100. Australia's population will still be growing, but through net migration rather than natural increase. By the end of the century, the top four countries by population will be India, China, Nigeria and the US (a reordering from the current China, India, US and Indonesia). The declining growth rates are directly linked to the declining birth rates and ageing populations of once fast-growing countries. By 2030, the median age in Japan will be fifty-one, in Italy it will be forty-nine and in China it will be forty-one, compared to Australia's thirty-nine, up from thirty-eight currently. The median age in fast-growing countries particularly in Africa, however, will be much younger: fifteen in Niger, eighteen in Nigeria and twenty in Kenya. This shows us that the future isn't necessarily a one-way street but a pendulum that swings.

Global generational change

The next decade will also bring significant generational change as well. By 2030, the largest generation globally will be Generation Alpha. They will comprise two billion people – nearly a quarter of the global population, compared to the Baby Boomers who will by then comprise less than 10 per cent, or 836 million people globally.

The impact of COVID-19

The global number of COVID-19 fatalities is tragically large, but as a contributor to total deaths, the impact of COVID-19 is not comparable to those of previous pandemics, such as the Spanish Flu. At 2.5 million annual deaths globally at the peak of COVID-19, this accounted for 4 per cent of the 60 million deaths annually.[314]

The biggest cause of death globally is heart disease (22 per cent of global annual deaths), followed by stroke (11 per cent) and respiratory diseases and infections (11 per cent), which is where COVID-19 deaths are categorised. However, if COVID-19 had a stand-alone category, it tragically trended to become the seventh biggest cause of death in 2020, after diarrhoeal diseases and preventable neonatal conditions.[315]

There has been and will continue to be an economic consequence of COVID-19, which Generation Alpha will have to foot the bill for, well into their working lives. But the impacts on their future are not just economic, and they are not just negative. As we explored in earlier chapters, we predict that COVID-19 will change the future of work for Generation Alpha, redefine who they see as heroes, integrate technology further into their lives, increase their resilience and see the rebirth of increased family time.

A thrill of hope

As a world, we are looking at this next generation and we are waking up to what Generation Alpha might 'grow up to be'. Generation Alpha represent a whole new generation, entirely born in a new century.

> 'My aim is to reassure parents that there are things we can do, and that there's much hope for Generation Alpha. Every generation has faced their struggles; past generations would have had wars, or famine or whatever it was, and it just looks different for this generation. And so, we're not unique in the sense that we will struggle in certain areas of our parenting – this is just our challenge. I really love working with young people, and my message to parents of Generation Alpha is, don't be afraid of the teen years. They have their own challenges, but teenagers are wonderful – they think deeply and want to make change. There's a lot of ways we can connect with them.'
> – *Collett Smart, psychologist*

Generation Alpha are being shaped in different times to generations past. They are more digital, global, mobile, social and visual than any generation before them. There's no doubt that Generation Alpha will come up against their challenges, their own storm clouds and uncertainty. We've touched on some of those challenges and uncertainties in this book. Others we haven't had the insight to forecast, but one thing is certain to us: their future is bright, and like every other generation they will find the tools they need to thrive in it. The future for Generation Alpha is exciting – full of creativity, innovation and opportunity. They're not only following the positive examples set by older generations but they are also empowered to take action, stand up for what they believe in and pave a new way forward. And it's here that we want to leave you with the anticipation of a great future for Generation Alpha, with the thrill of the new – the thrill of hope.

Endnotes

1. S. Covey, *The 7 Habits of Highly Effective People: Powerful lessons in personal change,* New York, Free Press, 2004.
2. 'Australians post COVID-19', S. Renton, McCrindle Research, 2020, accessed 12 March 2021. https://mccrindle.com.au/wp-content/uploads/reports/COVID19-Phase3-Report-2020.pdf
3. 'The World Factbook, "World"', Central Intelligence Agency, 5 February 2021, accessed 15 February 2021. https://www.cia.gov/the-world-factbook/countries/world/
4. 'World War II', J. Royde-Smith, *Britannica,* 23 August 1998, accessed 11 February 2021. https://www.britannica.com/event/World-War-II
5. 'The Second World War', RSL NSW, accessed 16 March 2021. https://www.rslnsw.org.au/commemoration/australias-military-heritage/the-second-world-war/#:~:text=One%20million%20Australians%2C%20both%20men,east%20Asia%20and%20the%20Pacific.
6. ibid.
7. H. Mackay, *Generations. Baby Boomers, their Parents and their Children,* Sydney, Pan Macmillan Australia, 1997.
8. M. McCrindle, *The ABC of XYZ; Understanding the Global Generations,* McCrindle; 3rd edition (28 April 2014).
9. '4102.0 Australian Social Trends, 2004', Australian Bureau of Statistics, 15 June 2004, accessed 15 March 2021. https://www.abs.gov.au/AUSSTATS/abs@.nsf/2f762f95845417aeca25706c00834efa/47f151c90ade4c73ca256e9e001f8973!OpenDocument
10. D. Coupland, *Generation X: Tales for an Accelerated Culture,* St. Martin's Griffin; 1st edition (March 15, 1991).
11. 'Who are Generation X?', *Business Australia,* accessed 12 February 2021. https://www.businessaustralia.com/how-we-help/be-a-better-employer/managing-people/who-are-generation-x-
12. 'Divorce rates in Australia', Australian Institute of Family Studies, accessed 15 March 2021. https://aifs.gov.au/facts-and-figures/divorce-rates-australia
13. 'Does Generation Y have it easier than the Baby Boomers?', M. McCrindle, McCrindle Research Blog, 13 April 2016, accessed 11 February 2021. https://mccrindle.com.au/insights/blogarchive/does-generation-y-have-it-easier-than-the-baby-boomers/
14. 'For Millennials, 9/11 and its aftermath shaped their view of the world', A. Wagman, *The Morning Call,* 11 September 2016, accessed 11 February 2021. https://www.mcall.com/news/local/mc-911-millenials-worldview-15-years-anniversary-20160911-story.html
15. 'Births, Australia', 9 December 2020, Australian Bureau of Statistics, Births, Australia, accessed 15 March 2021. https://www.abs.gov.au/statistics/people/population/births-australia/latest-release
16. 'How the global pandemic is shaping the sentiment, behaviour and outlook of Australians', S. Renton, McCrindle Research, 2020, accessed 12 March 2021. https://mccrindle.com.au/wp-content/uploads/reports/COVID19-Phase1-Report-2020.pdf
17. 'Underemployment: Reduced hours or prefers more hours', Australian Bureau of Statistics, 21 January 2021, accessed 16 March 2021. https://www.abs.gov.au/articles/underemployment-reduced-hours-or-prefers-more-hours
18. 'Recovering from COVID-19', S.Renton, McCrindle Research, 2020, accessed 12 March 2021. https://mccrindle.com.au/wp-content/uploads/reports/COVID19-Phase2-Report-2020.pdf

19. ibid.

20. 'The Future of Education', S.Renton, K. Stobbe, McCrindle Research, 2020, accessed 12 March 2021. https://mccrindle.com.au/wp-content/uploads/reports/Education-Future-Report-2020.pdf

21. C. Dweck, *Mindset: The Psychology of Success, How We Can Learn to Fulfil Our Potential,* Random House Publishing Group, 2008.

22. 'The Future of Education', S.Renton, K. Stobbe, McCrindle Research, 2020, accessed 12 March 2021. https://mccrindle.com.au/wp-content/uploads/reports/Education-Future-Report-2020.pdf

23. 'Climate change ranks highest as vital issue of our time Generation Z survey', K. Naidoo, Amnesty International, 10 December 2019, accessed 15 March 2021. https://www.amnesty.org/en/latest/news/2019/12/climate-change-ranks-highest-as-vital-issue-of-our-time/

24. 'The Future of Education Survey', [Nationally representative survey distributed to 1003 Australian parents], conducted by McCrindle Research, March 2020.

25. 'Baby Names Australia 2020', A. Fell, McCrindle Research, 2020, accessed 12 March 2021. https://mccrindle.com.au/wp-content/uploads/reports/Baby-Names-Australia-Report-2020.pdf

26. 'Recovering from COVID-19', S. Renton, McCrindle Research, 2020, accessed 12 March 2021. https://mccrindle.com.au/wp-content/uploads/reports/COVID19-Phase2-Report-2020.pdf

27. 'The Common Sense Census: Media Use by Tweens and Teens', V. Rideout and M. B. Robb, Common Sense Media, 2019, accessed 13 March 2021. https://www.commonsensemedia.org/sites/default/files/uploads/research/2019-census-8-to-18-full-report-updated.pdf

28. 'To grow up healthy, children need to sit less and play more', *The World Health Organization,* 24 April 2019, accessed 12 February 2021. https://www.who.int/news/item/24-04-2019-to-grow-up-healthy-children-need-to-sit-less-and-play-more

29. 'Children's screen time. From Growing Up in Australia: The Longitudinal Study of Australian Children', Australian Institute of Family Studies, September 2016, accessed 13 March 2021. https://aifs.gov.au/publications/childrens-screen-time

30. 'Research reveals shocking new statistics of Australia's bullying crisis', A. Fell, McCrindle Research blog, 15 March 2019, accessed 15 March 2021. https://mccrindle.com.au/insights/blog/three-in-five-australian-students-have-experienced-bullying/

31. 'How long does it take to hit 50 million users?', J. Desjardins, *Visual Capitalist,* 8 June 2018, accessed 11 February 2021. https://www.visualcapitalist.com/how-long-does-it-take-to-hit-50-million-users/

32. ibid.

33. 'Pokémon GO revenue and usage statistics (2020)', M. Iqbal, *Business of Apps,* 30 October 2020, accessed 11 February 2021. https://www.businessofapps.com/data/pokemon-go-statistics/

34. 'More than one billion animals killed in Australian bushfires', The University of Sydney, 8 January 2020, accessed 11 February 2021. https://www.sydney.edu.au/news-opinion/news/2020/01/08/australian-bushfires-more-than-one-billion-animals-impacted.html

35. 'Turnover and Retention Research Report', P. Begley and L. Dunne, Australian HR Institute, August 2018, accessed 13 March 2021. https://www.ahri.com.au/media/1222/turnover-and-retention-report_final.pdf

36. 'The Future of Jobs: Employment, Skills and Workforce Strategy for the Fourth Industrial Revolution, The World Economic Forum, January 2016, accessed 13 March 2021. http://www3.weforum.org/docs/WEF_Future_of_Jobs.pdf

37. '6-year-old made $11 million in one year reviewing toys on YouTube', S. Schmidt, *Washington Post*, 12 December 2017, accessed 11 February 2021. https://www.washingtonpost.com/news/morning-mix/wp/2017/12/11/6-year-old-made-11-million-in-one-year-reviewing-toys-on-you-tube/

38. 'YouTube's biggest star is a 5-year-old that makes millions opening toys', B. Popper, *The Verge*, 22 December 2016, accessed 11 February 2021. https://www.theverge.com/2016/12/22/14031288/ryan-toys-review-biggest-youngest-youtube-star-millions

39. 'About', *Ryan's World*, accessed 12 February 2021. https://ryans.world/about/

40. 'Mapping Pandemic Play Patterns', T. Aguilar, MarketCast Kids, 2020, accessed 16 March 2021. https://marketcast.com/wp-content/uploads/2020/11/MarketCast_Kidscreen_2022.pdf

41. 'Recovering from COVID-19', S. Renton, McCrindle Research, 2020, accessed 12 March 2021. https://mccrindle.com.au/wp-content/uploads/reports/COVID19-Phase2-Report-2020.pdf

42. C. Rogers, *On Becoming a Person: A Therapist's View of Psychotherapy*, Boston, Mariner Books, 1995

43. 'Are We There Yet? Today's Parents, Tomorrow's Kids', C. Kurz, J. Gurrier, ViacomCBS, 12 February 2020. https://insights.viacomcbs.com/categories/research-studies/are-we-there-yet/

44. C. Mackesy, *The Boy, The Mole, The Fox and the Horse*, London, Random House, 2019.

45. R. J. Palacio, *Wonder*, New York, Knopf, 2012.

46. M. McCrindle and A. Fell, *Work Wellbeing: Leading Thriving Teams in Rapidly Changing Times*, Sydney, Rockpool Publishing, 2020.

47. 'Constitution of The World Health Organization', The World Health Organization, 15 September 2005, accessed 12 February 2021. https://www.who.int/governance/eb/who_constitution_en.pdf

48. 'Wellbeing', Victoria State Government Better Health Channel, May 2020, accessed 11 February 2021. https://www.betterhealth.vic.gov.au/health/healthyliving/wellbeing

49. 'Youth Survey Report 2019', E. Carlisle, J. Fildes, S. Hall, B. Perrens, A. Perdriau and J. Plummer, Mission Australia, 2019, accessed 13 March 2021. https://www.missionaustralia.com.au/publications/youth-survey

50. M. McCrindle and A. Fell, *Work Wellbeing: Leading Thriving Teams in Rapidly Changing Times*, Sydney, Rockpool Publishing, 2020.

51. 'Australia's Physical Activity and Sedentary Behaviour Guidelines and the Australian 24-Hour Movement Guidelines', Australian Government Department of Health, 12 April 2019, accessed 12 February 2021. https://www1.health.gov.au/internet/main/publishing.nsf/Content/health-pubhlth-strateg-phys-act-guidelines

52. M. McCrindle and A. Fell, *Work Wellbeing: Leading Thriving Teams in Rapidly Changing Times*, Sydney, Rockpool Publishing, 2020.

53. ibid.

54. M. Walker, *Why We Sleep: Unlocking the Power of Sleep and Dreams*, New York, Scribner, 2017.

55. 'Sleep tips for children', Health Direct, January 2020, accessed 12 February 2021. https://www.healthdirect.gov.au/sleep-tips-for-children

56. 'Screens, man's new best friend', Mainstreet Insights, 28 September 2020, accessed 15 March 2021. https://mainstreetinsights.com.au/screens-mans-new-best-friend/

57. ibid.

58. 'What does too much screen time do to children's brains?', J. Cross, *Health Matters New York-Presbyterian*, accessed 11 February 2021. https://healthmatters.nyp.org/how-to-manage-kids-screen-time-during-the-covid-19-pandemic/

59. 'Healthy sleep tips', E. Suni, *Sleep Foundation*, 30 July 2020, accessed 11 February 2021. https://www.sleepfoundation.org/sleep-hygiene/healthy-sleep-tips

60. 'Mental Health: strengthening our response', The World Health Organization, 30 March 2018, accessed 12 February 2021. https://www.who.int/news-room/fact-sheets/detail/mental-health-strengthening-our-response

61. 'Mental illness', Health Direct, November 2020, accessed 11 February 2021. https://www.healthdirect.gov.au/mental-illness

62. 'Youth mental health report Youth Survey 2012–16', Mission Australia in association with Black Dog Institute, 2017, accessed 13 March 2021. https://www.blackdoginstitute.org.au/wp-content/uploads/2020/04/2017-youth-mental-health-report_mission-australia-and-black-dog-institute.pdf?sfvrsn=6

63. ibid.

64. F.M. Gore, P.J. Bloem, G.C. Patton, J. Ferguson, V. Joseph, C. Coffey, S.M. Sawyer and C.D. Mathers, 'Global burden of disease in young people aged 10–24 years: a systematic analysis', *The Lancet*, vol. 377, issue 9783, 18 June 2011, pp. 2093-102.

65. 'How the global pandemic is shaping the sentiment, behaviour and outlook of Australians', S. Renton, McCrindle Research, 2020, accessed 12 March 2021. https://mccrindle.com.au/wp-content/uploads/reports/COVID19-Phase1-Report-2020.pdf

66. 'Recovering from COVID-19', S. Renton, McCrindle Research, 2020, accessed 12 March 2021. https://mccrindle.com.au/wp-content/uploads/reports/COVID19-Phase2-Report-2020.pdf

67. ibid.

68. 'Stress in America 2020: A National Mental Health Crisis', *American Psychological Association*, October 2020, accessed 15 March 2021. https://www.apa.org/news/press/releases/stress/2020/report-october

69. 'R U OK? Day', the Australian Government Department of Health, January 2014, accessed 13 March 20221. https://www1.health.gov.au/internet/publications/publishing.nsf/Content/suicide-prevention-activities-evaluation~Appendices~appendixa~project31

70. 'Parenting and children's mental health, Health Direct, February 2020, accessed 11 February 2021. https://www.healthdirect.gov.au/parenting-childrens-mental-health

71. 'The Future of Education', S. Renton, K. Stobbe, McCrindle Research, 2020, accessed 12 March 2021. https://mccrindle.com.au/wp-content/uploads/reports/Education-Future-Report-2020.pdf

72. ibid.

73. 'Youth Survey Report 2020', E. Tiller, J. Fildes, S. Hall, V. Hicking, N. Greenland, D. Liyanarachchi, and K. Di Nicola, Mission Australia, 2020, accessed 13 March 2021. https://www.missionaustralia.com.au/publications/youth-survey

74. 'The Future of Education', S. Renton, K. Stobbe, McCrindle Research, 2020, accessed 12 March 2021. https://mccrindle.com.au/wp-content/uploads/reports/Education-Future-Report-2020.pdf

75. ibid.

76. ibid.

77. ibid.

78. ibid.

79. ibid.

80. M. Seligman, *Flourish*, New York, Simon and Schuster, 2011

81. 'Workplace Loneliness', Reventure, A Future that Works, 2019, accessed 13 March 2021. http://www.afuturethatworks.org.au/reports

82. 'Is your child lonely? (for parents)', Mental Health America, accessed 11 February 2021. https://mhanational.org/your-child-lonely-parents

83. ibid.
84. 'The Future of Education', S. Renton, K. Stobbe, McCrindle Research, 2020, accessed 12 March 2021. https://mccrindle.com.au/wp-content/uploads/reports/Education-Future-Report-2020.pdf
85. 'The Future of Education', M. McCrindle, McCrindle Research, 2019, accessed 12 March 2021. https://mccrindle.com.au/wp-content/uploads/reports/Education-Future-Report-2019.pdf
86. ibid.
87. 'The Future of Education', S. Renton, K. Stobbe, McCrindle Research, 2020, accessed 12 March 2021. https://mccrindle.com.au/wp-content/uploads/reports/Education-Future-Report-2020.pdf
88. 'Youth Survey Report 2019', E. Carlisle, J. Fildes, S. Hall, B. Perrens, A. Perdriau and J. Plummer, Mission Australia, 2019, accessed 13 March 2021. https://www.missionaustralia.com.au/publications/youth-survey
89. ibid.
90. ibid.
91. 'Building your resilience', American Psychological Association, 2012, accessed 11 February 2021. https://www.apa.org/topics/resilience
92. 'How the global pandemic is shaping the sentiment, behaviour and outlook of Australians', S. Renton, McCrindle Research, 2020, accessed 12 March 2021. https://mccrindle.com.au/wp-content/uploads/reports/COVID19-Phase1-Report-2020.pdf
93. F. Molloy, 'Dads play a role in preventing social anxiety in children', *Macquarie University The Lighthouse,* 10 October 2019, accessed 11 February 2021. https://lighthouse.mq.edu.au/article/october2/dads-play-a-role-in-preventing-social-anxiety-in-young-adults
94. ibid.
95. 'Parental touch may reduce social anxiety in children', The University of Amsterdam, *Medical Xpress,* 23 May 2018, accessed 11 February 2021. https://medicalxpress.com/news/2018-05-parental-social-anxiety-children.html
96. M. McCrindle and A. Fell, *Work Wellbeing: Leading Thriving Teams in Rapidly Changing Times,* Sydney, Rockpool Publishing, 2020.
97. 'All the words of the year, 1990 to present', American Dialect Society, accessed 11 February 2021. https://www.americandialect.org/woty/all-of-the-words-of-the-year-1990-to-present
98. 'The rise and fall of online platforms', *Mainstreet Insights,* 23 September 2020, accessed 15 March 2021. https://mainstreetinsights.com.au/the-rise-and-fall-of-online-platforms/
99. 'Labour Force Status of Families', Australian Bureau of Statistics, 16 October 2020, accessed 16 March 2021. https://www.abs.gov.au/statistics/labour/employment-and-unemployment/labour-force-status-families/latest-release
100. 'Recovering from COVID-19', S.Renton, McCrindle Research, 2020, accessed 12 March 2021. https://mccrindle.com.au/wp-content/uploads/reports/COVID19-Phase2-Report-2020.pdf
101. '4125.0 Gender Indicators, Australia, Jan 2013,' Australian Bureau of Statistics, 10 January 2013, accessed 15 March 2021. https://www.abs.gov.au/ausstats/abs@.nsf/Lookup/4125.0main+features4310Jan%202013
102. 'What does too much screen time do to children's brains?', J. Cross, *Health Matters New York-Presbyterian,* accessed 11 February 2021. https://healthmatters.nyp.org/how-to-manage-kids-screen-time-during-the-covid-19-pandemic/
103. ibid.

104. 'Screen time and the brain', D. Ruder, *Harvard Medical School,* 19 June 2019, accessed 11 February 2021. https://hms.harvard.edu/news/screen-time-brain

105. 'What screen time can really do to kid's brains', L. Margalit, *Psychology Today,* 17 April 2016, accessed 11 February 2021. https://www.psychologytoday.com/au/blog/behind-online-behavior/201604/what-screen-time-can-really-do-kids-brains

106. ibid.

107. 'Parenting is a balancing act', J. Guerrier, ViacomCBS, 03 June 2020, accessed 12 February 2021. https://insights.viacomcbs.com/post/parenting-is-a-balancing-act/

108. 'Recovering from COVID-19', S. Renton, McCrindle Research, 2020, accessed 12 March 2021. https://mccrindle.com.au/wp-content/uploads/reports/COVID19-Phase2-Report-2020.pdf

109. W. Parker, 'Tips for men on growing intimacy in marriage', *Very well mind,* 04 February 2020, accessed 11 February 2021. https://www.verywellmind.com/men-growing-intimacy-in-marriage-1270945

110. 'How the global pandemic is shaping the sentiment, behaviour and outlook of Australians', S. Renton, McCrindle Research, 2020, accessed 12 March 2021. https://mccrindle.com.au/wp-content/uploads/reports/COVID19-Phase1-Report-2020.pdf

111. 'Cyberbullying', eSafetyCommissioner, accessed 12 February 2021. https://www.esafety.gov.au/key-issues/cyberbullying

112. 'Research reveals shocking new statistics of Australia's bullying crisis', A. Fell, McCrindle Research blog, accessed 15 March 2021. https://mccrindle.com.au/insights/blog/three-in-five-australian-students-have-experienced-bullying/

113. 'Children are growing up with technology that blurs the line between animate and inanimate objects. How does this interaction affect kids' development?', S. Druga and R. Williams, *MIT Media Lab,* 06 June 2017, accessed 12 February 2021. https://www.media.mit.edu/posts/kids-ai-devices/

114. 'Children and parents: Media use and attitudes report 2018', Ofcom, 29 January 2019, accessed 13 March 2021. https://www.ofcom.org.uk/__data/assets/pdf_file/0024/134907/children-and-parents-media-use-and-attitudes-2018.pdf

115. ibid.

116. 'TikTok statistics', B. Doyle, Wallaroo Media, 06 February 2021, accessed 11 February 2021. https://wallaroomedia.com/blog/social-media/tiktok-statistics/

117. 'Children and parents: Media use and attitudes report 2018', Ofcom, 29 January 2019, accessed 13 March 2021. https://www.ofcom.org.uk/__data/assets/pdf_file/0024/134907/children-and-parents-media-use-and-attitudes-2018.pdf

118. 'Good habits start young', eSafety Commissioner, accessed 11 February 2021. https://www.esafety.gov.au/parents/skills-advice/good-habits-start-young

119. ibid.

120. 'Youth Portal', TikTok, accessed 12 February 2021. https://www.tiktok.com/safety/youth-portal?lang=en

121. ibid.

122. 'What parents need to know about Facebook Messenger Kids', L. Magid, ConnectSafely, accessed 12 February 2021. https://www.connectsafely.org/what-parents-need-to-know-about-facebook-messenger-kids/

123. 'Bluey', ABC iview, accessed 12 February 2021. https://iview.abc.net.au/show/bluey

124. C. Smart, *They'll Be Okay,* Sydney, Hachette Australia, 2019

125. American Greetings, 'American Greetings – World's Toughest Job' [video], American Greetings, 12 May 2015, accessed 12 February 2021.

126. 'Births, Australia', 0 December 2020, Australian Bureau of Statistics, Births, Australia, accessed 15 March 2021. https://www.abs.gov.au/statistics/people/population/births-australia/latest-release

127. The Melbourne Institute, The Household, Income and Labour Dynamics in Australia (HILDA) Survey, 2019, accessed 12 March 2021. https://melbourneinstitute.unimelb.edu.au/__data/assets/pdf_file/0011/3127664/HILDA-Statistical-Report-2019.pdf
128. ibid.
129. ibid.
130. 'The Importance of Fathers', D. Oliker, *Psychology Today,* 23 June 2011, accessed 11 February 2021. https://www.psychologytoday.com/au/blog/the-long-reach-childhood/201106/the-importance-fathers
131. ibid.
132. 'Clarke Gayford isn't the world's first stay-at-home dad – but he might be the most important', J. Adams, *The Telegraph,* 02 August 2018, accessed 11 February 2021. https://www.telegraph.co.uk/family/parenting/clarke-gayford-isnt-worlds-first-stay-at-home-dad-might-important/
133. '2016 Census Community Profiles Table 14. Dwelling Structure by Household Composition and Family Composition', Australian Bureau of Statistics, 23 October 2017, accessed 16 March 2021. https://quickstats.censusdata.abs.gov.au/census_services/getproduct/census/2016/communityprofile/036?opendocument
134. 'Births, Australia', Australian Bureau of Statistics, 9 December 2020, accessed 15 March 2021. https://www.abs.gov.au/statistics/people/population/births-australia/latest-release
135. 'Moving back in: the rise of multigenerational households', E. Liu, University of New South Wales, 10 January 2020, accessed 17 March 2021. https://www.be.unsw.edu.au/news/moving-back-rise-multigenerational-households
136. 'AHURI Essay: Multi-generation households in Australian cities', E. Liu and H. Easthope, Australian Housing and Urban Research Institute, February 2012, accessed 17 March 2021. https://www.ahuri.edu.au/__data/assets/pdf_file/0010/2080/AHURI_Final_Report_No181_Multi-generation_households_in_Australian_cities.pdf
137. 'Labour Force Status of Families', Australian Bureau of Statistics, 17 October 2020, accessed 15 March 2021. https://www.abs.gov.au/statistics/labour/employment-and-unemployment/labour-force-status-families/latest-release
138. 'Marriages and Divorces Australia', Australian Bureau of Statistics, 27 November 2020, accessed 16 March 2021. https://www.abs.gov.au/statistics/people/people-and-communities/marriages-and-divorces-australia/latest-release
139. 'Migration Australia', Australian Bureau of Statistics, 28 April 2020, accessed 16 March 2021. https://www.abs.gov.au/statistics/people/population/migration-australia/latest-release
140. ibid.
141. '2016 Census Community Profiles Table 1. Selected Person Characteristics By Sex [Time Series Profile], Australian Bureau of Statistics, 23 October 2017, accessed 16 March 2021. https://quickstats.censusdata.abs.gov.au/census_services/getproduct/census/2016/communityprofile/036?opendocument
142. 'Labour Force Status of Families', Australian Bureau of Statistics, 16 October 2020, accessed 16 March 2021. https://www.abs.gov.au/statistics/labour/employment-and-unemployment/labour-force-status-families/latest-release
143. 'Children should be seen and not heard', N. Parker, *The Spoke,* 06 January 2016, accessed 11 February 2021. http://thespoke.earlychildhoodaustralia.org.au/children-should-be-seen-and-not-heard/
144. 'The Household, Income and Labour Dynamics in Australia Survey: Selected Findings from Waves 1 to 17', R. Wilkins, W. Lab, P. Butterworth, E. Vera-Toscano, 2019, accessed 12 March 2021. https://melbourneinstitute.unimelb.edu.au/__data/assets/pdf_file/0011/3127664/HILDA-Statistical-Report-2019.pdf

145. 'These countries have the most expensive childcare', S. Fleming, World Economic Forum, 23 April 2019, accessed 12 February 2021. https://www.weforum.org/agenda/2019/04/these-countries-have-the-most-expensive-childcare/

146. 'Ryan's Rule', Queensland Health, accessed 12 February 2021. https://www.health.qld.gov.au/cairns_hinterland/html/ryan-home

147. 'What's the best way to discipline my child?', *American Academy of Pediatrics*, 11 May 2018, accessed 11 February 2021. https://www.healthychildren.org/English/family-life/family-dynamics/communication-discipline/Pages/Disciplining-Your-Child.aspx

148. D. Siegel and T. Payne, *The Whole-Brain Child: 12 Revolutionary Strategies to Nurture Your Child's Developing Mind, Survive Everyday Parenting Struggles, and Help Your Family Thrive*, New York, Scribe Publications, 2012

149. 'What's the best way to discipline my child?', *American Academy of Pediatrics*, 11 May 2018, accessed 11 February 2021. https://www.healthychildren.org/English/family-life/family-dynamics/communication-discipline/Pages/Disciplining-Your-Child.aspx

150. 'Fifteen reasons we need friends', S. Whitbourne, *Psychology Today*, 26 March 2013, accessed 11 February 2021. https://www.psychologytoday.com/us/blog/fulfillment-any-age/201303/fifteen-reasons-we-need-friends

151. ibid.

152. 'Getting to know your child's friends: tips for parents', *American Academy of Pediatrics*, 08 September 2016, accessed 11 February 2021. https://www.healthychildren.org/English/family-life/family-dynamics/communication-discipline/Pages/Getting-to-Know-Your-Childs-Friends.aspx

153. 'Parenting is a balancing act', J. Guerrier, ViacomCBS, 03 June 2020, accessed 12 February 2021. https://insights.viacomcbs.com/post/parenting-is-a-balancing-act/

154. R. Louv, *Last Child in the Woods: Saving Our Children from Nature-Deficit Disorder*, New York, Algonquin Books, 2008.

155. ibid.

156. 'Why Kids Need to Spend Time in Nature', D. Cohen, Child Mind Institute, accessed 15 March 2021. https://childmind.org/article/why-kids-need-to-spend-time-in-nature/

157. R. Louv, *The Nature Principle: Reconnecting with Life in a Virtual Age*, New York, Algonquin Books, 2012.

158. R. Louv, *Vitamin N*, New York, Atlantic PBS, 2017.

159. R. Louv, *Our Wild Calling, New York,* New York, Algonquin Books, 2019.

160. 'The Future of Education', S. Renton, K. Stobbe, McCrindle Research, 2020, accessed 12 March 2021. https://mccrindle.com.au/wp-content/uploads/reports/Education-Future-Report-2020.pdf

161. 'The Future of Education', M. McCrindle, McCrindle Research, 2019, accessed 12 March 2021. https://mccrindle.com.au/wp-content/uploads/reports/Education-Future-Report-2019.pdf

162. 'Schools', Australian Bureau of Statistics, 06 February 2020, accessed 12 February 2021. https://www.abs.gov.au/statistics/people/education/schools/2019

163. 'National, state and territory population', Australian Bureau of Statistics, 18 June 2019, accessed 12 February 2021. https://www.abs.gov.au/statistics/people/population/national-state-and-territory-population/dec-2019

164. 'The Future of Education', M. McCrindle, McCrindle Research, 2019, accessed 12 March 2021. https://mccrindle.com.au/wp-content/uploads/reports/Education-Future-Report-2019.pdf

165. ibid.

166. 'Programme for International Student Assessment (PISA) results from PISA 2018 (Australia)', A. Echazarra and M. Schwabe, OECD, 2018, accessed 15 March 2021. https://www.oecd.org/pisa/publications/PISA2018_CN_AUS.pdf

167. 'Alarm Bells': Australian students record worst result in global tests', J. Baker, *The Sydney Morning Herald*, 03 December 2019, accessed 11 February 2021. https://www.smh.com.au/education/alarm-bells-australian-students-record-w

168. 'Schools', Australian Bureau of Statistics, 06 February 2020, accessed 12 February 2021. https://www.abs.gov.au/statistics/people/education/schools/2019

169. McCrindle Research projection based on: 'Qualifications and Work', *Australian Bureau of Statistics,* 29 September 2020, accessed 14 February 2021. https://www.abs.gov.au/statistics/people/education/qualifications-and-work/latest-release

170. 'What is STEM?', Department of Education Western Australia, accessed 11 February 2021. https://www.education.wa.edu.au/what-is-stem

171. 'A learning secret: Don't take notes with a laptop', C. May, *Scientific American,* 03 June 2014, accessed 11 February 2021. https://www.scientificamerican.com/article/a-learning-secret-don-t-take-notes-with-a-laptop/

172. 'The Future of Education', M. McCrindle, McCrindle Research, 2018, accessed 12 March 2021. https://mccrindle.com.au/wp-content/uploads/reports/Education-Future-Report-2018.pdf

173. ibid.

174. ibid.

175. 'Teacher support readiness and the cons of classroom AI', K. Donaghey, *School News Australia,* 11 September 2018, accessed 11 February 2021. https://www.school-news.com.au/news/teacher-support-readiness-the-cons-of-classroom-ai/

176. 'How the global pandemic is shaping the sentiment, behaviour and outlook of Australians', S. Renton, McCrindle Research, 2020, accessed 12 March 2021. https://mccrindle.com.au/wp-content/uploads/reports/COVID19-Phase1-Report-2020.pdf

177. 'Recovering from COVID-19', S. Renton, McCrindle Research, 2020, accessed 12 March 2021. https://mccrindle.com.au/wp-content/uploads/reports/COVID19-Phase2-Report-2020.pdf

178. 'Understanding the Impact of COVID-19 on the Emerging Generations', A. Fell and M. McCrindle, McCrindle Research, May 2020, accessed 15 March 2021. https://mccrindle.com.au/wp-content/uploads/COVID19-Emerging-Generations-Report.pdf

179. 'The Future of Education', S. Renton, K. Stobbe, McCrindle Research, 2020, accessed 12 March 2021. https://mccrindle.com.au/wp-content/uploads/reports/Education-Future-Report-2020.pdf

180. 'How the Global Pandemic is Shaping the Sentiment, Behaviour and Outlook of Australians', S. Renton, McCrindle Research, 2020, accessed 12 March 2021. https://mccrindle.com.au/wp-content/uploads/reports/COVID19-Phase1-Report-2020.pdf

181. 'The Future of Education', S. Renton, K. Stobbe, McCrindle Research, 2020, accessed 12 March 2021. https://mccrindle.com.au/wp-content/uploads/reports/Education-Future-Report-2020.pdf

182. ibid.

183. 'The Future of Education', M. McCrindle, McCrindle Research, 2018, accessed 12 March 2021. https://mccrindle.com.au/wp-content/uploads/reports/Education-Future-Report-2018.pdf

184. ibid.

185. ibid.

186. ibid.

187. 'The Future of Education', S. Renton, K. Stobbe, McCrindle Research, 2020, accessed 12 March 2021. https://mccrindle.com.au/wp-content/uploads/reports/Education-Future-Report-2020.pdf

188. 'The Future of Education', M. McCrindle, McCrindle Research, 2018, accessed 12 March 2021. https://mccrindle.com.au/wp-content/uploads/reports/Education-Future-Report-2018.pdf

189. 'The Future of Education', M. McCrindle, McCrindle Research, 2019, accessed 12 March 2021. https://mccrindle.com.au/wp-content/uploads/reports/Education-Future-Report-2019.pdf

190. 'STEM Education: A review of the contribution of the disciplines of science, technology, engineering and mathematics', C. McDonald, *Science Education International*, Vol. 27, Issue 4, 2016, 530–569

191. 'The Future of Education', M. McCrindle, McCrindle Research, 2018, accessed 12 March 2021. https://mccrindle.com.au/wp-content/uploads/reports/Education-Future-Report-2018.pdf

192. 'STEM Education: A review of the contribution of the disciplines of science, technology, engineering and mathematics', C. McDonald, *Science Education International* Vol. 27, Issue 4, 2016, 530-569

193. '14 Generation Z quotes that expose their unique and high tech lives', R. Jenkins, *Ryan Jenkins blog,* accessed 12 February 2021. https://blog.ryan-jenkins.com/2016/05/16/14-generation-z-quotes-that-expose-their-unique-and-high-tech-lives

194. 'New Vision for Education: Unlocking the Potential of Technology', World Economic Forum, 2015, accessed 15 March 2021. http://www3.weforum.org/docs/WEFUSA_NewVisionforEducation_Report2015.pdf

195. 'The Future of Education', M. McCrindle, McCrindle Research, 2019, accessed 12 March 2021. https://mccrindle.com.au/wp-content/uploads/reports/Education-Future-Report-2019.pdf

196. 'The New Work Smarts: thriving in the new work order', AlphaBeta for Foundation for Young Australians, July 2017, accessed 15 March 2021. https://www.fya.org.au/wp-content/uploads/2017/07/FYA_TheNewWorkSmarts_July2017.pdf

197. 'The Future of Education', M. McCrindle, McCrindle Research, 2018, accessed 12 March 2021. https://mccrindle.com.au/wp-content/uploads/reports/Education-Future-Report-2018.pdf

198. 'The Future of Education', M. McCrindle, McCrindle Research, 2019, accessed 12 March 2021. https://mccrindle.com.au/wp-content/uploads/reports/Education-Future-Report-2019.pdf

199. 'The Future of Education', M. McCrindle, McCrindle Research, 2018, accessed 12 March 2021. https://mccrindle.com.au/wp-content/uploads/reports/Education-Future-Report-2018.pdf

200. 'Why schools should teach the curriculum of the future, not the past', H. Patrovi, *World Economic Forum,* 17 September 2018, accessed 11 February 2021. https://www.weforum.org/agenda/2018/09/why-schools-should-teach-the-curriculum-of-the-future-not-the-past/

201. 'National STEM School Education Strategy', Education Council, December 2015, accessed 15 March 2021. http://www.educationcouncil.edu.au/site/DefaultSite/filesystem/documents/National%20STEM%20School%20Education%20Strategy.pdf

202. 'The Future of Education', M. McCrindle, McCrindle Research, 2018, accessed 12 March 2021. https://mccrindle.com.au/wp-content/uploads/reports/Education-Future-Report-2018.pdf

203. ibid.

204. 'Future Skills', AlphaBeta for Google Australia, Future Skills Report, 2019, accessed 15 March 2021. https://alphabeta.com/wp-content/uploads/2019/01/google-skills-report.pdf

205. 'The Future of Education', M. McCrindle, McCrindle Research, 2019, accessed 12 March 2021. https://mccrindle.com.au/wp-content/uploads/reports/Education-Future-Report-2019.pdf
206. ibid.
207. ibid.
208. ibid.
209. ibid.
210. ibid.
211. 'The Future of Education', S. Renton, K. Stobbe, McCrindle Research, 2020, accessed 12 March 2021. https://mccrindle.com.au/wp-content/uploads/reports/Education-Future-Report-2020.pdf
212. 'Education and Work, Australia', Australian Bureau of Statistics, 11 November 2020, accessed 12 February 2021 . https://www.abs.gov.au/statistics/people/education/education-and-work-australia/latest-release
213. 'The Future of Education', S. Renton, K. Stobbe, McCrindle Research, 2020, accessed 12 March 2021. https://mccrindle.com.au/wp-content/uploads/reports/Education-Future-Report-2020.pdf
214. 'The Future of Education', M. McCrindle, McCrindle Research, 2019, accessed 12 March 2021. https://mccrindle.com.au/wp-content/uploads/reports/Education-Future-Report-2019.pdf
215. 'Insights into our School based Career Practitioners', M. McCrindle, *McCrindle Research Blog*, 21 June 2017, accessed 11 February 2021. https://mccrindle.com.au/insights/blogarchive/insights-into-our-school-based-career-practitioners/
216. 'The Future of Education', S. Renton, K. Stobbe, McCrindle Research, 2020, accessed 12 March 2021. https://mccrindle.com.au/wp-content/uploads/reports/Education-Future-Report-2020.pdf
217. 'Educating for the new world of work', M. McCullough, *KPMG, 15 June 2017*, accessed 14 February 2021. https://home.kpmg/au/en/home/insights/2017/06/australia-education-system-for-the-new-world-of-work.html
218. 'Qualifications and work', Australian Bureau of Statistics, 29 September 2020, accessed 12 February 2021. https://www.abs.gov.au/statistics/people/education/qualifications-and-work/latest-release
219. 'Australians pursuing higher education in record numbers [media release], Australian Bureau of Statistics, 23 October 2017, accessed 12 February 2021. https://www.abs.gov.au/AUSSTATS/abs@.nsf/mediareleasesbyReleaseDate/1533FE5A8541D66CCA2581BF00362D1D
220. ibid.
221. 'Dear Year 12 Student ... Take Heart', Eternity News, 02 September 2020, accessed 11 February 2021. https://www.eternitynews.com.au/australia/dear-year-12-student/
222. 'Crunching the number: Exploring the use and usefulness of the Australian tertiary admission rank (ATAR)', S. Pilcher and K. Torii, Mitchell Institute, 2018, accessed 12 February 2021. https://www.vu.edu.au/sites/default/files/crunching-the-number-exploring-use-and-usefulness-of-the-atar-mitchell-institute.pdf
223. 'Perceptions Are Not Reality', McCrindle Research for Skilling Australia Foundation, May 2017, accessed 15 March 2021. https://2qean3b1jjd1s87812ool5ji-wpengine.netdna-ssl.com/wp-content/uploads/work/Skilling-Australia-Vocation-Education-Report.pdf
224. ibid.
225. ibid.
226. 'The fast lane from school', TAFE NSW, accessed 11 February 2021. https://www.tafensw.edu.au/career-advice/blog/-/blogs/the-fast-lane-from-school

227. 'Future Skills', AlphaBeta for Google Australia, Future Skills Report, 2019, accessed 15 March 2021. https://alphabeta.com/wp-content/uploads/2019/01/google-skills-report.pdf

228. '15 more companies that no longer require a degree – apply now', *Glassdoor*, 10 January 2020, accessed 11 February 2021. https://www.glassdoor.com/blog/no-degree-required/

229. 'Bridging the gap: who takes a gap year and why', D. Curtis, P. Mlotkowski, M. Lumsden, National Centre for Vocational Education Research, 06 June 2012, accessed 15 March 2021. https://www.ncver.edu.au/__data/assets/file/0010/7102/bridging-gap-2494.pdf

230. ibid.

231. 'Future Skills', AlphaBeta for Google Australia, Future Skills Report, 2019, accessed 15 March 2021. https://alphabeta.com/wp-content/uploads/2019/01/google-skills-report.pdf

232. '2020 Graduate Outcomes Survey', Australian Government Department of Education, Skills and Employment, November 2020, accessed 16 March 2021. https://www.qilt.edu.au/docs/default-source/gos-reports/2020-gos/2020-gos-national-report.pdf

233. 'Recovering from COVID-19', S. Renton, McCrindle Research, 2020, accessed 12 March 2021. https://mccrindle.com.au/wp-content/uploads/reports/COVID19-Phase2-Report-2020.pdf

234. 'Future Skills', AlphaBeta for Google Australia, Future Skills Report, 2019, accessed 15 March 2021. https://alphabeta.com/wp-content/uploads/2019/01/google-skills-report.pdf

235. 'Population projections, Australia', Australian Bureau of Statistics, 22 November 2018, accessed 14 February 2021. https://www.abs.gov.au/statistics/people/population/population-projections-australia/latest-release

236. 'Chapter 1: How will Australia change over the next 40 years', The Treasury, 04 March 2015, accessed 14 February 2021. https://treasury.gov.au/publication/2015-igr/chapter-1-how-will-australia-change-over-the-next-40-years

237. M. McCrindle and A. Fell, *Work Wellbeing: Leading Thriving Teams in Rapidly Changing Times*, Sydney, Rockpool Publishing, 2020.

238. 'Cultural diversity increases – Australia's latest migration data', G. Brailey, McCrindle Research Blog, 10 June 2020, accessed 15 February 2021. https://mccrindle.com.au/insights/blog/cultural-diversity-increases-australias-latest-migration-data/

239. M. McCrindle and A. Fell, *Work Wellbeing: Leading Thriving Teams in Rapidly Changing Times*, Sydney, Rockpool Publishing, 2020.

240. ibid.

241. 'Young, smart, and kinda broke: What we learnt from our Census for Young People', ABC / Triple J Hack, Australian Broadcasting Corporation, 31 July 2018, accessed 15 March 2021. https://www.abc.net.au/triplej/programs/hack/whats-up-in-your-world-the-census-for-young-people/10051266

242. 'Turnover and Retention Research Report', P. Begley and L. Dunne, Australian HR Institute, August 2018, accessed 13 March 2021. https://www.ahri.com.au/media/1222/turnover-and-retention-report_final.pdf

243. 'Starbucks principles for upholding the third place: For our partners, our customers and our communities', Starbucks, accessed 11 February 2021. https://www.starbucks.com/responsibility/learn-more/policies/third-place

244. 'Youth unemployment: Gen Z rises to the challenge', H. Hawkes, *INTHEBLACK*, 01 September 2020, accessed 11 February 2021. https://www.intheblack.com/articles/2020/09/01/youth-unemployment-gen-z-rise-to-challenge

245. M. McCrindle and A. Fell, *Work Wellbeing: Leading Thriving Teams in Rapidly Changing Times*, Sydney, Rockpool Publishing, 2020.

246. 'Work-related Traumatic Injury Fatalities', Safe Work Australia, 2019, accessed 16 March 2021. https://www.safeworkaustralia.gov.au/sites/default/files/2020-11/Work-related%20traumatic%20injury%20fatalities%20Australia%202019.pdf

247. 'Workplace Loneliness', Reventure, A Future that Works, 2019, accessed 13 March 2021. http://www.afuturethatworks.org.au/reports

248. ibid.

249. M. McCrindle and A. Fell, *Work Wellbeing: Leading Thriving Teams in Rapidly Changing Times, Sydney,* Rockpool Publishing, 2020.

250. ibid.

251. ibid.

252. ibid.

253. 'The Regrets Survey', [Nationally representative survey distributed to 1,008 Australians], conducted by McCrindle Research, November 2019.

254. 'How the global pandemic is shaping the sentiment, behaviour and outlook of Australians', S. Renton, McCrindle Research, 2020, accessed 12 March 2021. https://mccrindle.com.au/wp-content/uploads/reports/COVID19-Phase1-Report-2020.pdf

255. M. McCrindle and A. Fell, *Work Wellbeing: Leading Thriving Teams in Rapidly Changing Times,* Sydney, Rockpool Publishing, 2020.

256. R. Greenleaf, *Servant Leadership: A Journey into the Nature of Legitimate* Power and Greatness, Paulist Press, 2002.

257. 'How the global pandemic is shaping the sentiment, behaviour and outlook of Australians', S. Renton, McCrindle Research, 2020, accessed 12 March 2021. https://mccrindle.com.au/wp-content/uploads/reports/COVID19-Phase1-Report-2020.pdf

258. M. McCrindle and A. Fell, *Work Wellbeing: Leading Thriving Teams in Rapidly Changing Times, Sydney,* Rockpool Publishing, 2020.

259. 'Recovering from COVID-19', S. Renton, McCrindle Research, 2020, accessed 12 March 2021. https://mccrindle.com.au/wp-content/uploads/reports/COVID19-Phase2-Report-2020.pdf

260. B. Brown, *Daring Greatly: How the Courage to Be Vulnerable Transforms the Way We Live, Love, Parent, and Lead,* New York, Penguin Life, 2015.

261. B. Brown, *Dare to Lead: Brave Work. Tough Conversations. Whole Hearts,* New York, Vermilion, 2018.

262. ibid.

263. S. Sinek, *Start with Why: How Great Leaders Inspire Everyone to Take Action,* New York, Penguin, 2011.

264. 'The power of imperfection', K. Catlin, Karen Catlin, 8 November 2012, accessed 16 March 2021. https://karencatlin.com/2012/11/08/power-of-imperfection/

265. Dr. Seuss, *Fox in Socks: Dr. Seuss's Book of Tongue Tanglers,* New York, Random House, 2011)

266. 'Household Size and Composition Around the World', The United Nations, 2017, accessed 15 March 2021. file:///C:/Users/ashle/Downloads/household_size_and_composition_around_the_world_2017_data_booklet.pdf

267. 'Population and households', Australian Institute of Family Studies, accessed 12 February 2021. https://aifs.gov.au/facts-and-figures/population-and-households

268. 'Household and Family Projections, Australia', Australian Bureau of Statistics, 14 March 2019, accessed 15 March 2021. https://www.abs.gov.au/statistics/people/population/household-and-family-projections-australia/latest-release

269. ibid.

270. 'Smart home Australia', *Statista,* accessed 14 February 2021. https://www.statista.com/outlook/dmo/smart-home/australia

271. 'The Renter of the Future' [Infographic]', McCrindle for Optus, 2016, accessed 15 March 2021. https://2qean3b1jjd1s87812ool5ji-wpengine.netdna-ssl.com/wp-content/uploads/images/Renter-of-the-Future_McCrindle_Optus.pdf

272. 'Average Weekly Earnings Australia', Australian Bureau of Statistics, 13 August 2020, accessed 15 February 2021. https://www.abs.gov.au/statistics/labour/earnings-and-work-hours/average-weekly-earnings-australia/may-2020

273. 'The Fading Australian Dream', M. McCrindle, McCrindle Blog, 22 March 2017, accessed 16 March 2021. https://mccrindle.com.au/insights/blogarchive/the-fading-australian-dream/

274. 'Renting Landscape in 30 countries around the world', RENTCafe blog, 12 February 2018, accessed 16 March 2021. https://www.rentcafe.com/blog/rental-market/renting-landscape-30-countries-around-world/

275. 'Renting an apartment/a house in Germany', European Consumer Centre Company Germany, 09 January 2020, accessed 11 February 2021. https://www.evz.de/en/living-in-germany/renting-in-germany.html

276. 'The New Australian Dream', McCrindle for Sekisui House, 2019, accessed 15 March 2021. https://2qean3b1jjd1s87812ool5ji-wpengine.netdna-ssl.com/wp-content/uploads/work/Sekisui-House-New-Australian-Dream-Report.pdf

277. '2071.0 – Census of Population and Housing: Reflecting Australia - Stories from the Census, 2016', Australian Bureau of Statistics, 28 June 2017, accessed 15 March 2021. https://www.abs.gov.au/ausstats/abs@.nsf/Lookup/2071.0main+features22016

278. 'Gender Indicators, Australia', Australian Bureau of Statistics, 15 December 2020, accessed 15 March 2021. https://www.abs.gov.au/statistics/people/people-and-communities/gender-indicators-australia/latest-release

279. '3101.0 – Australian Demographic Statistics, June 2019', Australian Bureau of Statistics, 19 December 2019, accessed 15 March 2021. https://www.abs.gov.au/ausstats/abs@.nsf/0/1CD2B1952AFC5E7ACA257298000F2E76

280. ibid.

281. 'Average salary in Brisbane, Queensland', *PayScale,* accessed 11 February 2021. https://www.payscale.com/research/AU/Location=Brisbane-Queensland/Salary

282. ibid.

283. 'OECD Better Life Index, 'Australia', OECD, accessed 14 February 2021. http://www.oecdbetterlifeindex.org/countries/australia/

284. 'Recovering from COVID-19', S. Renton, McCrindle Research, 2020, accessed 12 March 2021. https://mccrindle.com.au/wp-content/uploads/reports/COVID19-Phase2-Report-2020.pdf

285. 'Understanding the future consumer', M. McCrindle, A. Fell, K. Leung, P. Chi, McCrindle Research, 2020, accessed 12 March 2021. https://mccrindle.com.au/wp-content/uploads/reports/Analyse-Australia-2020-Understanding-the-Future-Consumer.pdf

286. 'The Future of Education Survey', [Nationally representative survey distributed to 1003 Australian parents], conducted by McCrindle Research, March 2020.

287. 'Kids and mobiles: how Australian children are using mobile phones', Australian Communications and Media Authority, 2020, accessed 30 July 2020. https://www.acma.gov.au/publications/2020-12/report/kids-and-mobiles-how-australian-children-are-using-mobile-phones

288. A. Maslow, *Motivation and Personality*, Hong Kong, Longman, 1987.

289. E. Hoffman, *The Right to be Human: A Biography of Abraham Maslow.* Jeremy P. Tarcher, Inc., 1988

290. 'Hackathon' [Facebook page], Facebook, accessed 14 February 2021. https://www.facebook.com/hackathon/?ref=page_internal

291. 'Favourite hacks of 2016', R. Zhang, *FACEBOOK Engineering,* 29 December 2016, accessed 11 February 2021. https://engineering.fb.com/2016/12/29/developer-tools/favorite-hacks-of-2016/

292. 'Future of Fresh', McCrindle for Woolworths, 2014, accessed 15 March 2021. https://www.woolworthsgroup.com.au/icms_docs/185017_The_Future_of_Fresh.pdf

293. ibid.

294. 'Aussies will pay more for sustainable products', R. Lucio, *Inside FMCG,* 29 August 2019, accessed 11 February 2021. https://insidefmcg.com.au/2019/08/29/aussies-pay-more-for-sustainable-products/

295. 'Future of Fresh', McCrindle for Woolworths, 2014, accessed 15 March 2021. https://www.woolworthsgroup.com.au/icms_docs/185017_The_Future_of_Fresh.pdf

296. 'The Online Store of the Future', IGD, 2018, accessed 12 March 2021. https://www.theconsumergoodsforum.com/wp-content/uploads/2018/05/201805-CGF-IGD-Online-Store-of-the-Future.pdf

297. 'What is a smart refrigerator, and is it worth it', M. Prospero, Tom's Guide, 26 March 2019, accessed 11 February 2021. https://www.tomsguide.com/us/what-is-a-smart-refrigerator,review-6307.html

298. 'Shoppers of the future', IGD, 2018, accessed 12 March 2021. https://www.igd.com/Portals/0/Downloads/Shoppers-of-the-Future.pdf

299. ibid.

300. 'Generation Influence: Reaching Gen Z in the new digital paradigm', The Center for Generational Kinetics for WP Engine, 2020, accessed 16 March 2021. https://wpengine.com/wp-content/uploads/2020/08/Generation-Influence-U.S.-Report.pdf

301. 'Cancel culture', Dictionary.com, accessed 14 February, 2021. https://www.dictionary.com/e/pop-culture/cancel-culture/

302. 'Cancel Ellen? The backlash against Ellen DeGeneres is about mor than #metoo', S. Cohen, *Forbes,* 01 August 2020, accessed 11 February 2021. https://www.forbes.com/sites/sethcohen/2020/08/01/cancel-ellen-the-metoo-backlash-against-ellen-degeneres/?sh=be690347f980

303. 'What is the cost of 'cancel culture'?', Z. Thomas, BBC, 08 October 2020, accessed 11 February 2021. https://www.bbc.com/news/business-54374824

304. 'The real truth about beauty: A global report', N. Etcoff, S. Orbach, J. Scott, H. Agostino, Commissioned by Dove, September 2004, accessed 15 March 2021. https://clubofamsterdam.com/contentarticles/52%20Beauty/dove_white_paper_final.pdf

305. 'Announcing the Dove Real Beauty Pledge', *Unilever,* 06 June 2017, accessed 11 February 2021. https://www.unilever.com/news/news-and-features/Feature-article/2017/Announcing-the-Dove-Real-Beauty-Pledge.html

306. 'Defining acceptance in modern day Australia', Mainstreet Insights, 18 December 2020, accessed 15 March 2021. https://mainstreetinsights.com.au/defining-acceptance-in-modern-day-australia/

307. 'What is the cost of 'cancel culture'?', Z. Thomas, BBC, 08 October 2020, accessed 11 February 2021. https://www.bbc.com/news/business-54374824

308. 'Advances in hip arthroplasty surgery: what is justified?', L. Zagra, *EFORT Open Rev.,* 2017 2(5): 171–178

309. 'Obesity and overweight', *The World Health Organization,* 01 April 2020, accessed 14 February 2021. https://www.who.int/news-room/fact-sheets/detail/obesity-and-overweight

310. 'Are We There Yet? Today's Parents, Tomorrow's Kids', C. Kurz, J. Gurrier, ViacomCBS, 12 February 2020. https://insights.viacomcbs.com/categories/research-studies/are-we-there-yet/

311. 'Screen time vs "green time": New research suggests parents are right to nag kids about playing outside', N. Kilvert, ABC News / ABC Science, Australian Broadcasting Corporation, 5 September 2020. https://www.abc.net.au/news/science/2020-09-05/screen-time-mental-health-kids-adolescents/12612454

312. 'Migration – Australian migration flows and population', J. Philips and J. Simon-Davies, Parliament of Australia, accessed 11 February 2021. https://www.aph.gov.au/About_Parliament/Parliamentary_Departments/Parliamentary_Library/pubs/BriefingBook45p/MigrationFlows

313. 'Fertility, mortality, migration, and population scenarios for 195 countries and territories from 2017 to 2100: a forecasting analysis for the Global Burden of Disease Study', S. Vollset, E. Goren, C. Yuan, J. Cao, A. Smith, T. Hsiao, et al., *The Lancet*, 2020, 396 (10258):1285-1306

314. 'WHO Coronavirus Disease (COVID-19) Dashboard,' The World Health Organization, 13 February 2021, accessed 14 February 2021. https://covid19.who.int/

315. ibid.

Acknowledgements

A big thank you to Fiona Hazard and the Hachette team both in Australia and the UK for your expertise, vision and pioneering spirit in publishing this book. You have all been incredibly kind to work with and a tremendous support. Thank you for welcoming us onboard, in the middle of a global pandemic no less!

Thank you to our survey respondents, focus group participants and our in-depth interviewees for your insights and stories. And a big thank you to the group of experts who willingly shared their expertise with us for this book; it is richer for having your contribution to it: Andrew Tolbert, Dr Anne Knock, Brendan Corr, Brett Murray, Collett Smart, Graeme Irwin, Jay Anderson, Dr Lindsay McMillan, Marilyn Cox, Melanie Karaca, Monica Dreger, Dr Scott Marsh, Dr Stephen Harris and Tony George. A special thank you to Hugh Mackay for reviewing this book and providing his endorsement. He has long been a mentor from afar to us and we are honoured to have this connection with the pioneer of social research in Australia.

To our amazing team at McCrindle, and there is none better, we want to say a huge thankyou. There would be no book without you: the research you provided, the data you analysed, the sources you checked, the manuscript you reviewed and the burden you took while we were out of action for these months will long be remembered. To spend each day doing meaningful work that we're passionate about with a team of friends whom we deeply respect and admire is an honour and a privilege. So thanks Ben, Geoff, Grant, Hannah, Hendrik, Jenna, Josh, Kevin, Kirstin, Luke, Marcelo, Natalie, Peter, Shannon, Sophie, Steph and Summer.

And here's to you, our reader – parent, caregiver, educator, manager, leader. We each play a part in raising Generation Alpha and our hope is that this book serves you to understand our children better so that you can help them to thrive.

Index

INDEX